Space and Time

Space and Time

*Essays on Visions of
History in Science Fiction
and Fantasy Television*

Edited by David C. Wright, Jr.,
and Allan W. Austin

McFarland & Company, Inc., Publishers
Jefferson, North Carolina, and London

LIBRARY OF CONGRESS CATALOGUING-IN-PUBLICATION DATA

Space and time : essays on visions of history in science fiction
    and fantasy television / edited by David C. Wright, Jr., and
    Allan W. Austin.
        p.   cm.
    Includes bibliographical references and index.

    ISBN 978-0-7864-3664-4
    softcover : 50# alkaline paper ∞

    1. Science fiction television programs — History and criticism.
    2. Fantasy telelvision programs — History and criticism.
    3. History on television.   4. Television and history.   I. Wright,
    David C., 1952–   II. Austin, Allan W.
    PN1992.8.S35S63   2010
    791.45'615 — dc22   2009054323

British Library cataloguing data are available

©2010 David C. Wright, Jr., and Allan W. Austin. All rights reserved

*No part of this book may be reproduced or transmitted in any form
or by any means, electronic or mechanical, including photocopying
or recording, or by any information storage and retrieval system,
without permission in writing from the publisher.*

Cover design by Mark Durr

Manufactured in the United States of America

*McFarland & Company, Inc., Publishers
    Box 611, Jefferson, North Carolina 28640
    www.mcfarlandpub.com*

Table of Contents

Introduction: Viewing the Past through Science Fiction and Fantasy Television
  DAVID C. WRIGHT, JR., AND ALLAN W. AUSTIN   1

1. Reflections of a Nation's Angst; or, How I Learned to Stop Worrying and Love *The Twilight Zone*
  NOVOTNY LAWRENCE   9

2. Beneath the Surface: *Voyage to the Bottom of the Sea* as Cold War Science Fiction
  RANDALL CLARK   29

3. Looking Glass War: The Topsy-Turvy World of *The Prisoner*
  BRYAN E. VIZZINI   43

4. The Limits of *Star Trek*'s Final Frontier: "The Omega Glory" and 1960s American Liberalism
  ALLAN W. AUSTIN   61

5. Lost in Translation: Autonomy, Agency, and Cybernetic Anxiety from Apollo to *The Six Million Dollar Man*
  DARYL LEE   82

6. It's About Tempus: Greece and Rome in "Classic" *Doctor Who*
  ANTONY KEEN   100

7. Constructing a Grand Historical Narrative: Struggles through Time on *Highlander: The Series*
  DAVID C. WRIGHT, JR.   116

8. The Future as Past Perfect: Appropriation of History in the *Star Trek* Series
  JUDITH LANCIONI   131

9. Too Close for Comfort? Exploring the Construction of Near Future Historical Narratives in Science Fiction Television
    KORCAIGHE P. HALE 156

10. "The Future Is the Past": Music and History in *Firefly*
    KENDRA PRESTON LEONARD 174

11. The Battle for History in *Battlestar Galactica*
    JANICE LIEDL 189

Suggested Readings in Science Fiction and Fantasy Television
    DAVID C. WRIGHT, JR. 209

Contributors 215

Index 219

Introduction:
Viewing the Past through Science Fiction and Fantasy Television

DAVID C. WRIGHT, JR., AND
ALLAN W. AUSTIN

From the years when television made the transition from black and white to color, with shows like *The Twilight Zone* and *Voyage to the Bottom of the Sea*, to the early twenty-first century, with shows like *Firefly* and the rebooted *Battlestar Galactica*, science fiction (sf) and fantasy series have provided audiences with more than just entertaining stories. They have also, consciously and unconsciously, articulated the hopes and fears of their times. These shows of speculative fiction — like all popular culture — have thus provided narratives embedded with social, cultural, and political meanings. Scholars have just begun to study these television shows, using an array of approaches as varied as the subject matter itself. This work reflects the scholarly diversity in this rapidly developing field, featuring eleven essays devoted to science fiction and fantasy television of the last half-century as well as a bibliography of suggested readings. Writing from diverse disciplinary perspectives, the authors address contemporary interest in the historical contexts of popular culture as well as the historical narratives presented in popular media, exploring science fiction and fantasy television to better understand the past and the ways in which viewers have tried to make it meaningful for themselves.

Although the study of moving images and history has come of age in the past two decades or so, and there are some studies of television and history, predominately of documentary programs (such as those produced by Ken Burns), scholarly works that examine representations of history in televised science fiction and fantasy are rare. While M. Keith Booker and Jan Johnson-Smith have published general histories of science fiction television that provide broad overviews of the subject and starting points for future research, neither provides the in-depth historical analysis of specific series (or even episodes) made possible by the nature of this anthology.[1] Beyond these general surveys, an increasing number of more focused studies are starting to appear that explore televised science fiction and fantasy, either thematically, by examining gender or race, for example, or topically, by studying a television series (for examples, see the suggested readings at the end of this book). Still, despite the exciting and important growth of the field, there remain few studies that specifically investigate the varied and complex relationships between televised science fiction and the history of the United States and the world.

Thus, despite a burgeoning moving images historiography, a few studies of televised history, and the growing number of studies of science fiction and fantasy television, the study of representations of history in sf and fantasy television remains quite undeveloped. The essays in this collection address this lacuna by contextualizing a particular program or series, discerning the ways in which a program or series depicts history, or, in some cases, doing both. The essays show how these works of televised speculative fiction played a significant role in not only the popular culture of their time but also our ability to understand it better.

As Peter Rollins and other scholars have noted, used as a primary source, moving images can provide revealing evidence about the society and culture that produce them.[2] This evidence, sometimes produced consciously but probably even more often unconsciously, can elucidate persistent concerns and enduring ideals of a past era and place. Thus, a close reading of science fiction and fantasy television can expand our understanding of the last fifty years of social and cultural history in important ways. A number of the essays in this book accomplish this, focusing on such topics as Cold War culture, renegotiations of race and gender, anxiety over the increasing role of technology, and the continuing legacies of colonialism.

Other essays herein study science fiction and fantasy television as secondary evidence. Examined this way, the popular medium of television allows scholars to better understand how narratives about past (and even current) events are constructed and communicated to the larger public. Investigating television as secondary evidence helps researchers and students gain a greater understanding of how the past has been interpreted and communicated by non-historians. This approach also can convey the reasons that constructing an understanding of past events is often a highly-contested endeavor. Thus, several of the essays examine differing types of historical narratives, such as a relatively traditional overarching narrative of struggle for social progress that champions the role of the individual in history to postmodern suggestions of indeterminate historical meaning and skepticism about human agency.

The essays cover television series that span five decades. The first four chapters consider, in order, *The Twilight Zone*, *Voyage to the Bottom of the Sea*, *The Prisoner*, and the original *Star Trek* series, all broadcast between 1959 and 1969. The next two essays study *The Six Million Dollar Man*, an iconic show of the 1970s, and *Doctor Who*, a long-running British series that started in the sixties, continued through the seventies, and lasted into the eighties. Chapters 7 and 8 reflect on how history is presented in *Highlander: The Series* and in the Star Trek franchise, with a close reading of *Star Trek: Deep Space Nine*, like *Highlander*, a series produced in the 1990s. The final essays analyze several near-future programs with short runs (*Space: Above and Beyond*, *seaQuest DSV/2032*, *Dark Angel*, and *Jeremiah*), the also short-lived *Firefly*, and, finally, the new version of *Battlestar Galactica*, all series produced since the mid–1990s.

In the first essay, "Reflections of a Nation's Angst; or, How I Learned to Stop Worrying and Love *The Twilight Zone*," Novotny Lawrence sets this classic of televised speculative fiction in the Cold War context of the late 1950s and early 1960s. After a brief recounting of Rod Serling's career and creation of the show, Lawrence examines several notable episodes in detail. He asserts that by working in the genres of science fiction and fantasy, Serling was able to bypass network concerns and present controversial material to a mass audience. Thus, the series could challenge common attitudes and behaviors of the time—including xenophobia, racism, and sexism—on network television. *The Twilight Zone* consequently forged a legacy of social critique to which subsequent speculative fiction, both on television and film, are indebted.

In the second chapter, Randall Clark argues in "Beneath the Surface: *Voyage to the Bottom of the Sea* as Cold War Science Fiction" that this long-lasting and popular show has not received the critical attention it deserves. According to Clark, the series epitomized a widespread mid–1960s political outlook that gave it great resonance with its audience members. While prominently featuring futuristic technology, many episodes focused on the protagonists battling threats to America. Analysis of this largely neglected series, then, provides a better understanding of the mixed emotions felt by viewers, who championed the use of technology to win the Cold War even while they worried about the increasing influence of shadowy government agencies and their possible loss of control over ever-more-powerful technologies.

With "Looking Glass War: The Topsy-Turvy World of *The Prisoner*," the third chapter, Bryan E. Vizzini scrutinizes the cult British show of the late 1960s. He finds that the short-lived series broke new formal, as well as ideological, ground. Vizzini asserts that the *The Prisoner* refused to take a side in the Cold War — a radical position at that time — by presenting the adversaries as mirror images of one another. He goes further, arguing that the show also deconstructed the futuristic spy genre itself, and even provided a postmodern reading of televisual narration. However, much of the show's thematic material reflected the cultural obsessions of the time, such as the advent of new technology, the use of hallucinogens, and the individual rebelling against conformity and authority. Thus, he positions *The Prisoner* as both an exemplary historical text that reveals the passions of a tumultuous era and a prescient cultural intervention that prefigured the critical attitude of post-modernism.

In chapter 4, Allan W. Austin provides a close reading of "The Omega Glory," an episode of the original *Star Trek* series. His examination of this episode paints the ideological tensions of the late 1960s in sharp relief by examining what its creator saw as a reformist social critique (that evolved, at least unconsciously, from the legacy of *The Twilight Zone*). Austin claims that even though the episode (and the series) acknowledged the widening criticism of the Cold War and the Vietnam War, as well as the growing struggles for racial and gender equality, *Star Trek* ultimately took an ambivalent stance, exemplifying the limits of sixties' liberalism. Thus, he suggests that this series, and perhaps most television programs, fail to escape reinscribing dominant ideological practices, despite proclamations by creators or fans to the contrary.

In chapter 5, "Lost in Translation: Autonomy, Agency, and Cybernetic Anxiety from Apollo to *The Six Million Dollar Man*," Daryl Lee situates this iconic seventies television series in the context of the Apollo Space Program and the early stirrings of cybernetic culture. He shows how the series articulated growing cultural anxieties about technology, much as *Voyage to the Bottom of the Sea* before it. While the Apollo space program could support familiar humanist narratives about technology by focusing on the astronaut as hero, Lee finds that this television series introduced a more ominous cybernetic narrative, one that presented the human as vulnerable to the expanding power of the technological. He pinpoints this era as pivotal in the development of a cultural discourse about how the emerging technological society was reshaping humanity. Thus, *The Six Million Dollar Man* is one of the first significant cultural presentations of the "cyborg," perhaps in some ways even a precursor of cyberpunk, bringing to the fore the themes of threats to human autonomy and agency by powerful hidden institutions and technology itself. The show enabled viewers to reflect upon their future, providing a more anxious and complex picture than the simple celebration of progress characteristic of the Apollo program.

In chapter 6, "It's About Tempus: Greece and Rome in 'Classic' *Doctor Who*," Antony Keen brings a classicist's knowledge and a fan's passion to an analysis of the original *Doctor Who* shows set in the Greco–Roman period or drawing upon the imagery of that era. Pointing out that the original purpose of the show was didactic, and thus historical or mythological story arcs were to be common, he examines the ways in which the stories based on historical events were presented as well as how the plots based upon classical mythology utilized and transformed the myths. Overall, Keen indicates that the producers' original didactic aims for the show were only occasionally achieved as other considerations and influences, such as that of Hollywood films, ultimately shaped most episodes.

In the seventh chapter, "Constructing a Grand Historical Narrative: Struggles through Time on *Highlander: The Series*," David C. Wright, Jr., examines a fantasy series that contained frequent and often lengthy flashbacks to earlier times in the lives of its immortal characters, especially its Scottish protagonist. Thus, over a six-year span the show conveyed substantial amounts of historical narrative that covered distant eras, such as the Bronze Age, but more commonly events that took place in recent centuries. Wright claims that *Highlander: The Series* constructed a grand historical narrative of moral progress forged over the centuries by the struggle of the oppressed against those with the power to hurt and deprive others. Thus, by rejecting the postmodern search for ambiguous or multiple narratives, the series imparted a strong moral message and embraced the efficacy of human action.

In chapter 8, "The Future as Past Perfect: Appropriation of History in the *Star Trek* series," Judith Lancioni examines various readings of the *Star Trek* franchise, especially noting how the historical process is presented. Then, by focusing on certain episodes of *Star Trek: Deep Space Nine*, she further explores Star Trek's use of history and finds that this particular series provokes a rewarding consideration of the role of human agency in history.

Through close analysis of episodes about the protagonist's displacement in time, Lancioni finds the series broaches postmodern conceptualizations of texts, time, and consciousness. Thus, in contrast to the *Highlander*'s endorsement of the importance of the individual in history, Lancioni locates ambiguity about the role of the individual in this particular iteration of *Star Trek*.

In the ninth chapter, "Too Close for Comfort? Exploring the Construction of Near Future Historical Narratives in Science Fiction Television," Korcaighe P. Hale looks at several science fiction shows set in the near future. She argues that although different in a variety of ways, their proximity to the present might be a significant reason none of them had a successful, lengthy run. Hale examines *Space: Above and Beyond, seaQuest DSV/2032, Dark Angel,* and *Jeremiah* to discover the historical memory shared by the characters in each show. She concludes that the dissonance between viewers' own "memory" of the future's past, that is, the present and about-to-happen, and of that presented in the shows might cause too many to reject the shows.

With chapter 10, "'The Future Is the Past': Music and History in *Firefly*," Kendra Preston Leonard analyzes the recent series that portrayed life on a future frontier in outer space as similar to that in the nineteenth-century American West. However, the show also featured elements of Asian culture as well. Leonard elucidates how this social/cultural composite was conveyed through the show's music, as well as its narrative and visual presentation. Thus, although the setting (and its political context, in particular) might be foreign to most viewers, she claims that much of the soundscape of the show provides cultural familiarity to North Americans. Yet, just as the show has themes drawn from what has been identified by Edward Said, among others, as Orientalism, so does some of the music of the series.[3] Therefore, Leonard concludes that the dichotomous musical elements fail to mesh, and the privileging of the Western material results in an evocative and perhaps even credulous view of colonialism.

In the final chapter, "The Battle for History in *Battlestar Galactica*," Janice Liedl finds that the central conflict in this reimagined version of the 1970s series centered on the meaning of history and who gets to define it. She shows that undergirding this struggle in the far future is the early twenty-first century anxiety over the loss of humanity. Liedl argues that the new Galactica asks: what preserves human identity as technology progresses toward the construction of human-like non-humans? Then, she suggests that history and religion might be significant fields of contention as antagonists proffer differing answers.

Through these eleven essays from scholars in a variety of disciplines, *Space and Time* initiates an interdisciplinary dialogue about how sf and fantasy television can articulate people's aspirations and fears for the future, thereby providing an outstanding means for accessing the social imaginary of an era. The book also addresses how these televised series transmit narratives about the past, shaping the audience's collective memory. Thus, sf and fantasy television can be seen as constructing historical consciousness, not as a poor version of what is done by professional historians, historical films, or even television documentaries, but in different, sometimes subtle and complex, ways. These essays demonstrate that the study of science fiction and fantasy television can indeed make an important contribution to historical knowledge and to debates about historical meaning.

NOTES

1. M. Keith Booker, *Science Fiction Television: A History* (Westport, CT: Praeger, 2004; Jan Johnson-Smith, *American Science Fiction TV: Star Trek, Stargate, and Beyond* (Middletown, CT: Wesleyan University Press, 2005).

2. Peter C. Rollins, ed., *Hollywood as Historian: American Film in a Cultural Context* (Lexington: University Press of Kentucky, 1983) (revised ed., 1998).

3. Edward Said, *Orientalism* (New York: Pantheon, 1978).

1

Reflections of a Nation's Angst; or, How I Learned to Stop Worrying and Love *The Twilight Zone*

NOVOTNY LAWRENCE

Rod Serling's *The Twilight Zone* (1959–1964) is an iconic series in the annals of television history. During its five-year run, Serling used the show to critique society, reflecting the fear and paranoia that existed in the 1950s and 1960s as a result of the Cold War, as well as the bourgeoning civil rights and feminist movements. Although the series explored these issues under the guise of science fiction and fantasy, a brief overview of Serling's career and then a close examination of key episodes can reveal anxieties that permeated the U.S. due to its changing social, economic, and political climate.

A thorough study of *The Twilight Zone* necessarily begins with the show's creator, Rod Serling, who had become one of television's most prolific writers prior to developing the series. Serling built his reputation as a screenwriter during the 1950s, writing dramatic teleplays for *Kraft Television Theater* (1947–1958) and *Playhouse 90* (1956–1961), both of which aired programs live. In *A Critical History of Television's The Twilight Zone, 1959–1964*, Don Presnell and Marty McGee assert that Serling "helped define television as a dramatic art form with 'Patterns,' a powerful dramatization of a corporate power struggle that aired January 12, 1955, on *Kraft Television Theater*, and 'Requiem for a Heavyweight,' a touching story of an over-the-hill boxer that aired October 11, 1956, on *Playhouse 90*."[1] Both teleplays showcased Serling's penchant for commenting on the social order. The former focused on "the values of a society that places great stock in success and has little interest in morality once success is attained," while the latter used a boxer's career as a metaphor to suggest that "when a person's career is finished, their profession discards them."[2]

Serling won Emmy Awards for "Patterns" and "Heavyweight" which positioned him among notable teleplay writers such as Paddy Chayefsky and Robert Allan Arthur.[3] During the following years he strengthened his reputation as one of TV's most acclaimed writers, continuing to work for *Playhouse 90*. He won a third Emmy for his adaptation of Ernest Lehman's short story "The Comedian" (1957), and received critical praise for scripts such as "The Dark Side of the Earth" (1957), "A Town Has Turned to Dust" (1958), and "The Rank and File" (1959).[4]

Unfortunately, Serling's ascendance as a writer coincided with commercial changes within the television industry. As the medium evolved during the 1950s, it became a profit-driven entity rather than a tool to educate and promote social change. With this new strategy, network executives became more concerned with appeasing the advertisers that provided revenue to sponsor programs than with creating content that examined relevant issues. On several occasions this became a major point of contention between network executives and Serling, whose teleplays were often altered to conciliate program sponsors. In *The Twilight Zone Companion*, Marc Scott Zicree notes that prior to the initial broadcast of the highly successful "Requiem for a Heavyweight," Serling was forced to make adjustments to his work. The script initially contained the line "got a match?"; however, it was removed because the show's sponsor was Ronson lighters.[5] In another instance, the set of a different Serling teleplay was transformed when "it was decided that the Chrysler building had to be painted out of a New York skyline as seen through an office window on the set because the sponsor of the show was the Ford Motor Company."[6]

The television networks' preoccupation with satisfying advertisers directly contrasted with Serling's ideals about how the medium should be used. In *Rod Serling: Submitted for Your Approval* (1995), a documentary chronicling *The Twilight Zone*, Serling recalled, "TV didn't want to offend by showing controversy, but TV offended by showing commercials during dramas. No dramatic art form should be dictated by men whose training and instincts are cut from an entirely different cloth. The fact remains that these men sell consumer goods, not an art form."[7]

As networks went to extreme lengths to appease program sponsors, television content was changing as well. By the late 1950s, live series like *Playhouse 90* and *Kraft Television Theatre* were a dying form. As Zicree argues, "The basic economic reality was inescapable: a live show could be aired only once while a show on film could be shown again and again."[8] With that in mind, networks cancelled approximately ten live shows each year as they transitioned to filmed series.[9]

In response to these changes, in 1959 Serling announced that he was developing a weekly series of science fiction and fantasy stories. His decision to leave dramatic television for the seemingly "less important" world of sci-fi surprised those familiar with his work. Presnell and McGee contend, "To many the decision seemed impulsive and illogical, a step down."[10] During an appearance on *The Mike Wallace Show*, Serling was asked by the famous television interviewer why he no longer planned to write "anything important" for television.[11] He responded: "I don't have to fight anymore. I don't want to battle sponsors and agencies. I don't want to fight for something I want and have to settle for second best. I don't want to have to compromise all the time, which is in essence what a television writer does if he wants to take on controversial themes."[12]

While Serling suggested that his series would be devoid of significant material, he recognized that the genre provided him with more flexibility to explore controversial sociopolitical themes. From his past experiences, Serling had learned that "network censors would not allow two senators to engage in current political debate, but they could not stand in the way of two Martians saying the same things in allegorical terms."[13] He effectively duped the censors, who "left him alone because they didn't understand what he was doing or truly believed he was in outer space."[14] This artistic freedom allowed him to effectively critique American society under the guise of science fiction and fantasy.

Although Serling formally announced that he planned to create *The Twilight Zone* in 1959, he actually began developing the program in 1957 when he submitted a script that he intended to be the pilot episode titled "The Time Element" to CBS's vice president of programming, William Dozier.[15] "Element" tells the story of Pete Jensen, who has a recurring dream in which he is in Honolulu on December 6, 1941—the day before the Japanese attack on Pearl Harbor. He tries to warn people of the impending air strike, but no one believes him. Terrified, Jensen explains the dreams to a psychiatrist, insisting that the events are real and that he has traveled back in time with this prophecy. Like everyone else, the psychiatrist is skeptical of the time travel theory.

Jensen then falls asleep on the psychiatrist's couch. His dream picks up where it last left off. It is the morning of December 7, 1941, and he cries out "I told you! Why wouldn't anybody listen to me?" as an explosion rocks the building he is in. Suddenly the psychiatrist awakens to find that he has dreamt the entire scenario and that it is present-day 1958. In an attempt to calm his nerves following the nightmare, he visits a bar where he notices a photograph of Pete Jensen on the wall. He looks vaguely familiar, but the psychiatrist cannot place him. When he inquires about the man's identity, the bartender explains that he was a former barkeep who had been killed at Pearl Harbor.[16]

"The Time Element" contained many of the themes that would later define *The Twilight Zone*. The science fiction/fantasy script centered on a significant event, and it concluded with a captivating twist. Although CBS expressed skepticism about the format, when "The Time Element" premiered on November 24, 1958, it was well received, garnering more phone calls, telegrams, and letters than any other CBS drama.[17] In addition, "The Time Element" received a glowing review from *New York Times* critic Jack Gould, who wrote that "the humor and sincerity of Mr. Serling's dialogue made 'The Time Element' consistently arresting. And Mr. Serling wisely left the individual viewer to work out for himself whether the play's meaning was that even with fresh knowledge of the past no one will heed its lesson, that to be out of step with the crowd is to only invite ridicule."[18]

After witnessing the success of "The Time Element," CBS offered Serling a contract to create *The Twilight Zone*. The pilot episode, "Where Is Everybody?", premiered October 2, 1959. "Everybody" tells the story of an amnesiac who finds himself alone in a small town. He searches for others, but always seems to be just minutes behind those he seeks. For example, in one scene he enters a room where a cigar is still burning, while he finds a cup of warm coffee in another. He continues to search until madness sets in. At this point the show reveals that he is locked in a chamber as part of a military experiment, which tests the effects of isolation on soldiers.

"Everybody" was well received by critics after its debut. Cecil Smith of the *Los Angeles Times* called the show "the finest weekly series of the season, the one clear and original light in a season marked by the muddy carbon copies of dull westerns and mediocre police shows."[19] Furthermore, Terry Turner of the *Chicago Daily News* noted: "*The Twilight Zone* is about the only show now on the air that I actually look forward to seeing. It's the one series that I will let interfere with other plans."[20]

After *Zone*'s successful premier, Serling immediately began injecting the series with social, economic, and political commentary that reflected issues plaguing late 1950s and early 1960s Americans. The program addressed prominently the anxieties caused by the Cold War. In *Nightmare in Red: The McCarthy Era in Perspective*, Richard M. Fried contends that while scholars remain divided on the exact origins of the Cold War, in the 1950s few Americans doubted that the Communist Soviet Union was to blame for inciting the conflict.[21] The actions taken by the Soviets while fighting against the Axis Powers during World War II were viewed as callous and met with disdain by the U.S. Thus, it was widely believed that "as the Soviets rolled back the Nazis in 1944–1945, they treated ruthlessly the goods, governments, and lives of the peoples who lay in their path."[22]

Tensions between the U.S. and the Soviet Union only increased after World War II, during which the countries established themselves as the most powerful nations in the world.[23] In *America Divided: The Civil War of the 1960s*, Maurice Isserman and Michael Kazin note that in the aftermath of the war, the superpowers "employed the force of arms and ideological conviction to persuade the vast majority of nations and their citizens to choose up sides."[24] Isserman and Kazin further contend that in order to garner support for their respective pursuits, "the two superpowers fought with sophisticated propaganda, exports of arms and military advisers, and huge spy services...."[25]

The Cold War gained greater momentum in 1949 when the Soviet Union equaled the U.S.'s military power, exploding its first atomic bomb. In the ensuing years, the U.S. and USSR continued testing nuclear weapons in the open air, exposing both military personnel and civilians to harmful doses of radiation from fallout.[26] These acts created a looming fear of a nuclear holocaust that permeated the fabric of American society.[27]

Several episodes of *The Twilight Zone* capture the essential anxieties of the Cold War period.[28] "Third From the Sun," which originally aired on January 8, 1960, perfectly articulated the angst and desperation caused by the widespread fear of nuclear annihilation. "Sun" tells the story of scientist William Sturka (Fritz Weaver) and test pilot Jerry Riden (Joe Maross), who learn that their planet will be destroyed by all-out nuclear war in 48 hours. In an effort to escape the impending catastrophe, Sturka and Riden plan to steal an experimental spacecraft and flee their doomed planet with their families. A coworker named Carling (Edward Andrews), however, discovers their plot and attempts to thwart their escape. "Sun" reaches its climax when, arriving at the airfield, Carling confronts Sturka, Riden, and their families at gunpoint. In an act of desperation, Riden wrestles the gun away from Carling, allowing the conspirators to secure the spacecraft and flee the planet. The episode ends with the men looking at their destination through the window of the craft. Riden says, "It's the third planet from the sun ... It's called Earth. That's where we're going, a place called Earth."

In 1959, "Third from the Sun" clearly played upon the audience's ambivalence about the Cold War by introducing a setting that appeared to be Earth, despite the fact that subtle clues in the diegesis suggest that the characters actually inhabit another planet. For example, Sturka uses a cordless and sleek phone in his home, while the car that the families drive to the airfield sounds like a rocket. Perhaps the greatest indication of the alien nature of their planet is the spacecraft used to escape. The ship's capability far surpasses American space technology at the time. Specifically, the craft can carry human passengers and is capable of traveling outside of the atmosphere, a feat that the U.S. would not accomplish until 1961 as part of the Mercury Project.[29]

While the aforementioned elements allude to the otherworldliness of the planet, it does closely resemble Earth. The characters look, sound, and dress like Americans. The picturesque neighborhood in which Sturka and his family reside resembles a suburban community. More importantly, the fictional space resembles the U.S. during the 1950s because its inhabitants are consumed by the same fear — nuclear holocaust. Cinematographer Harry Wild emphasizes this angst throughout the episode by utilizing canted angles, which make the backgrounds appear tilted. This cinematographic technique subtly, but effectively, suggests that while things appear fine on the surface, fear of nuclear devastation has made life in the suburban neighborhood crooked and awry.

Not only is the psychological angst of nuclear war implied, it is also addressed directly. In a conversation between Sturka and his daughter Jody (Denise Alexander), the nuclear terror that has consumed her friends explicitly appears:

> JODY: Everyone I talk to lately, they've been noticing that something's wrong. Something's in the air. Something's going to happen and everybody's afraid. Why, dad, why?
> STURKA: People are afraid because they make themselves afraid. They're afraid because they subvert every great thing discovered. Every fine idea, every thought, every marvelous invention ever conceived, they subvert it. They make it crooked and devious. And then too late, far too late they ask the question why.

This interaction significantly shifts the focus from the weapons of destruction to the people who create and use them. Thus, this story suggested to 1950s audiences that technology was not inherently bad; instead, peoples' misuse of their advancements could potentially harm or destroy civilization.

The Twilight Zone addressed other topics in addition to nuclear annihilation. Rod Serling also commented upon the anticommunist movement, which was inextricably linked to the Cold War. According to Isserman and Kazin, anticommunists had been active since the onset of the Cold War, partly due to the Soviet Union's development of nuclear weapons, which in the minds of politicians, military leaders, and many ordinary U.S. citizens solidified the foreign power as a significant threat to the American way of life.[30] Therefore, the fear of Communist influence in the U.S. heightened as the USSR's military power grew. Fried notes that other factors contributed to the growing fear of a "Red" takeover, including the victory of the Communist Party in China, the Korean War, and "the pressures building at all levels of politics and in the life of the nation's major public institutions."[31]

The fear of Communist influence reached its peak in the early 1950s when Senator Joseph R. McCarthy became the seminal leader in the campaign to expose subversive members of the Party. Fried asserts that during those years "McCarthy personified the search for Communist influence throughout American life."[32] His crusade against the Communist infiltrators began February 9, 1950, in a speech he delivered at the Lincoln Day celebration in Wheeling, West Virginia. McCarthy was reported to have pronounced, "I have here in my hand a list of 205 ... a list of names that were made known to the Secretary of State and who nevertheless are still working in and shaping the policy of the State Department."[33] During the years following the speech, McCarthy held hearings in which he attempted to expose suspected Communists working in the government, leveled false charges of subversion at other individuals, and waged a campaign against the U.S. Army that he claimed was "infested with Reds."[34] McCarthy was eventually thwarted on December 2, 1954, when the Senate censured him for "disruptive behavior and violations of decorum."[35] Unfortunately, his radical anticommunist crusade was infectious, extending beyond the confines of the U.S. government and into arenas such as the educational system and the entertainment industry. In the case of the former, conservatives feared that Communists had infiltrated the educational system as part of a mission to corrupt the minds of impressionable youths. According to Fried, anticommunists believed that "the influence of 'Reducators' and of subversive ideas ranged ... from outright communism to 'progressive education.'"[36] Not surprisingly, the search to expose alleged educators teaching a Communist-infused curriculum coincided with the rise of McCarthy's government probes.

As previously mentioned, the quest to expose "Reds" also reached Hollywood when the House Un-American Activities Committee (HUAC) probed the film industry in an attempt to cleanse it of subversive activity. The motion picture industry was a logical, albeit easy, target for anticommunists. According to Fried:

> Hollywood did serve as an oasis for the Communist Party, providing both the funds to grease Party causes and the glamour to grace them. The movie industry backed the standard 1930s leftist crusades — civil rights and sharecroppers, anti-fascism, and Spanish Loyalists. Some actors flirted with Communism, but the screenwriters, Hollywood's intelligentsia, were primarily the ones who joined the Party.[37]

Furthermore, in *The Committee: The Extraordinary Career of the House on Un-American Activities*, Walter Goodman contends, "Of some three hundred members of the Party's 'talent branches' almost half were screenwriters."[38]

HUAC's probe of Hollywood initially began in October 1947 with testimony by "friendly" witnesses who "defended the Americanism of their trade and its product."[39] The list included studio heads such as Jack Warner of Warner Bros. and Louis B. Mayer of MGM.[40] Notable actors like Ronald Reagan, Robert Taylor, and Gary Cooper also testified, speaking against the influence of the Communist Party.[41]

After the testimonies of the "friendly" witnesses, the "unfriendly" witnesses, who would become known as the Hollywood Ten, testified. The group was composed of screenwriters Lester Cole, Alvah Bessie, Ring Lardner, Jr., John Howard Lawson, Albert Maltz, Samuel Ornitz, Adrian Scott, and Dalton Trumbo as well as directors Herbert Biberman and Edward Dmytrk.[42] All of the ten were or had once been members of the Communist Party, but they adamantly declined to discuss their political views or affiliations, invoking the protection of the First Amendment. As a result, the Ten were cited for contempt of Congress.[43] Although they appealed the decision to the Supreme Court, Congress's ruling was upheld. Subsequently, in an attempt to distance themselves from the Hollywood Ten, motion picture studio heads held a meeting at which they decided to frame a policy. As Fried has written, "The Ten had 'impaired their usefulness to the industry' and were forthwith suspended or fired, not to be rehired until they had purged themselves of contempt, been acquitted, or sworn they were not Communists. Hollywood was on notice that Communists would not knowingly be employed."[44] Significantly, the studio executives' decision to indefinitely suspend or fire members of the Hollywood Ten calls attention to another disturbing aspect of the anticommunist crusade. Beyond actually belonging to the Party, associating with known Communists or appearing sympathetic to their plight was considered equally un-American.

The *Twilight Zone* featured several episodes that reflected the paranoia, fear, and discrimination that consumed Americans as a result of the McCarthy era. "The Monsters are Due on Maple Street," Serling's spin on Arthur Miller's play *The Crucible*, serves as a prime example.[45] Miller's work featured a hero who welcomed death rather than implicating others in the seventeenth-century Salem witch trials.[46] Originally aired March 4, 1960, "The Monsters" shared a similar theme and content, perfectly encapsulating the period.

"The Monsters" takes place on a peaceful suburban street on a sunny afternoon. As the episode begins, the residents go about a range of daily activities, enjoying the peace and tranquility of their neighborhood. However, their lives are interrupted when an unidentified flash of light, that they initially believe a meteor, flies overhead. Soon after, Maple Street experiences a power failure that affects the residents' appliances, including lights, lawn mowers, and motor vehicles. Resident Pete Van Horn (Ben Erway) sets off on foot to discover the cause while Tommy (Jan Handzlik), a young boy obsessed with science fiction comics, informs the neighbors that he believes that human-looking aliens have infiltrated Maple Street and caused the disturbance. The neighbors dismiss his theory until Mr. Goodman's (Barry Atwater) car inexplicably starts on its own. Suspicion falls upon him until another neighbor's porch light turns on by itself. Finger-pointing and false accusations ensue until the residents are in a state of alarm. Steve Brand (Claude Atkins) tries to restore order, but when a shadowy figure walks toward the residents in the dark, panic breaks out. Charlie Farnsworth (Jack Weston) fires a rifle at the figure, instantly killing it. The residents descend upon the fallen menace and are stunned to find that Farnsworth has actually murdered the returning Mr. Van Horn. At this point, madness consumes the residents, who accuse each other of being linked to the alien menace as the lights on various houses flash on and off. A full-scale riot ensues and the camera pans out, revealing two aliens watching the activity from a nearby hilltop.

> ALIEN 1: Understand the procedure now. Just stop a few of their machines, and radios, and telephones, and lawn mowers. Throw them into the darkness for a few hours and sit and watch the pattern.
> ALIEN 2: And this pattern is always the same?
> ALIEN 1: With few variations. They pick the most dangerous enemy they can find and it's themselves. All we need do is sit back and watch.
> ALIEN 2: Then I take it this place, this Maple Street is not unique?

ALIEN 1: By no means. Their world is full of Maple Streets. And we will go from one to the other and let them destroy themselves.

"The Monsters Are Due on Maple Street" functions as a powerful metaphor for the McCarthy era by demonstrating the madness that can ensue as of result of suspicion and false accusations. In both the Communist witch hunts and the fictional story, the paranoia derives from a foreign menace. In the former, the main concern is Communists hailing from the Soviet Union, while the latter literally depicts aliens from outer space infiltrating planet Earth. In "Monsters," Serling again focuses his investigation on the ugliness of humankind to expose the dangers of such unwarranted suspicion. Significantly, during the McCarthy years and in "Maple Street," the accusers become the monsters, transforming once peaceful communities into spaces encompassed by concern and mistrust.

The events that occurred on Maple Street and in Hollywood when HUAC returned in 1951 to resume its Communist hearings are eerily similar. When actress Gale Sondergaard was subpoenaed to testify, she asked the Screen Actors Guild (SAG) for help. The union turned her away out of concern that they would appear sympathetic to an accused Communist.[47] Other performers such as Serling Hayden and Edward G. Robinson saved themselves by naming others who had been or were members of the Communist Party.[48] The Screen Directors Guild avoided suspicion by making its members take a loyalty oath that specified that they were not and had never been members of the Communist Party, while studio executives protected themselves by refusing to hire persons whose names appeared on blacklists, which contained the names of actors, screenwriters, directors, and others who were either confirmed or suspected members of the party or "Red sympathizers." According to Fried, studios also checked the *Red Channels*,[49] "a compendium listing 151 entertainers and their Communist-front links," before hiring personnel.[50]

The events that unfold in "Maple Street" parallel the activities that occurred in Hollywood. When the meteor initially flies overhead, the neighbors share the same curiosity about the anomaly. However, after Tommy explains that someone in the neighborhood might be an alien, the neighbors turn on one another out of both fear of the potential extraterrestrial menace as well as trepidation of being accused of being the alien threat. First, the residents of the neighborhood become suspicious of Les Goodman when his car starts on its own. Their suspicion is heightened when a neighbor reveals that she has often seen Goodman standing in his yard late at night staring at the stars. Although Goodman attributes his behavior to insomnia, he quickly finds himself under the watchful eyes of his neighbors. Sympathetic to Goodman's plight, Steve Brand suggests that they leave him alone and quickly finds himself accused by Charlie Farnsworth who warns, "You best watch who you're seen with Steve. Until we get this all straightened out you ain't exactly above suspicion yourself!" Brand responds to the residents' behavior, saying:

> Stop telling me who's dangerous and who isn't and who's safe and who's a menace! And you're with him all of you! You're all standing out here set to crucify somebody! You're all set to find a scapegoat! You're all set to point some kind of a finger at a neighbor! Believe me friend, the only thing that's going to happen is we're going to eat each other up alive!

Unfortunately, Brand's warning falls on deaf ears and the suspicion and finger pointing escalates much like it did during the McCarthy era. The destruction of Maple Street functions as a powerful metaphor for the people whose lives were affected or damaged by the anti–Communist witch hunts. In addition to addressing McCarthyism symbolically, Serling frankly denounces this behavior in the show's epilogue:

> The tools of conquest do not necessarily come with bombs and explosions and fallout. There are weapons that are simply thoughts, attitudes, prejudices — to be found only in the minds of men. For the record, prejudices can kill and suspicion can destroy, and a thoughtless, frightened search for a scapegoat has a fallout its own — for the children, and the children yet unborn. And the pity of it is that these things cannot be confined to *The Twilight Zone.*

In addition to Cold War anxieties and McCarthyism, *The Twilight Zone* also reflected the struggle for black equality that gained momentum during the 1950s and continued into the 1960s. On December 2, 1952, in Topeka, Kansas, black attorney Thurgood Marshall argued the case of Oliver Brown, a turning point in the Civil Rights Movement.[51] Brown "sought to enjoin enforcement of state law that permitted cities to maintain segregated schools, which forced his eight-year-old daughter Linda to travel a mile by bus to reach a black school even though she lived only three blocks from an all white school."[52] *Brown vs. the Topeka Board of Education* was actually filed on behalf of several plaintiffs from South Carolina, Delaware, and the District of Columbia. Risking their jobs and lives, the plaintiffs sought equality under Marshall's leadership.[53]

Although the case was initially heard in December 1952, several factors delayed the verdict, forcing the plaintiffs to wait until May 17, 1954, for the Supreme Court's final decision.[54] Reasons for the setback included the sudden death of presiding Chief Justice Fred Vinson (who was replaced by Earl Warren), division among the judges, and a demand that the litigants prepare a re-argument "pertaining to the intentions of the framers of the Fourteenth Amendment, the power of the court to abolish segregation in the schools, and, if the tribunal did have such a right and choose to exercise it, whether the Supreme Court could permit gradual desegregation or did it have to order an instant end to segregation."[55] After rearguing the case, Marshall and the plaintiffs patiently awaited the outcome, ultimately claiming victory one and a half years after the case was originally heard when Chief Justice Earl Warren announced: "We conclude that in the field of public education the doctrine of separate, but equal has no place."[56]

The *Brown* case marked a significant victory for blacks and white liberals who advocated an end to racial discrimination. After the landmark decision, the Civil Rights Movement gained momentum with protests occurring throughout the South. There were sit-ins, voter registration campaigns in Mississippi, marches in Selma, Alabama, "Freedom Rides" on Trailways and Greyhound buses that attempted to end segregation in interstate travel terminals, and a host of other important measures taken to put an end to inequality. While protestors often suffered verbal and physical abuse at the hands of hostile whites, they followed the nonviolent stance advocated by the Reverend Dr. Martin Luther King, Jr., who outlined a strategy to capture the brutality on camera so that it could be broadcast into American homes. Significantly, King noted, "We are here today to say to the white men that we will no longer let them use their clubs in dark corners. We are going to make them do it in the glaring light of television."[57] The strategy was effective as television captured and broadcast footage of civil rights advocates being spat upon and punched while trying to desegregate lunch counters. Television also showed images of the violence that ensued in Montgomery, Alabama, following the integration of the city's Central High School and the March on Washington where thousands rallied for civil rights in 1963.

Much like King, Rod Serling utilized television as a platform in the crusade against prejudice, which he considered "the most innate evil in our society."[58] While writing for *Playhouse 90*, Serling had initially attempted to address racial discrimination in a script that he wrote about Emmett Till, a fourteen-year-old Chicago native who was lynched by two white men, Roy Bryant and J.D. Milam, while visiting his uncle in Mississippi. Despite an overwhelming amount of evidence against the two men, an all-white jury acquitted them. Serling's teleplay attempted to address the immorality of the Till case, but network executors drastically changed it before it aired. The story, set in a western town in the 1800s, changed the Till character from black to Mexican. The tale still centered on a lynching and a sheriff who did little to stop it, "but it was so far removed from the contemporary scene that it simply didn't have the real strength that the original did."[59]

The Twilight Zone provided Serling the opportunity to create material that advocated equality, capturing the essence of the Civil Rights Movement. "The Big Tall Wish," which originally aired April 8, 1960, provides a perfect example of how the series was used to press for equality. "Wish" tells the story of Bolie Jackson (Ivan Dixon), an aging boxer preparing for a comeback fight that he does not believe he can win. Bolie's biggest fan, a young boy named Henry (Steven Perry), encourages him, informing him that he will make a "big tall wish" for him to win the fight. Despite breaking his hand before the brawl, Bolie wins, but refuses to believe in magic, insisting that he won on his own. Henry pleads with Bolie: "If you don't believe, it won't be true!" His begging falls on deaf ears and Bolie suddenly finds himself back in the ring, flat on his back and counted out. When he returns to Henry after suffering the defeat, the child tells him that he will not be making any more wishes.

> HENRY: I'm too old for wishes. And there ain't no such thing as magic, is there?
> BOLIE: Maybe there is magic. Maybe there's wishes too. I guess the trouble is, there's not enough people around to believe.

"The Big Tall Wish" presented a progressive message at the time of its broadcast because it featured one of television's first predominantly black casts in a dramatic program. Prior to "Wish," black performers had been featured in situation comedies such as *Beulah* (1950–1953) and *Amos 'n' Andy* (1951–1953), which fell back upon the traditional hackneyed stereotypes — the loyal Tom, buffoonish coon, tragic mulatto, the overbearing mammy, and the savage buck — that had crossed over to television from minstrel shows, vaudeville, motion pictures, and radio programs.[60] For example, *Beulah* featured Hattie McDaniel in the title role as a dimwitted domestic servant of a white family, while *Amos 'n' Andy* starred Alvin Childress and Spencer Williams as lazy buffoons always plotting schemes in an attempt to acquire wealth.

"Wish" worked in direct opposition to *Beulah* and *Amos 'n' Andy*. While the aforementioned shows featured one-dimensional black caricatures, "Wish" depicted multifaceted black characters. This fresh approach cut against Hollywood's practice of relegating black performers to comedic roles devoid of significant exploration of black life. Furthermore, unlike their predecessors, Bolie and Henry spoke proper English rather than the stereotypical "slang" utilized by McDaniel, Williams, and Childress, whose lines often included quips like "If marriages are made in heaven, my guardian angel's sho' been loafin' on the job!"; "Splain dat to me!"; and "Now ain't dat sumptin!"[61] Thus, "The Big Tall Wish" broke important barriers in depicting black actors on equal terms with white performers.

The major theme of "wish" also functioned as a powerful commentary regarding the struggle for civil rights. During the movement, King, Fannie Lou Hamer, Thurgood Marshall, June Johnston, Oliver Brown, and a host of others stood in harm's way in the attempt to abolish racial discrimination. However, the struggle for equality was largely predicated upon hope. As protestors took action, they had to hope that schools and lunch counters could be integrated, hope that television would capture the brutality that they endured at the hands of whites, and hope that the government would change the Jim Crow laws that systematically oppressed blacks.

In "Wish" the Bolie character stood as a symbol of those struggling for civil rights, while Henry represented hope. Bolie's success relied upon his ability to believe that wishing or hoping can exact positive change. When he rejected Henry's pleas to believe in the wish that he made, Bolie finds himself back in the ring being counted out. After losing the fight, he realized the error of his ways, understanding that more people need to hope that change is possible. In 1960, this powerful statement urged those engaged in the struggle for equality to persevere and remain faithful to hope.

Serling continued to examine racial discrimination in ensuing episodes of *The Twilight Zone*, including "Death's Head Revisited" (1961), "A Quality of Mercy" (1961), "The Gift" (1962), and "I Am Night — Color Me Black" (1964) among others. These installments examined prejudice against various ethnicities, advocating an end to all discrimination. Specifically, the shows addressed anti–Semitism, discrimination against Asians, Latinos, and Blacks, respectively. Each show functioned as an important call for Americans to reevaluate and change their racial politics.

The Twilight Zone also reflected changes occurring in the U.S. as a result of the Women's Liberation Movement, which reemerged in the 1960s, challenging traditional sexual politics governed by binary oppositions that placed men in superior and women in inferior roles. In *America Divided*, Isserman and Kazin write that Betty Friedan played a major role in the revival of the movement. In the 1950s, Friedan, a graduate of Smith College, retired from a ten-year career as a labor journalist to focus on raising her three children. She continued to freelance as a writer, contributing to women's magazines. At the end of the decade, on the occasion of the fifteenth reunion of her graduating class, Friedan conducted a survey of her classmates, measuring how they felt about their achievements.[62] Nearly 90 percent of the respondents were housewives, and many expressed dissatisfaction at their failure to better use their education. After compiling the survey results, Friedan argued that the women's unhappiness stemmed from the unequal relations between men and women in American society.[63] She began writing about these issues for women's magazines and presented her conclusions in a book titled *The Feminine Mystique* (1963).

According to Daniel Horowitz, Friedan's text asserted that "a sexual counterrevolution" had taken place in the 1950s, "a moratorium during which many millions of women put themselves on ice and stopped growing."[64] Hence, "they accepted the notion — or 'mystique'— that the true glory of womanhood lay in the role of wife and mother, and nowhere else."[65] Friedan argued that the solution to this problem was in the re-creation of mutually enhanced lives of men and women in a new world of gender equality. As she wrote, "Who knows of the possibilities of love when men and women share not only children, home, and garden, not only the fulfillment of their biological roles, but the responsibilities and passions of the work that creates the human future and the full human knowledge of who they are?"[66]

While some people scoffed at Friedan's politics, public-opinion polls demonstrated that women and men embraced the "second wave" of American feminism. Feminist goals included "equal pay for equal work, equal responsibility of men and women for housework and child rearing, an end to domestic violence, an end to the 'glass ceiling' that kept women out of managerial positions, and an end to sexual harassment in the work place."[67] This struggle for gender equality occurred in conjunction with the Civil Rights Movement and the Gay Liberation Movement among others. Thus, during the tumultuous 1960s, great strides were made on a multitude of social, political, and economic fronts, including the Women's Movement, which "in the 1960s and 1970s realized many of its goals with astonishing rapidity."[68]

During *The Twilight Zone*'s five-year run, the series featured a number of episodes that contained feminist themes, contradicting depictions of women as content housewives that were staples of popular programs like *Father Knows Best* (1954–1960) and *Leave It to Beaver* (1957–1963). Episodes such as "The Invaders" (1961), "Ring-a-Ding Girl" (1963), and "The Living Doll" (1963) serve as prime examples. Each of the aforementioned installments portrayed strong female characters in complete control while overcoming seemingly insurmountable odds. Specifically, "The Invaders" depicted a woman's struggle and eventual victory over an alien presence, while "Ring-a-Ding Girl" told the story of a successful actress who willingly gives her own life to save the lives of her loved ones. Finally, "The Living Doll" features the toy, "Talking Tina," who exacts revenge upon an abusive husband and father.

While such episodes promoted gender equality, perhaps the installment that best reflected the politics of the Women's Movement was "Number Twelve Looks Just Like You," which originally aired January 24, 1964. "Twelve" is set in the year 2000 and tells the story of a totalitarian society in which at the age of nineteen its inhabitants undergo a surgical process called the "transformation," making them "beautiful" and identical to everyone else. Furthermore, the operation suppresses the patients' ability to develop emotion. This utopia is disturbed when, in an effort to remain unique, eighteen-year-old Marilyn (Collin Wilcox) attempts to reject the impending procedure. Her mother, best friend, and uncle cannot understand her opposition to the surgery. They criticize, question, and finally admit Marilyn to a clinic for psychological evaluation. She attempts to escape, but is captured and forced to undergo the transformation. When Marilyn emerges she is assimilated and "beautiful."

"Twelve" was a powerful and haunting episode that detailed society's obsession with appearance, particularly as it pertained to women who had historically been pressured to fulfill the standards of conventional beauty. In the attempt to emphasize the significance of Marilyn's decision to reject such messages, *The Twilight Zone* producers cast Suzy Parker, one of the most famous models at the time "Twelve" aired, as the character's mother. According to *Zone* producer William Froug, "She was the superstar of models. She wasn't much of an actress, but she was gorgeous to look at. It was my notion that if you were going to do a show about everybody looking as beautiful as possible use *her* [sic]."[69] Therefore, when audiences familiar with Parker viewed "Twelve," they witnessed Marilyn reject the real-life pinnacle of beauty in favor of her own individuality. Such a bold statement fell directly in line with feminist politics.

Significantly, Marilyn's attempts to avoid the "transformation" fail. The fact that she ultimately has no choice in the matter exposes the totalitarian nature of the society in which she lives, while alluding to the fact that America's biased gender politics operate in a similar fashion. As Betty Friedan argued in *The Feminine Mystique*, equality between men and women is tantamount to achieving more fulfilling lives. Thus, women must have the freedom to choose to function as stay-at-home mothers, join the work force, and share domestic responsibilities with their husbands. If that was not the case and women were forced into fulfilling traditional gender roles without freedom of choice, then they live in a society much like the one presented in "Twelve."

The Twilight Zone remains a seminal and iconic series. Working under the guise of science fiction and fantasy, Rod Serling used mainstream TV to successfully critique society demonstrating that the medium could indeed function as entertainment, while serving as a means to challenge the status quo. This strategy was so effective that since *Zone*'s cancellation in 1964, the show has garnered continued interest from fans, critics, and entertainment industry executives who have made several attempts to reincarnate the series. For example, in 1983 directors such as Joe Dante and John Landis collaborated on the production of the theatrical feature, *The Twilight Zone: The Movie*, while new versions of the series, *The New Twilight Zone* (1985–1989) and *The Twilight Zone* (2002–2003), were created for television. Furthermore, scholars, including Marc Scott Zicree and Peter Wolfe among others, have written articles and books acknowledging the value of the series.

Zone's importance transcends the 1950s as well as the many attempts to reinvent the program. While the series explored McCarthyism, the Cold War, the Civil Rights Movement, and the Feminist Movement, subsequent science-fiction and fantasy TV programs and films successfully implemented the formula that Serling perfected to address pressing issues of the day. Notable examples include *Star Trek* (1966–1969), *Soylent Green* (1973), and *Alien* (1979), which explore racial discrimination, the government, and gender politics, respectively. More recently, *Battlestar Galactica* (2004–present), *Equilibrium* (2002), *V for Vendetta* (2005), *The Happening* (2008), and a host of other films and TV programs, have utilized science-fiction and fantasy to explore contemporary sociopolitical issues such as racism, politics, the war in Iraq, and global warming. Thus, *The Twilight Zone* remains as influential today as it was during its original television run and is integral in creating a holistic examination of the significance of the science fiction and fantasy genre.

Notes

1. Don Presnell and Marty McGee, *A Critical History of Television's* The Twilight Zone (Jefferson, NC: McFarland, 1998), 11.
2. *Rod Serling: Submitted for Your Approval*, dir. Susan Lacy, perf. Mike Dan, Kim Hunter, and Saul David, 86 min., CBS Entertainment, 1995, DVD.
3. In *Tube of Plenty: The Evolution of American Television*, 2d ed. (New York: Oxford University Press, 1990), Erik Barnouw explains that Chayefsky's work "had wide influence on anthology drama-its successes and failures" (159). Chayefsky's work included teleplays

such as "Holiday Song" (1953), "Bachelor's Party" (1954), and "A Catered Affair" (1959) (Barnouw 159). Chayefsky's work paved the way for writers such as Aurthur whose teleplays "Man on a Mountain Top" (1954) and "A Man Is Ten Feet Tall" (1955) appeared on the *Philco-Goodyear Television Playhouse* (1948–1955) series.

4. Marc Scott Zicree, The Twilight Zone *Companion*, 2d ed. (Los Angeles: Silman-James Press, 1989), 13.
5. Ibid., 14.
6. Ibid.
7. *Rod Serling: Submitted for Your Approval.*
8. Zicree, 15.
9. Presnell and McGee, 12.
10. Ibid., 11.
11. Ibid.
12. Quoted in Zicree, 96.
13. Presnell and McGee, 12.
14. Arlen Schumer, *Visions from* The Twilight Zone (San Francisco: Chronicle, 1990), 149.
15. Presnell and McGee, 12.
16. Plot summary from Presnell and McGee, 12–13.
17. Ibid., 13.
18. Jack Gould, "Triumph by Serling: Writer's 'Time Element' Stars William Bendix on *Desilu Playhouse*," *The New York Times*, November 25, 1958, 67.
19. Quoted in Zicree, 96.
20. Ibid. Despite garnering favorable critical reviews, ratings for *The Twilight Zone* were below expectations. This plagued the series during its entire five-year run and it was always on the verge of cancellation.
21. Richard M. Fried, *Nightmare in Red: The McCarthy Era in Perspective* (New York: Oxford University Press, 1990), 7.
22. Ibid., 7.
23. Maurice Isserman and Michael Kazin, *America Divided: The Civil War of the 1960s* (New York: Oxford University Press, 2000), 9.
24. Ibid.
25. Ibid.
26. Ibid.
27. Jane Loader and Kurt Raffety's *Atomic Café* (1982) provides an interesting look at the Cold War Era. The film uses stock footage from educational films as well as footage from military testing ranges to demonstrate the paranoia that permeated the country during the Cold War.
28. "Time Enough at Last" (1959), "One More Pallbearer" (1962), and "The Old Man in the Cave" (1963) serve as other notable examples of episodes that addressed the fear of nuclear holocaust. Adapted from a short story written by Lynne Venable that in 1953 had been published in *If* magazine, "Time Enough at Last" is a seminal episode because it holds the distinction of being the first TV program to depict the detonation of a nuclear bomb on U.S. soil (Zicree 67). "Time" is a frequently discussed episode. More detailed examinations can be found in Schumer, Presnell and McGee.
29. Francis French and Colin Burgess, *Into That Silent Sea: Trailblazers of the Space Era, 1961–1965* (Lincoln: University of Nebraska Press, 2007).
30. Isserman and Kazin, *America Divided*, 210.
31. Fried, 119.
32. Ibid., 6.
33. Ibid., 120, 123.
34. Ibid., 137. According to Fried, the exact words from McCarthy's speech were lost and he later denied stating that he knew of 205 known Communists working in the State

Department. Instead, he claimed that the number was 57 and used that figure in later talks. It was eventually discovered that McCarthy had no list containing the names of Communists working in the State Department (Fried 123).
  35. Ibid., 140–141.
  36. Ibid., 153.
  37. Ibid., 73.
  38. Walter Goodman, *The Committee: The Extraordinary Career of the House on Un-American Activities* (New York: Farrar, Straus, and Giroux, 1968), 86.
  39. Fried, 75.
  40. "Friendly" witnesses were those that belonged to Hollywood's conservative Right. They were exempt from suspicion because they proclaimed staunch American values and despised subversive activity just as much or more than the members of HUAC. David Bordwell and Kristin Thompson, *Film History: An Introduction* (New York: McGraw Hill, 1994), 373.
  41. Bordwell and Thompson, 372.
  42. Fried, 76.
  43. Ibid.
  44. Ibid., 77–78.
  45. Presnell and McGee, 55.
  46. Fried, 156.
  47. Ibid., 154.
  48. Bordwell and Thompson, 373.
  49. American Business Consultants, which was founded by three ex–FBI agents, published the *Red Channels* (Fried 157). Their former service to the United States as Federal Agents lent credibility to the document, making it appear even more accurate than the blacklist.
  50. Fried 157.
  51. Harvard Sitkoff, *The Struggle for Black Equality: 1954–1992* (New York: Hill and Wang, 1993), 20.
  52. Ibid.
  53. Ibid.
  54. Ibid., 22.
  55. Ibid., 20.
  56. Ibid., 22. While *Brown vs. the Topeka Board of Education* was a landmark case in the struggle for civil rights, it is important to note that the Supreme Court did not order an instant and total end to school desegregation. Instead, the justices adopted the "gradual" approach, "assigning the responsibility for drawing up plans for desegregation to local school authorities and left it to local federal judges to determine the pace of desegregation, requiring that a 'prompt and reasonable' start toward full compliance be made and that desegregation proceed with all deliberate speed" (Sitkoff 23).
  57. Quoted in David J. Garrow, *Protest at Selma* (New Haven: Yale University Press, 1978), 198.
  58. *Rod Serling: Submitted for Your Approval.*
  59. Ibid.
  60. Donald Bogle, *Toms, Coons, Mammies, Mulattos, and Bucks: An Interpretive History of Blacks in American Films* (New York: Viking, 1973), 3–10.
  61. Donald Bogle, *Primetime Blues: African Americans on Network Television* (New York: Farrar, Straus, and Giroux, 2001), 20, 27.
  62. Isserman and Kazin, 122.
  63. Ibid.
  64. Daniel Horowitz, *Betty Friedan and the Making of the Feminist Mystique: The American Left, the Cold War, and Modern Feminism* (Amherst: University of Massachusetts Press, 1998), 217.

65. Isserman and Kazin, 122–123.
66. Betty Friedan, *The Feminine Mystique* (New York: Norton, 1963), 378.
67. Isserman and Kazin, 122.
68. Ibid., 122.
69. Quoted in Zicree, 401.

Bibliography

Barnouw, Erik. *Tube of Plenty: The Evolution of American Television*, 2d ed. New York: Oxford University Press, 1990.
Bogle, Donald. *Primetime Blues: African Americans on Network Television*. New York: Farrar, Straus, and Giroux, 2001.
_____. *Toms, Coons, Mammies, Mulattos, and Bucks: An Interpretive History of Blacks in American Films*. New York: Viking, 1973.
Bordwell, David, and Kristin Thompson. *Film History: An Introduction*. New York: McGraw Hill, 1994.
French, Francis, and Colin Burgess. *Into That Silent Sea: Trailblazers of the Space Era, 1961–1965*. Lincoln: University of Nebraska Press, 2007.
Fried, Richard M. *Nightmare in Red: The McCarthy Era in Perspective*. New York: Oxford University Press, 1990.
Friedan, Betty. *The Feminine Mystique*. New York: Norton, 1963.
Garrow, David J. *Protest at Selma*. New Haven: Yale University Press, 1978.
Goodman, Walter. *The Committee: The Extraordinary Career of the House on Un-American Activities*. New York: Farrar, Straus, and Giroux, 1968.
Gould, Jack. "Triumph by Serling: Writer's 'Time Element' Stars William Bendix on *Desilu Playhouse*." *The New York Times*, November 25, 1958, 67.
Horowitz, Daniel. *Betty Friedan and the Making of the Feminist Mystique: The American Left, the Cold War, and Modern Feminism*. Amherst: University of Massachusetts Press, 1998.
Isserman, Maurice, and Michael Kazin. *America Divided: The Civil War of the 1960s*. New York: Oxford University Press, 2000.
Presnell, Don, and Marty McGee. *A Critical History of Television's* The Twilight Zone. Jefferson, NC: McFarland, 1998.
Rod Serling: Submitted for Your Approval. Dir. Susan Lacy. Perf. Mike Dan, Kim Hunter, and Saul David. DVD. CBS Entertainment, 1995.
Schumer, Arlen. *Visions from* The Twilight Zone. San Francisco: Chronicle, 1990.
Sitkoff, Harvard. *The Struggle for Black Equality: 1954–1992*. New York: Hill and Wang, 1993.
Zicree, Marc Scott. *The* Twilight Zone *Companion*, 2d ed. Los Angeles: Silman-James Press, 1989.

2

Beneath the Surface
Voyage to the Bottom of the Sea as Cold War Science Fiction

RANDALL CLARK

A crew of men with vaguely defined military ties, on a submarine called the *Seaview*, traveling around the world under the sea to fight an assortment of monsters, megalomaniacs, and natural disasters may sound like a simple premise for a television series, but it gave the ABC television network one of its first hit series, *Voyage to the Bottom of the Sea*, in 1964. During its time on the air, the program achieved many noteworthy accomplishments. The series ran for four seasons, making it the longest running science fiction television series of the 1960s.[1] *Voyage to the Bottom of the Sea* was also the first science fiction television series by film producer and director Irwin Allen and thus became the foundation for Allen's fondly remembered slate of science fiction series, which include *Lost in Space*, *The Time Tunnel*, and *Land of the Giants*. Based on a successful theatrical film of the same title from 1961 and produced and directed by Allen, the project became the first science fiction television series to be adapted from a motion picture. Not for another twenty-five years would another television series based on a film, *Alien Nation*, make it into even a second season; in the meantime, television viewers witnessed multiple high-profile failures such as small-screen versions of *Planet of the Apes*, *Logan's Run*, *Starman*, and *Westworld* (the series was titled *Beyond Westworld*), Indeed, if one ignores genres altogether and simply looks at television series based on motion pictures, *Voyage to the Bottom of the Sea*'s four year run, while certainly not placing it in the same category as a blockbuster like *M*A*S*H*, makes it one of the ten most successful series adapted from a film.

Clearly *Voyage to the Bottom of the Sea* had something special going for it, but today, for several reasons, many overlook its accomplishments. The series has never had the dedicated fan base of *Star Trek* or many other science fiction TV shows; in fact, it does not even have the following of Allen's *Lost in Space,* and may not even be as well remembered as *The Time Tunnel* and *Land of the Giants.* Apart from the four standards of 1960s TV show tie-ins — comic books, lunch boxes, board games, and model kits — *Voyage to the Bottom of the Sea* has never been highly merchandised, not even when the series was still on network television. The show will probably never receive the same treatment as *Lost in Space,* a series reworked as a 1997 big budget film with an Oscar-winning actor playing the male lead. Furthermore, the program rarely appears in reruns in syndication or on cable television. At the time of this writing, in fact, the series remains the only one of Allen's series not to have all of its episodes released on DVD. The once popular series has been largely forgotten while series that were less successful at the time are better remembered: there are more than twice as many episodes of *Voyage to the Bottom of the Sea* as there are the original *Outer Limits,* but which evokes a stronger memory today?

Television series fall out of favor with viewers after several decades for many reasons, including the obvious explanation that audience tastes almost inevitably change over time, but perhaps the major reason that *Voyage to the Bottom of the Sea* is not particularly popular today is the same reason for its undeniable popularity in the mid–1960s: *Voyage to the Bottom of the Sea,* more than almost any other science fiction series of the period, remained very much rooted in a specific place and time. Despite being set in the then near future of the 1970s and the 1980s, the series was so immersed in the Cold War era that it could not be translated easily into another; to watch *Voyage to the Bottom of the Sea* is to witness a perfect fusion of 1960s fears, hopes, idealism, and pragmatism. Moreover, unlike *The Twilight Zone,* the series did not mask its social commentary as allegory. With *Voyage to the Bottom of the Sea,* viewers knew that, to use an idiom from the period, "what you see is what you get." This program presented a series of episodes in which Americans overtly fought both agents from other countries and monsters to preserve their freedom.

To fully understand *Voyage to the Bottom of the Sea,* the series must be placed in the larger context of mid–1960s American popular culture. Seen this way, the series was a by-product of two social phenomena that had sweeping and powerful effects on the country — the space age and the Cold War. (For the most part, *Voyage to the Bottom of the Sea* largely ignored a third significant cultural phenomenon of the decade, rock music and youth culture, although it did add a young surfer character in seasons two and three.) The crew of the *Seaview* routinely fought enemy agents from countries that, while rarely identified, clearly represented the primary foreign threats to the United States at the time, specifically the Soviet Union, "Red" China, and Cuba. The *Seaview* triumphed over foreign powers it encountered by employing technology a bit more advanced than any science actually available to military or intelligence agencies at the time, with military discipline.

But the exploits depicted on *Voyage to the Bottom of the Sea*, with their fusion of espionage and science fiction, were hardly unique to the series and in fact could be found in every popular mass medium. Similar fictional heroes appeared in the James Bond movies, the unnamed secret agent protagonist of Len Deighton's novels, Adam Hall's Quiller novels, and a host of paperback series featuring Bond imitations with names like Matt Helm, Ed Noon, and Joe Gall. Hollywood featured the Bond and the Derek Flint films as well as film versions of the Helm and Quiller series, along with three films adapted from Deighton's novels. The comic pages starred Modesty Blaise, who also appeared in novels and in one film. T.H.U.N.D.E.R. agents, the Doom Patrol, Nick Fury and the agents of S.H.I.E.L.D., Doctor Solar, Nukla, and Judomaster appeared in comic books. *Voyage to the Bottom of the Sea* shared some key characteristics with these other works. The protagonists in all these stories worked for their countries to save the world from Communists or some other oppressive group, usually from a foreign nation. Furthermore, both heroes and villains were dependent upon scientific gadgets and weaponry to achieve their goals. Finally, all of these science fiction vehicles emphasized the protagonists' human side, despite their amazing feats (admittedly more in the Bond novels than the movies and not at all in the Flint films).

The futuristic genre dominated television, too. Espionage and science fiction abounded in 1964, the year *Voyage of the Bottom of the Sea* launched. That fall, in addition to seeing spies defeated by advanced technology on *Voyage to the Bottom of the Sea*, viewers could watch *The Man from U.N.C.L.E.*, arguably the most science-fiction oriented of the many spy series that appeared on television during the 1960s. Rod Serling's symbol-laden *The Twilight Zone* had ended its five-year run earlier in the year, but *The Outer Limits*, less allegorical than Serling's program but still inclined to address Cold War paranoia more indirectly than *Voyage to the Bottom of the Sea*, had just started its second season. *My Favorite Martian* (which had its characters fight enemy spies more than once) allowed viewers to laugh at the concept of alien invasion. The witty and hip *That Was the Week That Was* regularly joked about both the Cold War and the space race. Children could watch another series about a technologically advanced submarine, Gerry and Sylvia Anderson's marionette show *Stingray,* and *Jonny Quest,* the action-adventure cartoon from I-producers William Hanna and Joseph Barbera, which frequently featured young Jonny and company fighting Eurasian villains. In addition many espionage and science fiction episodes appeared in series that did not have an espionage and science fiction basis — Rob Petrie, Herman Munster, Fred Flintstone, and the castaways of *Gilligan's Island,* among others, all had encounters, real or imagined, with spies.[2] And this was just in 1964; the number of espionage-science fiction hybrids would continue to grow during the four years that *Voyage to the Bottom of the Sea* was on the air, all focusing in a similar fashion on scientific progress and secret government-controlled technology.

Amid this outburst of science fiction programming, *Voyage to the Bottom of the Sea* was developed as the adaptation of the 1961 movie, which provided the premise for the series in general and the plot for the series' pilot in particular. The Cold War themes of the television show echoed those found in the film, albeit in muted form. In the movie, the Earth faces a crisis after meteors penetrate the Van Allen belt, which catches fire and causes the planet's temperature to rise, threatening the extinction of humankind. Admiral Nelson (Walter Pidgeon), the designer of the *Seaview,* takes the submarine on an unauthorized mission to launch an atomic missile into the belt, an action which he believes will extinguish the fire. Quickly the crew and the audience learn that an unidentified saboteur exists onboard; she is finally identified as the submarine's psychologist, who offers no specific explanation for attempting to sabotage this important mission but who could be viewed as the agent of a foreign government. Still, the film merely hints of the Cold War, and the saboteur is actually somewhat less important to the plot than another character, a religious fanatic who wants to stop the *Seaview* because he believes the fire in the Van Allen belt is the result of an act of God.[3]

In adapting *Voyage to the Bottom of the Sea* from film to television producers placed greater emphasis on the *Seaview* itself. A notoriously thrifty producer, Allen routinely reused costumes, sets, and stock footage from one project to another; he had had three different-sized models of the *Seaview* constructed for the film, along with some rather elaborate sets representing the interior of the submarine that he did not want to waste.[4] In the series' first season, in particular, Allen tried to film as many scenes as possible in the submarine because the movie's salvaged sets alone were worth forty thousand dollars.[5] In this way, the *Seaview* became as important a character on the program as any of the human cast members.

But what began as a cost-saving venture eventually enhanced the show, both as a drama and as a reflection of the Cold War era. First, it allowed *Voyage to the Bottom of the Sea* to explore the use of submarines as Cold War weaponry. While subs had been used for warfare as far back as World War I, developments of the late 1950s and early 1960s had put submarines back into the public imagination and tied them directly to Cold War tensions. Nuclear-powered subs and the ability to extract oxygen from the ocean's water made it possible for submarines to stay submerged for long periods of time and travel great distances; an American submarine, the USS *Nautilus*, had sailed under the North Pole in 1959 and another, the USS *Triton*, had sailed around the entire globe one year later. By this time both the United States and the Soviet Union were arming their submarines with ballistic missiles. In the eyes of many Americans, submarines had suddenly been altered from archaic leftovers of World War II into a cutting-edge technology, rather like a spaceship that just happened to travel under water.

Set ten years into the future, the technology of the television series' *Seaview* was even more advanced than was shown in the film. In the pilot, the vessel is described as "the most extraordinary submarine in all the seven seas" and "the mightiest weapon afloat." While the submarine is well known to Americans, its full purpose is not, a concept perfectly designed to play upon Cold War fears that a lot of the scientific devices viewers saw were not exactly what they appeared to be. In the series' pilot, viewers are told that the *Seaview*'s "public image is that of an instrument of marine research" but that it is "secretly assigned to the most dangerous of missions against the enemies of mankind." Like a superhero, the *Seaview* has a secret identity with a secret hideaway as well — the submarine's loading dock has been carved into stone in the California coast. As the pilot episode succinctly explains, "Few men know of its [the loading dock's] existence. And fewer men even suspect its purpose." Undoubtedly a strong part of *Voyage to the Bottom of the Sea*'s appeal lay in the fact that it presented the United States as the leader in submarine technology and overtly stated that Americans used that technology only for good causes (even if the *Seaview* must be presented to the public behind a cover story, with its true missions a secret). Unlike the film, the television program does not establish direct ties between the *Seaview* and the U.S. military. In the series, the submarine is owned by

Admiral Nelson's private research institution. Cooperation with the Navy and indeed with the American government is clear: the *Seaview* receives most of its missions from the military, and the submarine's captain, Lee Crane, is a naval officer on loan to Nelson's institute. The blending of the military and private sector was familiar to audiences because of the space race. This portrayal of military/civil cooperation allowed the producers of *Voyage to the Bottom of the Sea* to show the crew of the *Seaview* as acting in an official manner without actually implying that the American government itself was engaging in any covert activity.

The use of a submarine as the primary setting had other impacts on the series, some that were perhaps subtler and more psychological. According to series star David Hedison, who portrayed Crane, the producers of *Voyage to the Bottom of the Sea* did their best to exploit the claustrophobic atmosphere inherent in a television program that took place on a submarine.[6] While some characters, and especially Captain Crane, left the *Seaview* fairly often, a majority of the crew spent most of their time aboard the submarine. Tensions could run high in almost any episode, even when there was no particular threat to the crew's safety, and the series captured the isolation and helplessness the men (and they were men; unlike the movie, the television series had no women aboard the *Seaview*) often felt while at sea. Crew tension is indicated as heightened by the lack of women. For instance, in one episode, a crewman attacks a superior officer who will not grant him leave to visit his pregnant and ailing wife.[7]

The crew was also shown as having to worry about sudden attack. To emphasize the state of danger in which the crew served — and to save Allen some money — the producers quickly created a recurring gimmick they nicknamed "rock and roll": to simulate an attack on the *Seaview*, cast members were told to throw themselves to the left of the sets while the cameras filming the episode were swung to the right.[8] The obviously staged "rock and roll" scenes have become somewhat fondly remembered by the series' fans and even inspired some jokes and parodies, but they did create the essential feeling that the crew of the *Seaview* were always at risk. Watching the men in their state of confinement must have resonated with the audience, who themselves must have felt somewhat trapped in a world that had recently offered them Sputnik, the Cuban Missile Crisis, John Kennedy's assassination, the Viet Nam War, and urban unrest. If it was difficult to get a leave from the *Seaview*, it was impossible to get one from mid–1960s America. But even on a less abstract level, watching a television series set on a submarine and the tensions that these men experienced week after week could only remind viewers of the tensions between America and other nations, even if viewers were not aware of this at the time.

The claustrophobic *Seaview* could, however, travel almost anywhere — as viewers were reminded every week, this was a voyage to the bottom of the sea — and in the four-year run of the program, the submarine went on missions to the Arctic, the Antarctic, and many locations in between. While the military nature of the program, essential to its Cold War background, means that the characters on the series were not exactly free to come and go at will, they did have overall control over where the vessel went. Significantly, this quality directly contrasted with all the other Irwin Allen series from the 1960s. *Lost in Space*, *The Time Tunnel*, and *Land of the Giants* were all about characters who are trapped in a place — or in the case of *The Time Tunnel*, a time — that they do not wish to be.[9] The emphasis in these series is placed first on survival, then on returning home. Furthermore, the advanced technology that forms the bases for these programs also played a part in leaving the protagonists stranded in the first place.

In *Voyage to the Bottom of the Sea*, on the other hand, the emphasis is not on escape but on control. Beginning in the pilot episode, in which Crane sneaks onboard the submarine as a means of testing the *Seaview*'s security, episodes consistently depict the submarine as a powerful device, capable of great feats, that is under the authority of the United States and must remain so at any cost. Many episodes of the program show enemies attempting to gain control of the *Seaview*, either through manipulating the crew or through seizing the submarine outright. But even though the crew members of the *Seaview* may sometimes lose control over their circumstances, they always regain it. There is never a hint, as there always was on Allen's other programs, that this technology (developed by and owned by Americans) could become a problem for those who had been entrusted to employ it. *Voyage to the Bottom of the Sea* is an unabashedly pro-science series, with the sleek and impressive *Seaview* at the heart of that positive attitude towards science.

The program is also unabashedly pro-scientist. Throughout the series' run, Admiral Nelson repeatedly identifies himself as a man of science who uses rational thought when making important decisions. In fact, Nelson sometimes comes into conflict with the military, whose leaders want to act out of instinct and distrust of the unknown; by presenting Nelson as correct in almost every conflict, the program endorses the United States' scientists over its military, perfectly natural for an era during which astronauts were heroes and soldiers were beginning to become objects of controversy.

The always rational Nelson has no parallel in Allen's other series, which tended to present characters who were more impetuous and administrators who were less effective. The characters in *The Time Tunnel*, for example, are stranded in the past because one of the scientists who invented the time travel device tests it prematurely in response to a senator's threat to cut off the projects' funding. It is impossible to imagine a similar situation occurring on *Voyage to the Bottom of the Sea*.[10]

Another major change that was made in the transition from Hollywood movie to television series was a greater awareness of the Cold War. Communist villains, along with a few unreformed Nazis, appear throughout the series' run, particularly in the first season. The changes can be seen as early as the series' pilot; although the same framework was used as the basis for the movie and the pilot, some significant changes were made to the story. Notably, greater emphasis was placed on the Cold War, which had done nothing but intensify in the three years between film and television program. Instead of meteors hitting the Van Allen belt, the potential disaster here comes from earthquakes in the Arctic Circle that will produce massive tidal waves. The entire world is no longer at risk; the tidal waves pose threats to both American coasts and to Western Europe. Significantly, Eastern Europe and Asia, Communist strongholds at the time, are not endangered and in fact it is a mysterious individual from this region, who refers to the United States and Western Europe as "our enemies" and intends to prevent Admiral Nelson from accomplishing his mission. This villain, who is seen only from behind and who has no name, was intended by Allen to be the recurring nemesis of the *Seaview*, but ABC did not want to feature such a character on a regular basis.[11] The fortuitous decision by the network freed the series' writers to dream up as villains a variety of megalomaniacs in a wider range of settings than a single character would have allowed; nevertheless, these villains always hinted of Russia or China. This time the reason for opposing the mission is clearly stated: foreign powers will seize control of free nations in the chaos that follows the tidal waves. Finally, instead of a saboteur on the *Seaview*, a spy in the upper echelons of the U.S. military reports to the unidentified foreign powers.[12]

Although the series is set in the 1970s and 1980s, the producers made no attempt to create a futuristic tone for the program. Characters wear clothing of the 1960s, speak slang from the 1960s, and most important of all, face the political concerns of the 1960s. Plot points from the series sound like a checklist of America's political issues at that time: an attempt to assassinate the president, the *Seaview*'s being ordered to launch a nuclear missile, brainwashing, nerve gas used against the crew, a peace conference disrupted by Communist agents, the apparent death of everyone on Earth except for the crew of the *Seaview*, and an American nuclear weapon falling into the wrong hands.

To illustrate these concerns, two episodes from early in the series' run merit particularly close examination. The first to be considered, "The Mist of Silence," the series' fourth episode, is a surprisingly political piece; in his book *Irwin Allen Television Productions, 1964–1970*, author Jon Abbott calls it "the darkest, grimmest episode of the entire series."[13] The plot is clearly inspired by the story of Che Guevara and Fidel Castro in Cuba. The episode begins with an assassination attempt against President Alejandro Fuente, who recently seized control of an unnamed Latin American nation. As a result of the failed attempt, Fuente, who has been outspoken in his hatred for the United States and "a friend to any of its enemies," surprises the American government by asking to defect to America. A government official identified only as "the Chairman" arranges for the *Seaview* to transport Fuente to Washington, D.C., but warns Nelson that Fuente may not be sincere in his desire to defect and further adds that the man might be carefully manipulated by his nation's military, the real power behind his puppet government that keeps Fuente alive only because of his propaganda value with his people, who view him as "a hero of the revolution." Joining the crew members of the *Seaview* as they transport Fuente to the United States is the leader of the government in exile, Ricardo Galdez, who is in fact the unsuccessful assassin from the opening scene. In a scene that echoes the relationship between Guevara and Castro, Galdez explains that he and Fuente had fought together but became bitter enemies after the revolution because "Alejandro hated tyranny only so long as someone else was the tyrant." In the attempt to reach Fuente, several members of the *Seaview* crew are captured and ordered to make anti–American statements. When Captain Crane refuses, several of his men are executed. Reportedly, ABC opposed the executions as being too potent for television audiences but Allen insisted on including this plot element.[14] These scenes are quite powerful and the sight of Americans being systematically taken before the firing squad in a foreign country must have had an incredibly dramatic impact.

Just over a month later the series aired its ninth episode, "Hot Line." This episode centers on possible accidental nuclear detonation, a topic that had already been impressed upon the public mind by the release of the films *Dr. Strangelove, Or: How I Learned to Stop Worrying and Love the Bomb* and *Fail Safe* earlier that year. The episode also drew upon public interest in the "hotline" that connected the White House and the Kremlin that had been installed just over a year before following the Cuban Missile Crisis. In this episode, the Soviet Union has lost control over one of its satellites; unable to destroy it, the Kremlin determines that the satellite will splash down into the ocean off the coast of California. Should the nuclear reactor on the satellite detonate, the resulting radiation will kill tens of thousands of Americans. It is up to the *Seaview* to transport two Soviet experts who can defuse the satellite before detonation. One of those experts, however, has been replaced by a double agent who has been ordered to sabotage the *Seaview*'s mission. The episode is noteworthy not just because it seems remarkably similar to genuine societal concerns of the time but because it is actually somewhat sympathetic to the Soviets. The premier seems genuinely horrified when he learns the satellite will land so close to California, and one of the experts who defuses the satellite joins the crew of the *Seaview* in a toast after the mission has succeeded: "To our homes," he says, "wherever they may be." As a symbol of his overcoming unwavering Cold War loyalties, he acknowledges that he has come to prefer champagne to vodka.

The espionage stories that were so commonplace in the first season of *Voyage to the Bottom of the Sea* did not disappear at any point in the series' run but certainly became less prominent in seasons two through four. Jon Abbott suggests that such a change was necessary to continue to attract viewers, as audiences were being bombarded by spy stories by 1965.[15] Whatever the reason, producers decided to emphasize science fiction more, asking writers to come up with scripts featuring monsters or creatures as often as possible. But even the program's episodes with heavy science fiction elements continued to reflect Cold War concerns. A doppelgänger theme became a recurring plot motif throughout the series' final seasons, with the *Seaview* crew either facing evil versions of themselves or facing other crew members who had in some way become possessed by an outside presence, thus altering their thoughts and behavior. This sort of possession story is of course a staple of science fiction but became particularly prominent during the Cold War, when it became a perfect metaphor for Soviet subversion. The doubles that viewers see on the *Seaview*, whether actual duplicates or the genuine crew members in a possessed state, are cold, disloyal, and incapable of thinking for themselves. In other words, these doubles have all the disagreeable characteristics that Americans attributed to Communists, and they can be seen as representing Americans who were converted into Communists.

The first of the "double" stories, season two's "The Cyborg," in many ways set the tone for the other such episodes to follow. Certainly it is appropriate that the double in this case be a robot, as a robot not only echoed viewers' fears that they might someday become mechanical in their behavior, but also represented fears of technology that was misused by enemies. A scientist named Tabor intends to use his cyborgs to create a "one world government"; he believes that the cyborgs are perfect for running such a government because, unlike humans, they are not motivated by love, hate, or friendship. As part of his plan, the scientist intends to use the *Seaview* to launch a nuclear attack — to accomplish this, he kidnaps Nelson and replaces him with a cyborg. The scientist and Nelson have some revealing discussions about the merits — or flaws — of the unemotional cyborgs. When told that the cyborgs are superior to humans, Nelson replies, "Mechanically, you mean." The evil scientist acknowledges, "Well, they've never written a sonnet." The rogue scientist is himself particularly interesting.[16] His name, Tabor, is very close to "robot" spelled backwards, indicating, perhaps, his disaffection from humankind. "Cyborg" ends when one of the cyborgs develops emotions and helps Nelson; Tabor is killed. At the conclusion, Nelson notes that emotions can be both a human's greatest strengths and weaknesses.

Over the next three seasons, the crew of the *Seaview* would be taken over by aliens in the episodes "Monster from Space" and "Shadowmen" and by a sea creature in "The Creature." Nelson was possessed by an alien in "Day of Evil," as was Crane in "The Deadly Cloud." Duplicates of the crew would appear in "Deadly Dolls" and "The Wax Men." The latter seems particularly relevant to the Cold War as it presented Crane, the only crew member who had not been replaced by a double, as fighting for freedom against the sinister duplicates. The series even featured two tales of supernatural possession as a ghost attempted to take over the body of Admiral Nelson in "The Phantom Strikes" and "The Return of the Phantom." Significantly, the ghost was the spirit of a German U-boat commander. Although World War I–era Germans did not pose a genuine threat to Americans in the 1960s, East Germans were certainly seen as enemies. In each of these episodes the crew of the *Seaview* persevered and individualism triumphed, either because the possessed characters asserted themselves and regained their personalities or because they fought and overcame the duplicates who would usurp their rightful place.

As frequent as the doppelgänger stories were, they were not as common as the monster stories that the program began to rely on in the second season. But even the monster stories, while usually devoid of espionage, still reflected Cold War concerns. Giant creatures are in fact another staple of science fiction in post–World War II America. The giant creatures seen in many science fiction films — and with increasing frequency on *Voyage to the Bottom of the Sea*— were usually the result of some sort of encounter with radiation and can be interpreted as the embodiment of viewers' fears of nuclear war. The *Seaview*'s first encounter with such a monster actually occurred during the first season, and the show explicitly states that the monster is the result of a scientific experiment gone awry. In "The Village of Guilt" a scientist has been using an extract from the pituitary gland to experiment on sea life in the hopes of creating enormous creatures that could be slaughtered and used to feed the entire planet. Thus, the *Seaview* encounters a school of catfish bigger than small boats that were produced by these experiments. But one creature has gotten out of control and killed three men; it is up to Admiral Nelson to bring the experiment to an end. This episode is a fairly typical science fiction cautionary tale warning that humanity must not interfere with nature. Another first season episode, "The Amphibians," would make the same point a bit more strongly by having its scientists experiment on humans. Subsequent episodes would not offer a scientific explanation for the existence of the threatening creatures; they would simply arrive and pose a threat to the *Seaview*. This lack of explanation actually strengthened the episodes in certain ways by adding to their sense of paranoia; if audiences did not know exactly why these creatures existed, then they had to assume that these monsters could attack at any time or any place — much like a nuclear weapon.

The series understandably has a more ambivalent attitude towards aliens than towards monsters, since its aliens are more intelligent and therefore capable of rational behavior. Unfortunately, as any science fiction fan knows, that rational behavior does not necessarily preclude the aliens posing a threat to Earth. *Voyage to the Bottom of the Sea* presented several episodes with alien characters, most of which had titles like "The Heat Monster" or "Deadly Invasion," and centered on alien beings as menaces. Occasionally, however, an alien would be, if not friendly to Earth, at least not hostile either. In "The Sky Is Falling," an alien's ship has crash landed on Earth and needs to refuel. Nelson attempts to assist the alien while the military prepares to attack it. This episode stands with "Hot Line" as one of the few pacifist episodes broadcast during the series' run.

Despite, or perhaps due to these types of imaginative episodes, the show's audience was decreasing, and *Voyage to the Bottom of the Sea* was cancelled at the end of its fourth season. It was just one of many science fiction and/or espionage programs to leave the airwaves that year; audience tastes had changed and escapist television shows undergirded by anxiety about foreign threats were now out of favor, replaced by programs that had more social relevance. After launching *Land of the Giants*, producer Allen largely moved on from the science fiction genre, becoming famous for his disaster movies in the 1970s.

Today, most discussions of influential television series of the 1960s do not dwell on *Voyage to the Bottom of the Sea*, if it is mentioned at all. But for four years, years in which America itself went through some astonishing changes, the *Seaview* was a constant presence on television. The show, week in and week out, told audiences exactly what they wanted to hear — that there was a foreign enemy abroad, that the nation was strong, and that science could be their salvation.

Notes

1. Displaying the sort of precision that series fans had long come to expect from the crew of the *Seaview*, *Voyage to the Bottom of the Sea* ran almost exactly four years to the day, premiering on September 14, 1964, and airing its last episode on September 15, 1968.

2. Also, three series set during World War II — *Combat*, *McHale's Navy*, and *Twelve O'Clock High* — may have lacked science fiction elements but certainly shared *Voyage to the Bottom of the Sea*'s respect for the fighting capability of the military and its habit of questioning the efficacy of military procedure.

3. *Voyage to the Bottom of the Sea*, DVD, directed by Richard Fleischer and Irwin Allen (1961; 20th Century–Fox Home Entertainment, 2003).

4. Gary Gerani, *Fantastic Television* (New York: Harmony Books, 1977), 63.

5. Jon Abbott, *Irwin Allen Television Productions, 1964–1970* (Jefferson, NC: McFarland, 2006), 11.

6. *The Fantasy Worlds of Irwin Allen*, Van Ness Films, 1995.

7. See episode 10, "Submarine Sunk Here."

8. *The Fantasy Worlds of Irwin Allen*.

9. The fact that the family on *Lost in Space* is named Robinson has caused many to see it as a sort of science fiction version of *Swiss Family Robinson*, and in 1975 Allen actually did produce a *Swiss Family Robinson* television series for ABC.

10. Even when the characters are taken someplace against their will — echoing Allen's other series, Crane and another crew member find themselves lost on Venus in one episode and the entire crew travels back in time to the Revolutionary War in another — they do not remain stranded but find a way to return home.

11. Abbott, 20.

12. The film's script was followed more closely in the series' fiftieth episode, titled "The Sky's on Fire," which credited the motion picture screenplay as its source.

13. Abbott, 23.

14. tv.com/voyage-to-the-bottom-of-the-sea.

15. Abbott, 12.

16. The villains on *Voyage to the Bottom of the Sea* are often depicted as somewhat decadent, and this character certainly falls into that category; as portrayed by the corpulent

actor Victor Buono, he always dresses in solid white, is constantly eating, and may be the first villain in television history to be shown drinking Perrier.

BIBLIOGRAPHY

Abbott, Jon. *Irwin Allen Television Productions, 1964–1970.* Jefferson, NC: McFarland, 2006.
The Fantasy Worlds of Irwin Allen. DVD. Directed by Kevin Burns. 1995. Van Ness Films, 2000.
Gerani, Gary. *Fantastic Television: A Pictorial History of Sci-Fi, the Unusual and Fantastic from* Captain Video *to the* Star Trek *Phenomenon and Beyond.* New York: Harmony Books, 1977.
tv.com. http://www.tv.com/voyage-to-the-bottom-of-the-sea.
Voyage to the Bottom of the Sea. DVD. Directed by Richard Fleischer and Irwin Allen. 1961. 20th Century–Fox Home Entertainment, 2003.

3

Looking Glass War
The Topsy-Turvy World of The Prisoner

BRYAN E. VIZZINI

> PRISONER: *Has it ever occurred to you that you're just as much a prisoner as I am?*
> NUMBER 2: *My dear chap, of course, I know too much. We're both Lifers. I am definitely an optimist, that's why it doesn't matter who Number 1 is....It doesn't matter which side runs the Village.*
> PRISONER: *It's run by one side or the other.*
> NUMBER 2: *Oh certainly, but both sides are becoming identical. A perfect blueprint for World Order. When the sides facing each other suddenly realize that they're looking into a mirror, they'll see that this is the pattern for the future.*
> —"The Chimes of Big Ben" (season one, episode two)

For seventeen swiftly paced episodes in 1967–68, *The Prisoner* challenged the official version of the Cold War to a degree unparalleled in television before or after its brief run. While the competition—in England, *The Avengers* and *The Saint*; in America, *The Man from U.N.C.L.E.*, *Mission: Impossible*, and *The Wild, Wild West*—remained true to the norms of the spy genre and to the conformist narratives forged in the post-war period, *The Prisoner*, as pop culture expert Chris Gregory has argued, deconstructed both, offering in their stead an alternative geopolitical narrative that eschewed Manichean platitudes and calls for conformity.[1] Moreover, as the series drew to a close, *The Prisoner* delivered an uncompromising indictment of viewers' collective assumptions and the Orwellian mechanisms by which they had been instilled and maintained—to wit, the medium of television itself. The show's concept was straightforward. Patrick McGoohan played a former British intelligence agent whose sudden resignation triggered his kidnapping and imprisonment in a place known only as The Village. There, stripped of their names and known only by their assigned numbers, McGoohan (Number 6) and his counterparts sought answers to the most basic of questions. Who, or which side, oversaw The Village? Who was the mysterious off-screen Number 1, and what was his/her/its agenda? Who could be trusted?

Number 6 was hardly alone in asking questions. Each week, his captors relentlessly grilled him in the effort to discover why precisely he had resigned. And, each week, Number 6 struggled to escape his captors, only to find himself still imprisoned at episode's end, a point that the closing sequence (barred gates slamming shut in front of McGoohan) punctuated. So much for moral clarity and happy endings!

For nearly two decades previously, film (and later television) had peddled the Establishment line of the Cold War as an epic struggle between good and evil, on one level, and cooperation and nonconformity on another.[2] Whether as a carefully calculated response to the intense political scrutiny that culminated with the Alger Hiss and Julius Rosenberg trials, the Hollywood Ten hearings, and the Army-McCarthy Hearings, or a cynical attempt to capitalize on them (or both), the 1950s and early 1960s entertainment industry routinely exploited popular fears of enemies living both outside and inside one's national borders. The depiction of domestic nonconformity (political and sexual) as an ideological and material threat all too often served as ammunition for those who sought to rationalize the invasion of privacy and violation of civil liberties, ironically reflecting George Orwell's stark warnings regarding precisely such behavior in his contemporary masterpiece *1984*.[3] Perhaps the spy genre's embrace of anti-communist and/or conformist motifs throughout the 1950s (and, to a much lesser extent, the 1960s) is fitting, then, given Toby Miller's argument that spying is an inherently undemocratic (even Orwellian) undertaking.[4] Not until *The Prisoner* would television producers dare to make that point.

Mid-1960s film and television spy dramas, to be sure, marked a shift away from the heavy-handed black and white world of their predecessors, but their increasing emphasis on humor, science fiction, and satire — most notably in TV programs like *Get Smart* and *The Avengers*— only reinforced the pop culture industry's reluctance to challenge directly the assumptions underlying the official story, especially on the small screen.[5] Enter *The Prisoner*. When Patrick McGoohan first pitched his idea for a bold new television spy drama to ITV head Lew Grade in 1966, he brought considerable capital to the meeting. At the time McGoohan was the highest paid actor in British television and star of the network's immensely popular *Danger*

Man (a.k.a. *Secret Agent Man*). Even so, McGoohan's dark tale of an unknown agency imprisoning retired intelligence agents in an escape proof village (filmed entirely at one location no less) hardly boded well for a genre in which audiences had become accustomed to exotic locales, heroes with Houdini-like escape skills, and a fairly clear view of what distinguished the good guys from the bad. McGoohan's international star appeal notwithstanding, *The Prisoner* was a tough sell.

While Grade allegedly concluded that it was "so crazy, it might work," the concept's success arguably owed more to a specific confluence of timing, location, and need than it did to Grade's gut feeling. By 1966, unpopular conflicts in Vietnam, Burma, Algeria, and elsewhere had done much to sour popular attitudes toward authority and the government. Protest movements proved especially strong in England and France, and within a few years would dominate U.S. politics as well. The ideology of revolution, the antithesis to conformity, similarly proved appealing to those at odds with their governments' policies at home and abroad. Moreover, John Frankenheimer's *Manchurian Candidate* and *Seven Days in May*, along with Stanley Kubrick's *Doctor Strangelove*, already had proved that challenging the conventional Cold War wisdom could prove successful with critics and profitable with audiences.[6] In short, by the late 1960s the timing was right for *The Prisoner* to challenge authority and conformity on the small screen.

That *The Prisoner* was essentially a British production, Wesley Britton contends, was no accident either. British culture in general, and television in particular, reflected sensibilities quite different from those of their American counterparts.[7] Whether as a result of England's front-line position in both world wars, the realization that Soviet missiles would strike London long before reaching Washington, or simply a heightened sense of realism when it came to the gritty nature of conflict, British writers like John Le Carré generally offered a far darker (and less black and white) view of the Cold War.[8] If a show like *The Prisoner* stood any chance of reaching production, it would be in England, not America.[9]

Finally, as the network executive in charge, Grade faced a real dilemma. Two episodes into the 1966 season, lead actor Patrick McGoohan, in an interesting case of art imitating life, had resigned from *Danger Man*.[10] At the very moment that *Danger Man*, along with *The Avengers* and *The Saint*, had begun to resonate with American audiences, the prospective time slot (on both sides of the Atlantic) stood empty. Simply put, without McGoohan onscreen, Grade and the network were losing money. Gambling that McGoohan's presence alone might transform financial loss into financial gain, Grade may well have decided to roll the dice. Besides, if *The Prisoner* proved to be a disaster, he could always pull the plug.

Still, *The Prisoner*'s chances seemed good. The show had a bona fide star in McGoohan and, behind the scenes, former *Danger Man* director David Tomlin and writer George Markstein stood ready to continue in their earlier roles. The addition of *Avengers* director Don Chaffey rounded out McGoohan's dream team and production began in December 1966.

"Arrival," the series' first episode, aired in October 1967 and set the tone for all that would follow. The title sequence, to be repeated for each of the subsequent sixteen episodes, provided the backstory. T*he Prisoner* opens as British intelligence agent McGoohan races his Lotus 7 sports car down the motorway and through the streets of London. After storming through the passageways of headquarters, he angrily slams a resignation letter on the desk of his superior (played by series writer and co-creator George Markstein). Viewers cannot hear what he says, but McGoohan is quite animated, gesturing righteously. He then races back to his apartment, followed in the distance by a hearse. Unnoticed, the hearse pulls up to the front of McGoohan's apartment just moments after the ex-agent's arrival. The driver steps up to the front door and sprays some sort of knockout gas through the keyhole. McGoohan, surprised in the midst of packing, succumbs, and awakes some time later amidst unfamiliar surroundings — The Village.

The Village's role as prison is readily apparent, even if chains and bars are nowhere in evidence. When McGoohan looks out upon the landscape surrounding him, he finds only open water and vast expanses of empty land. When he tries to make a phone call, The Village operator politely informs him that he may make local calls only. Finally, his meeting with the mysterious Number 2 confirms that he will not be leaving The Village anytime soon.

What does Number 2 and his equally nebulous superiors want? Why, information, old boy! In particular, Number 2 (and his endless chain of successors) wants to know exactly why McGoohan (now called Number 6) resigned. Number 6, as the following, oft-repeated (it appears in the title credits for the remainder of the series) exchange reveals, for his own part simply wants to know his captors' identity:

PRISONER: Where am I?
NUMBER 2: The Village...
PRISONER: What do you want?
NUMBER 2: Information...
PRISONER: You won't get it!
NUMBER 2: By hook or by crook, we will!

> PRISONER: Whose side are you on?
> NUMBER 2: That would be telling....[11]

This bit of dialog reaffirms the conventional Cold War narrative and yet begins the process by which *The Prisoner* will proceed to undermine its every assumption. Number 6 clearly thinks that Number 2 must represent *either* "Us" or "Them," and that his principal task is to discover which. While such black and white, either/or thinking certainly reflected the way the Establishment (and the mass media) portrayed the geopolitical situation — and, consequently, hardly challenged much of anything — the repartee between Number 2 and Number 6 offered hints of things to come, in particular the discomforting possibility that the story's protagonist is being held captive by his own side, what most pop cultural Cold War representations would have labeled (tritely perhaps) the "good guys."

Still, having been exposed to nearly twenty years of anti-communist propaganda, audiences might assume that the unseen jailors represented the other side. *The Prisoner* provides no such comfort. At the end of "Arrival," Number 6 confronts a new Number 2 over the tactics that led one of the prisoners to commit suicide:

> NUMBER 2: What we do here has to be done. It's the law of survival, it's either them or us.
> NUMBER 6: You imprison people, steal their minds, destroy them....
> NUMBER 2: It depends whose side you're on, doesn't it?
> NUMBER 6: I'm on your side.
> NUMBER 2: Then we'll have to find out where your sympathies lie....
> NUMBER 6: You know where they lie.
> NUMBER 2: Subject shows great enthusiasm for his work. He is utterly devoted and loyal. Is this a man that suddenly walks out?
> NUMBER 6: I didn't walk out. I resigned.
> NUMBER 2: People change, exactly. So do loyalties.

Number 6 already has concluded that his captors likely are from "our" side, not "theirs," and that in the quest for information, they are more than willing to drug, deceive, imprison, break, and ultimately kill. These actions hardly constitute bragging rights for organizations and governments that sought to distinguish themselves from an enemy they charged with precisely such offenses — a point to which *The Prisoner* would return in "The Chimes of Big Ben."

A fan favorite, and a key chapter in the ongoing development of *The Prisoner*, "The Chimes of Big Ben" shows Number 6's seemingly successful escape and return to London. Upon arriving, he immediately returns to headquarters to inform his former employers of a shadowy organization imprisoning former intelligence agents. However, the quotation that opens the episode suggests that the two sides have become virtually indistinguishable in their methods. "The Chimes of Big Ben" takes this point to its logical, albeit extreme, conclusion. In his meeting with his former director, Fotheringay, and another known only by his military rank of colonel, Number 6's unease grows:

> NUMBER 6: Are you sure you haven't got a village here?
> COLONEL: Where is the Village?
> NUMBER 6: Lithuania, on the Baltic. Thirty miles from the Polish border.
> COLONEL: How did you find out?
> NUMBER 6: Nadia told me.
> COLONEL: How did she know?
> NUMBER 6: She worked for their government ... she came across a secret file....
> COLONEL: On how to catch a spy in six lessons.
> NUMBER 6: I risked my life and hers to come back here because I thought it was different ... it is, isn't it, isn't it different?

The episode's climax begins with Number 6 prepared to explain why he resigned. No sooner does he begin to speak than he hears Big Ben chime eight times in the background. Glancing at his watch, a gift from an apparent confederate in Poland, Number 6 notices that it too is set to eight o'clock despite what should have been a one hour time difference — wherever he is, it is not London and, likely, not even Poland. Sure enough, when Number 6 springs forward and opens a nearby cabinet, he discovers a tape recorder playing background noise of London. Number 6 is still in The Village. The episode closes with Fotheringay being sent away, perhaps to London for his next assignment. Already having challenged the most conventional of narrative assumptions through its suggestion that neither side had a monopoly on dirty tricks and bad behavior, with this episode *The Prisoner* had just taken a particularly radical turn. The two sides now appeared to be working together in *disappearing* their own operatives — a notion that even fans of John Le Carré and *Danger Man* (both of which had begun to explore the earlier possibility of the two sides being more alike than different) would have found shocking.[12]

If, as *The Prisoner* suggested, the chief conflict lay not between East and West, communism and democracy, where did it lie? McGoohan argued that the principal struggle in society was one between conformity and individualism. Proponents of the official narrative similarly saw this particular struggle as a front line in the ongoing confrontation. The difference lay in McGoohan's contention that conformity, not individualism, posed the greatest threat to Western values and that, paradoxically, this very quest for conformity was responsible for the increasing similarities between the two sides in the Cold War.[13]

Having dismissed traditional geopolitical explanations of conflict as illusory, *The Prisoner* subsequently spent much of its run indicting society's emphasis on conformity as the principal means for maintaining just such an illusion. This subject featured prominently in the episodes "Free for All" and "Dance of the Dead," challenging the very essence of traditional "family programming" with its emphasis on conformity to social and political mores that characterized contemporary shows like *Father Knows Best, The Adventures of Ozzie and Harriet,* and *Leave It to Beaver*.[14] "Free for All" provides an especially damning portrait of conformity, freedom, and the democratic process. In the heroes and villains, black and white world of conventional Western Cold War narratives, democratic principles are the antithesis to the political values that uphold the communist state. McGoohan, who wrote the episode, maintains his earlier contention that the two sides are, in fact, more or less identical in their behavior. In democratic societies, he argues, political ritual serves as just another means of instilling and enforcing conformity, one that ultimately results in the same lack of political freedom that characterized the Eastern bloc societies.

The episode begins with the new Number 2 urging Number 6 to run for the office of Number 2 in The Village. "There is," he notes, "a lack of opposition in the matter of free elections. This is not good for our community and reflects an acceptance of things as they are." Number 6 accepts the challenge, running on a platform of "Free, for all."

McGoohan devotes the remainder of the episode to casting democracy as nothing more than a puppet show, its "strings" visible from the very start. Village photographers and journalists manipulate interviews and campaign speeches to produce the messages, issues, and quotes already printed in their news organs. Crowds of enthusiastic supporters follow Number 6 everywhere, their applause drowning out his words. They applaud anything that he utters, even when he angrily charges that most of them will remain in The Village until they die "like rotten cabbages." The seemingly enthusiastic participation of Village inhabitants *en masse* at the debates and public speeches reaffirms the democratic process as both all-inclusive and harboring the real possibility of change. Or does it?

On Election Day, Number 6's ballot box fills to overflowing. Unfortunately, Number 6's celebration is cut short. In what fast is becoming a staple of the series, Number 2 orders Number 6 drugged. Upon awakening in Number 2's control room, Number 6 rushes to the microphone to address his would-be constituents. What he discovers is complete and total apathy. He "won" the election, but Number 2 continued to hold power and everyone in The Village simply returned to going about his or her business. The Village's democratic process was the greatest farce of them all, a grand showing of conformity in which every member of the community, long conditioned to cooperate and conform, willingly participated. The electoral process was no longer a means to an end; it had become an end in itself. If the villagers were indeed prisoners, as the program contends, they were complicit in their own imprisonment. The episode concludes with Number 6 receiving a savage beating at the hands of Village guards — one of the few instances where Number 6 suffers violence at the hands of his captors — perhaps a warning to those who seek true change and freedom.

"Dance of the Dead" takes the message a step further, exploring the extent to which an individual's freedom of choice can conflict with society's demands for conformity and suggesting that the point is a moot one, the latter already having vanquished the former. The episode begins with Number 6 receiving an invitation to a Village dance and carnival. As he watches other Villagers prepare for the upcoming festivities, Number 6 receives a visit from Number 2 that sets the tone for the story about to unfold:

> NUMBER 2: You've got your invitation for the Carnival tomorrow…. You'll come.
> NUMBER 6: I have a choice?
> NUMBER 2: You'll do as you want.
> NUMBER 6: As long as it's what you want.
> NUMBER 2: As long as it's what the majority wants. We're democratic in some ways.

True to form, Number 6, already determined to exercise his freedom of choice by not attending, seeks to persuade others to do the same. Shortly after his conversation with Number 2, he addresses a young lady:

> NUMBER 6: Don't go.
> GIRL: I must.
> NUMBER 6: There's a reason?
> GIRL: Reason?

The episode continues in this vein. After secluding himself in his apartment in frustration, Number 6 receives an unexpected delivery of flowers.

> NUMBER 6: Supposing I don't want any flowers.
> DELIVERY MAN: Everybody has flowers. For carnival tomorrow. Be seeing you.

So it goes. The unexpected flowers are just the first such occurrence. Shortly thereafter, his maid presents him with a package containing his carnival attire.

NUMBER 6: Don't I get a choice?
MAID: Other people choose. It's a game.

Ultimately, Number 6 attends, if for no other reason than the carnival affords Number 6 access to the otherwise forbidden Town Hall and its levers of power. Upon noticing that all the other Village inhabitants are dressed in expressive regalia, Number 6 asks why he is the only person present without a costume. In a particularly telling, and chilling, remark, Number 2 responds, "Perhaps because you don't exist."

The carnival celebrations climax with a surreal scene in which Village members dressed as kings and generals conduct a mock trial, charging Number 6 with murder. In the trial and its aftermath — the "judges" find Number 6 guilty and sentence him to death, which in this case simply means chasing him hysterically throughout The Village. This episode, thus, reaffirms that, in The Village at least, all life is a stage, and all people actors simply playing their pre-assigned roles.

The Prisoner made abundantly clear its thesis that conformity undermined, rather than upheld, such traditionally Western concepts as free will, choice, and self-determination. By the standards of mid-to-late-1960s film and television, this was pretty radical. Not until the early 1970s would the anti-hero — Billy Jack, Dirty Harry, Popeye Doyle, Serpico, and others — transform nonconformity into a virtue on a more or less regular basis. Even the counterculture classic *Easy Rider*, the archetypical tale of nonconformity and anti-heroes, did not appear until 1969.

The Prisoner subsequently featured two back-to-back episodes that pushed the conformity issue ever further. "Living in Harmony" and "The Girl Who Was Death" refused to conform even to the narrative structure and conventions *The Prisoner* itself had established. As noted earlier, *The Prisoner*'s willingness to challenge authority and conformity so overtly onscreen was borderline revolutionary, at least within the confines of the proverbial box. In a move that would prefigure post-modernism, *The Prisoner* now stepped outside the confines of the box.

"Living in Harmony" transfers *The Prisoner* from the realm of spy dramas to that of the Western (nearly nine months before the similarly styled *Star Trek* episode "Specter of the Gun" moved the *Enterprise* crew to the O.K. Corral). The episode opens with Number 6 riding his horse, in full cowboy attire. The title credits, for once, do not appear and The Village is nowhere to be seen. Rather, the episode takes place within the confines of a stereotypical Western town replete with saloons, jails, and the like.

While the setting has changed, key components of the story have not.

Within minutes of its opening, the episode follows Number 6 as he rides into town, storms into the jail, and angrily throws his sheriff's badge on the desk. He then departs the jail and begins to ride across the great wide Western opens. In the distance, a gang of men dressed in black give pursuit. They overtake and beat Number 6 unconscious. He awakes in a strange town where a Mexican promptly greets him.

> MEXICAN: Welcome to Harmony, stranger!
> NUMBER 6: Harmony? Never heard of it.
> MEXICAN: Not many people have señor. It's sorta expensive.
> NUMBER 6: So am I. Where is this town?
> MEXICAN: You'll find out señor, it's wise not to ask too many questions.

Sound familiar? For its duration, "Living in Harmony" transposes elements of the classic *Prisoner* formula into a format readily familiar to viewers of the ubiquitous Western television dramas. In the town saloon, Number 6 meets the Judge, who immediately asks Number 6 why he resigned his position as sheriff. "What were your reasons?" the Judge asks. "My reasons?" Number Six replies. The remainder of the episode revolves around the Judge trying to persuade Number 6 to take up the badge and gun again. Number 6 eventually takes the badge but refuses the gun. Only after a gunfighter known as "The Kid" strangles a young barmaid, does Number 6 break down, going off to confront the murderer in traditional Western style. Still, while he takes his gun to the showdown, he very pointedly leaves behind his badge. The episode climaxes as viewers accustomed to television Westerns would expect, with a duel between Number 6 and "The Kid," followed by a gunfight with the Judge and his henchmen. The dust settles, only to reveal Number 6 in Village attire, his adversaries similarly clothed. The town of Harmony exists as a series of cardboard cutouts. Number 6 is still in The Village. The coda explains that Number 6's Western adventure was the latest attempt to break him, this time through a drug-induced hallucination.

"Living in Harmony" had the distinction of being the only *Prisoner* episode banned in the U.S. during the series' initial run. The official explanation was that the U.S. networks dropped the episode due to concerns over the use of mind-altering drugs. Given the number of earlier episodes that prominently featured Village pharmaceuticals, the more likely reason is Number 6's ongoing refusal to pick up his badge and gun — i.e., to serve — a message of particular political sensitivity in the Vietnam War era.[15]

Just as "Living in Harmony" opens in an unfamiliar fashion, so too does "The Girl Who Was Death," which begins with the opening of what appears to be a children's book. Cut to Number 6, again in a setting outside The Village, this time in ordinary clothing, attending a cricket match with former *Danger Man* confederate Agent Potter. The initial implication is that Number 6 either has returned to his former life, his escape from The Village taking place entirely off screen, or that he is reliving events that took place prior to his resignation. In typical *Prisoner* fashion, the reality is far, far more complicated.

The episode shifts gears quickly, changing the plot and setting from one closely resembling that of *Danger Man* to one more akin to that of *The Avengers* or *The Wild, Wild West*. A comely blonde who identifies herself as Death (we soon learn that her name is Sonia) leads Number 6 on a merry old chase, from a relatively mundane pub to the Tunnel of Love at a local amusement park to a Turkish bath (with Number 6 in Sherlock Holmes attire no less) to a high-speed car chase in the British countryside. Every step of the way, Sonia taunts Number 6, offering such choice observations as "I love the way your hair curls on the back of your neck. You'll make a beautiful corpse." Number 6, for his part, departs from form in a big way, engaging each new absurd challenge with a sly grin and with tongue firmly in cheek. Gone, for the moment at least, is the brooding anti-hero.

Eventually Sonia lures Number 6 into a deserted village where she attacks him with a machine gun, mortar, and grenades. Ever resourceful, Number 6 escapes courtesy of a conveniently placed bulldozer and an even more conveniently placed manhole. Finally, Number 6 follows Sonia to an isolated lighthouse that serves as a base of operations for her deranged father, who dresses like Napoleon and calls himself the Emperor. Sonia and the Emperor plan to unleash death upon London in the form of a missile cleverly concealed in the lighthouse itself. After setting a trap for his adversaries, Number 6 makes good his own escape and watches as the rocket explodes upon takeoff, presumably killing both Sonia and the Emperor.

Abruptly, the scene changes. Number 6, back in The Village, sits with a group of children and closes the book that viewers last saw just after the opening credits. "And that," he concludes, "is how I saved London from the mad scientist." The entire episode stands revealed as a series of nods and winks to various other spy programs, contained all the while within the broader rubric of a fairy tale, itself imbedded in the context of Number 6's ongoing rebellion against his Village captors.

"Living in Harmony" and "The Girl Who Was Death" succeeded in calling attention to, and then erasing, somewhat tenuous distinctions between seemingly disparate genres. Westerns and the spy dramas alike shared a formula rooted in the geopolitical dualism (good guys versus bad guys) that *The Prisoner* had tackled from the very first episode. The Kid and the Judge prove virtually interchangeable with media stereotypes of the Soviets and their ilk — both are nemeses ideologically different from, and opposed to, Number 6 himself. Resolution may occur only with the hero vanquishing his opponents. "The Girl Who Was Death" suggests that even children's stories operate in much the same manner and from the same assumptions. Sonia and the Emperor are clear stand-ins for any number of Cold War stereotypes. Yet, they also can represent Number 2 and his retinue, a point made clear in the closing moments when viewers see that the Emperor and Sonia *are* Number 2 and his associate. The two episodes are not without irony. After all, on the most obvious level, Number 6 ultimately succumbs to conformity, playing the role that the underlying narrative structure assigns him. In "Living in Harmony," he takes up the gun and kills the bad guys. In "The Girl Who Was Death," he performs a similar duty. At no other point in the series does Number 6 so closely resemble the archetypical Cold War hero as in these two episodes. On another level, though, *The Prisoner* had reached a new high in nonconformity. "Living in Harmony" and "The Girl Who Was Death" represent a narrative breakthrough in the history of television. Viewers might change the channel or the program but, as *The Prisoner* now confirmed, the essential story remained the same. In making viewers cognizant of how a single basic storyline drives nearly all of their onscreen entertainment, *The Prisoner* has pulled back the curtain on the means by which popular culture often aids the Establishment in sustaining the social, political, and economic status quo.[16]

With both the box and the metanarrative it contains sitting in plain view, *The Prisoner* launched into a controversial two-part finale that would leave neither intact. The penultimate episode, "Once Upon a Time," does not so much break new ground as provide an overview of the series to date. Number 2 — the inimitable Leo McKern in an encore performance — attempts yet again to break Number 6, this time through hypnotic regression. In a succession of highly charged scenes, Number 2 and the omnipresent butler force Number 6 to relive formative episodes in his life, in the hopes that he eventually will reveal the reasons for his resignation. They will, of course, prove unsuccessful. To the extent that "Once Upon a Time" breaks any new ground, it does so through the sheer intensity of its acting. McKern and McGoohan turn in superb performances, the demands for which proved so high that, in another instance of life imitating art, McKern (like his character Number 2) suffered a heart attack during filming. Plotwise, the episode offers little that viewers have not seen before and simply serves as a bridge to the truly revolutionary "Fall Out."

The most surreal episode of the whole series, "Fall Out," opens with one of Number 2's underlings conceding the long struggle to Number 6, who, he notes, finally has earned the right to meet Number 1. Together with the butler, the trio proceeds down a long passageway to the accompaniment of the Beatles' "All You Need Is Love." The episode would grow only stranger. Number 6 enters a vast underground chamber made up to resemble Parliament. Robed and hooded figures, features hidden beneath black and white masks, bear placards identifying them only by their role in society—"Defectors," "Pacifists," "Reactionaries," etc. Number 6 sits on a throne facing the assembly while the "president" marks the opening of a trial of sorts. First up is Number 48, a ragtag young man charged with "the most serious breach of social etiquette—total defiance of the elementary laws which sustain our community, questioning the decisions of those who voted to govern us, unhealthy aspects of speech and dress not in accordance with general practice...." Next up is, surprisingly, Number 2 (again Leo McKern), last seen as the apparent victim of a heart attack during his final confrontation with Number 6. Number 2's subsequent monologue suggests that he represents the polar opposite of Number 48:

> NUMBER 2: It has been my lot, in the past, to wield a not inconsiderable power. Nay, I have had the ear of a statesman, kings and princes of many a land. Governments have been swayed, policies defined and revolutions nipped in the bud at a word from me in the right place and at the propitious time. Not surprising, therefore, that this community should find a use for me. Not altogether by accident that one day I should be abducted and wake up here amongst you.

The president momentarily confirms that Numbers 48 and 2 represent "the two forms of revolt. The first, uncoordinated youth rebelling against nothing it can define. The second, an established, successful, secure member of the Establishment turning upon and biting the hand that feeds him." Turning his attention to Number 6, the president notes, "At the other end of the scale we are honored to have with us a revolutionary of a different caliber. He has revolted. Resisted. Fought. Held fast. Maintained. Destroyed resistance. Overcome coercion. The right to be a Person, Someone, or Individual." The president turns to Number 6 and offers him his freedom. He asks only that Number 6 first take the stand and address the assembly. "I," Number 6 begins before the assembly drowns out his next words in a chorus of "Aye, aye, aye." The scene continues in this vein for several moments, reminiscent of Number 6's campaigning experience in "Free for All." The president finally silences the assembly and leads Number 6 to a chamber containing a large rocket. Inside the rocket Number 6 confronts another robed and hooded figure — the mysterious Number 1. Like the assembly members, Number 1's face remains hidden behind a black and white mask. Number 6 rips the mask from his face only to find another mask, that of a monkey. Incensed, Number 6 tears this mask away. The face leering maniacally back at him is none other than his own. Now things get downright unusual! After a brief chase, Number 1 locks himself away in the rocket's nosecone, leaving Number 6 to make good his escape. For once, though, he has allies. Toting submachine guns, the butler, Number 2, and Number 48 join Number 6 in a pitched gun battle with Village guards. Once again, "All You Need Is Love" pours from the omnipresent Village loudspeakers, in apparent juxtaposition to the unprecedented levels of violence consuming The Village. People lay dead, others flee, and, all the while, an ominous voice counts backward as the rocket prepares for liftoff. In a stolen truck, Number 6 and his allies lead the exodus from The Village, crashing through barred gates just as the rocket lifts into the sky, reducing all behind it to ash and cinder. Pedal to the floor, the truck winds out of the countryside and onto the motorway, Numbers 6, 2, and 48, in the bed of the truck, laugh, dance and sing "Dry Bones." The butler, alone at the wheel, remains ever silent. Back in London, the quartet part ways, Number 6 and the butler returning together to Number 6's residence.

Free at last? By now viewers should know that *The Prisoner* abhors easy answers. Parked in front of his residence is the Lotus 7 sports car, seen repeatedly in the series' opening credits. As Number 6 climbs in, we see another familiar vehicle approaching from behind — the black hearse, which slows before passing Number 6 and the butler, both of whom seem oblivious to its presence. The butler mounts the stairs, but before he can insert his key in the lock the door opens on its own, just like all the doors in The Village. Cut to Number 6 racing his Lotus down the motorway, the scene identical in every respect to the opening shot of the title credits. The end?

The Prisoner finale arguably raises as many questions as it answers. Number 6, to be sure, remains a nonconformist to the very end. And, as the assembly president concedes, Number 6's persistence has paid off — he has won. But the nature or meaning of his victory is anything but clear.

Prisoner fans argue to this day over the episode's meaning. More than a few, notably those expecting the clear and tidy conclusions to which they are accustomed, feel cheated. Is Number 1 really Number 6? (Viewers see Number 1's face for less than two seconds of screen time — blink and you miss it.) Does the appearance of the hearse and the image of Number 6 driving his Lotus suggest that Village authorities will once again snatch him, that Number 6, like Sisyphus, is doomed to repeat eternally a cycle of imprisonment and escape?[17] Does the opening of the automatic door (the house number "1" plainly visible) at his residence mean that he is still in The Village, or at least in *a* village?[18]

Its steady indictment of both the conventional Cold War narrative and its means of delivery notwithstanding, *The Prisoner* well might have saved its most ominous point for last. Confronted with a metanarrative woven into every social institution (government, schools, media, entertainment), members of society, *The Prisoner* suggests, subconsciously internalize the narrative and its underlying assumptions. Thus, for example, people without hesitation divide the world into two spheres, "us" and "them," good and evil. A more pernicious implication, though, is that in internalizing the narrative, citizens begin to police their own behavior, becoming their own captors. That Number 6 might be Number 1, and consequently complicit in his own imprisonment, is another one of many fairly obvious nods to Orwell's *1984*, where the lead character Winston lives in a society full of walls and bars, the dimensions and realities of which he himself helps to sustain. *The Prisoner* offers no easy solutions to these existential conundrums; it simply calls them to viewers' attention.

From a historical perspective, *The Prisoner* warrants attention for a number of reasons. *The Prisoner* broke with the then current convention and repeatedly took to task conventional Cold War assumptions in episodes like "Arrival," "Free for All," and "Dance of the Dead." With "The Chimes of Big Ben," where the two sides are revealed to be working as one, *The Prisoner* upended the prevailing narrative of the Cold War as a conflict between two ideological opposites. "Living in Harmony" and "The Girl Who Was Death," for their parts, revealed the extent to which the Establishment, the media, and pop culture work collectively to impart a single official narrative (or, in Toby Miller's words, a "ruling ideology") in the guise of various forms of programming. Viewers might think that they have a choice when they change the channel or pick up a newspaper. In reality, they do not. Whether they change the channel or not, viewers conform. Not until decades later would television programmers attempt to suggest anything so remotely risky.

The Prisoner is of historical significance for other reasons as well. The show's approach to narrative and meaning proved extremely cutting edge for the time (and remains so to this day). The very notion of a metanarrative, as well as the argument that the narrative and its assumptions were encoded in popular entertainment, drew heavily upon and even prefigured elements of post-modernism that would not become widespread in Anglo-American academia until the 1970s and 1980s. Roland Barthes' study of semiotics and popular culture, for example, would not be translated into English until 1972. Michel Foucault's *Discipline and Power*, which dealt in part with the notion that "language is oppression," did not appear until 1975. Jean Baudrillard's observations on media-created realities, for their part, appeared in English only in 1996.[19] Finally, *The Prisoner* is a classic example of pop culture's ability to serve as a historical text, providing revealing glimpses and insights into the world of 1967–68. From the widespread use of hypnotics and hallucinogens featured in many of the episode plotlines, to its general disdain for authority and conformity, to its ambivalence with respect to technology (which generally served to monitor and enforce), *The Prisoner* captured onscreen the political turmoil and angst that characterized the period out of which it emerged. Although the past may not repeat itself, it does live on, in *The Prisoner*.

Notes

1. Chris Gregory, *Be Seeing You: Decoding* The Prisoner (Bloomington: Indiana University Press, 1997).
2. See, for example, Teresa Alves, "'Some Enchanted Evening': Tuning in the Amazing Fifties, Switching Off the Elusive Decade," *American Studies International* (2001): 25–40; Tino Balio, ed., *The American Film Industry* (Madison: University of Wisconsin Press, 1985); Roger A. Berger, "'Ask What You Can Do for Your Country': The Film Version of H.G. Wells's *The Time Machine* and the Cold War," *Literature / Film Quarterly* (1989): 177–187; Peter Biskind, "Pods, Blobs, and Ideology in American Films of the Fifties," *Shadows of the Magic Lamp: Fantasy and Science Fiction in Film*, eds. Georg Slusser and Eric S. Rabkin (Carbondale: Southern Illinois University Press, 1985), 58–72; David Caute, *The Great Fear* (New York: Simon and Schuster, 1978); Ronald L. Davis, *Celluloid Mirrors: Hollywood and American Society Since 1945* (Fort Worth: Harcourt Brace College Publishers, 1997); Linda K. Fuller, "The Ideology of the 'Red Scare' Movement: McCarthyism in the Movies," *Beyond the Stars*, eds. Paul Loukides and Linda K. Fuller (Bowling Green, OH: Bowling Green University Popular Press, 1990), 229–248; Cyndy Hendershot, *Paranoia, the Bomb, and 1950s Science Fiction Films* (Bowling Green, OH: Bowling Green State University Popular Press, 1999); Daniel J. Leab, "How Red Was My Valley: Hollywood, the Cold War Film, and I Married a Communist," *Journal of Contemporary History* (January 1984): 59–88; Patrick Lucanio, *Them or Us: Archetypal Interpretations of Fifties Alien Invasion Films* (Bloomington: Indiana University Press, 1987); and Victoria O'Donnell, "Science Fiction Films and Cold War Anxiety," *Transforming the Screen, 1950–1959*, ed. Peter Lev (New York: Charles Scribner's Sons, 2003).
3. Michael Rogin, in his study of motherhood and domesticity in Cold War films, showed that from 1943 through 1964 filmmakers often equated strong-willed and/or inde-

pendent women and mothers with threats to the fabric of American society. Whether as seductresses (e.g., *Kiss Me Deadly*, 1955; *Jet Pilot*, 1957) or domineering wives and mothers capable of emasculating the men in their lives (e.g., *My Son John*, 1952; *The Manchurian Candidate*, 1962), women who strayed from the traditional norms American society had set for them either lead good men astray or raise sons too weak to avoid conscription into the ranks of domestic communists. See Michael Rogin, "Kiss Me Deadly: Communism, Motherhood, and Cold War Movies," *Representations* 6 (Spring 1984): 1–36.

4. Toby Miller, *Spyscreen: Espionage on Film and TV from the 1930s to the 1960s* (New York: Oxford University Press, 2003), vi.

5. Wesley Britton provides a clever, yet appropriate, description of such shows, referring to them as "Spy Fi." See Wesley Britton, *Spy Television* (Westport, CT: Praeger, 2004), 13.

6. See, for example, Jonathan Kirshner, "Subverting the Cold War in the 1960s: *Dr. Strangelove*, *The Manchurian Candidate*, and *The Planet of the Apes*," *Film & History* (2001): 40–44.

7. Ibid., 94.

8. Ibid.

9. Worth noting is Mark Bould's argument that *The Prisoner* is less the product of British, or any other national, sensibilities, than those of creator Patrick McGoohan. See Mark Bould, "This Is the Modern World: *The Prisoner*, Authorship, and Allegory," *Popular Television Drama*, eds. Jonathan Bignell and Stephen Lacey (Manchester: Manchester University Press, 2005).

10. Gregory, *Be Seeing You*.

11. All quotes are from the referenced episodes as reproduced on DVD by A&E.

12. Two particularly good examples are Le Carré's *The Spy Who Came In from the Cold* (both the novel and the film) and the *Danger Man* episode entitled "The Colony."

13. Chris R. Tame, "Different Values: An Analysis of Patrick McGoohan's *The Prisoner*," *Libertarian Alliance* (1983).

14. The family sitcom was hardly alone in its emphasis on conformity. Ever popular Westerns and crime dramas — *The Lone Ranger*, *Have Gun Will Travel*, *The Untouchables*, and *Gangbusters* to name but a few — monopolized airtime, and further etched in viewers' consciences the existence of a Manichean world in which obedience to authority (legal and social) was paramount.

15. Gregory, *Be Seeing You*, 147.

16. In a particularly insightful essay on pop culture, narratives, and the State, Toby Miller draws upon the theories of Michel Foucault, explaining that "storylines become the ruling ideology of a place and era." As such, they become key tools in the creation and manipulation of "reality." Entertainment is no longer simply entertainment; rather, it is part of the Orwellian machine so frighteningly depicted in *1984*.

17. This is the essence of Chris Gregory's argument — i.e., that *The Prisoner* is a cyclical tale, and one modeled on Joseph Campbell's mythic hero, who must endlessly repeat a pattern of separation, initiation, and return *ad infinitum*. See Gregory, *Be Seeing You*.

18. McGoohan himself has suggested as much, noting in one interview, "We all live in a little Village." He goes on to explain that The Village was an external symbol of something that lay within us all. Warner Troyer Interview, March 1977, reproduced at http://www.cultv.co.uk/mcgoohan.htm. Accessed 7 September 2007.

19. See Jean Baudrillard, *Simulacra and Simulation* (Ann Arbor: University of Michigan Press, 1996).

BIBLIOGRAPHY

Bould, Mark. "This Is the Modern World: *The Prisoner*, Authorship, and Allegory." In *Popular Television Drama*, eds. Jonathan Bignell and Stephen Lacey. Manchester: Manchester University Press, 2005.
Britton, Wesley. *Spy Television*. Westport, CT: Praeger, 2004.
Carraze, Alain, and Helene Oswald. The Prisoner: *A Televisionary Masterpiece*. London: Virgin, 2005.
Gregory, Chris. *Be Seeing You: Decoding* The Prisoner. Bloomington: Indiana University Press, 1997.
Miller, Toby. *Spyscreen: Espionage on Film and TV from the 1930s to the 1960s*. New York: Oxford University Press, 2003.
Rakoff, Ian. *Inside* The Prisoner. Somerset: Butler and Tanner, 1998.
Tame, Chris R. "Different Values: An Analysis of Patrick McGoohan's *The Prisoner*." *Libertarian Alliance* (1983).
White, Matthew, and Jaffer Ali. *The Official* Prisoner *Companion*. New York: Grand Central, 1988.

4

The Limits of *Star Trek*'s Final Frontier
"The Omega Glory" and 1960s American Liberalism

ALLAN W. AUSTIN

Americans found themselves and their country at a crossroads in 1968. Confronted by Cold War conflict abroad and intensifying social upheaval at home, historian William Chafe argues that Americans struggled in 1968 to discern what common identity — if any — held them together as a community. A vexing question throughout the history of the United States, Americans found the issue of identity further complicated in the late 1960s by growing opposition to the misbegotten war in Vietnam and increasing criticism about how unsuccessful the nation had been in applying the ideals of the Constitution to all Americans, especially minorities and women. Framed by the Cold War, these debates seemed to be tearing the American polity apart.[1]

Gene Roddenberry and his collaborators produced the *Star Trek* television series as this cultural crisis climaxed. Roddenberry had chosen the genre of science fiction, in fact, because he hoped it would allow him to address pressing social issues, including the gap between ideals and the American reality, from a liberal perspective.[2] Science fiction, in theory, allowed *Star Trek*'s makers to imagine any future they wanted; in reality, however, the society and culture of the late 1960s decisively shaped and limited their imagination. As a result, despite the good intentions of the series, *Star Trek* ultimately reflected the limits of liberalism in the late 1960s. While the show suggested that at least some progress had occurred, it also demonstrated the continuing hold of long-established stereotypes and the difficulty that most Americans had in imagining a future of peace and true equality.

"The Omega Glory" and the U.S. in 1968

The makers of *Star Trek* attempted to solve the problems of the late 1960s by creating a better future just as Cold War anxiety peaked. Abroad, by 1968, long-simmering questions about the advisability and even viability of an interventionist foreign policy had reached a boil. The war in Vietnam reminded Americans daily of potential problems with the bipartisan global activism initiated by Harry S Truman and subsequently pursued, albeit in different ways, by Dwight D. Eisenhower, John F. Kennedy, and Lyndon B. Johnson. Indeed, the Tet Offensive at the start of the year exacerbated doubts about the Vietnam War when the enemy achieved substantial, if shortly held, military successes throughout the South. Coming just as Johnson and his generals had lauded significant progress in the war and promised "a light at the end of the tunnel," the Tet Offensive amplified the public's already significant distrust of the government. In the aftermath of Tet, more Americans worried that the U.S. was losing the Cold War competition with the Soviet Union in the Third World, while others began to question the proper role of the U.S. in world affairs.

At the same time that Americans' doubts about U.S. foreign policy grew, some activists involved in various 1960s reform movements became disillusioned with the possibility of accomplishing real social change from within the system as Americans, in the words of Chafe, "witnessed both the greatest triumphs — and the sharpest defeats — of postwar liberal democracy."[3] The civil rights movement, while certainly achieving important progress, had not eliminated racism, a reality highlighted by white, working-class anger directed at both African Americans and the liberal white establishment. In response, the civil rights movement accelerated its drift toward radical "black power." At the same time, the student movement peaked as more American youth expressed a deep sense of betrayal by the U.S. government. Simultaneously, a women's movement that had begun to build over the course of the decade (spurred on in part by discriminatory treatment within the civil rights and student movements) exploded into the national consciousness with the provocative protest of the Ms. America contest in Atlantic City.

A series of crises in 1968 further exacerbated the tensions among Americans while challenging "the very viability of their collective identity."[4] As distrust of the government grew, the assassinations of Martin Luther King, Jr., and Robert F. Kennedy added to the sense that change within the system was no longer possible. Johnson's decision not to run for reelection both shocked and relieved many Americans, but it did not calm national tensions, which peaked with the police riot at the Democratic National Convention in Chicago. According to historian Walter LaFeber, the national election that followed "exemplified, and helped climax, the most domestically dangerous, chaotic American era since the Civil War."[5] The madness of 1968 culminated with the election of Richard Nixon on a platform promising law and order, causing Americans to miss a real opportunity, Chafe concludes, for genuine social reform achieved from within the system.

Amid this broad turmoil, "The Omega Glory" debuted on March 1, 1968. While seemingly a trivial event in light of the wide crises engulfing the United States, this *Star Trek* episode assumes increased importance when examined as primary evidence of the broader culture that both produced and consumed it. Gene Roddenberry, the creator of *Star Trek* and author of "The Omega Glory," had in fact consciously decided to use television as a medium to explore contemporary political and social issues. In the process, Roddenberry not only critiqued contemporary American society but also "revitalized American myths by displacing them into a futuristic, quasi-scientific setting."[6]

A closer reading of "The Omega Glory" elucidates a tense moment in the U.S. past that intimately connected domestic and foreign policy as well as one liberal American response to the deep anxieties unleashed by the onset of the Cold War more than two decades earlier. Roddenberry clearly set out to highlight and critique contemporary American society, questioning what he saw as an increasingly mindless nationalism that blinded Americans to the dangers of technology and to problematic American relations with the rest of the world. In doing so, "The Omega Glory" reflected widely held concerns; its proposed solution also mirrored a popular liberal response to these problems that simultaneously included both progressive and reactionary elements. Rooted firmly in deep American anxieties and well-known liberal solutions, the episode implicitly suggested that, in order to overcome Cold War fears and to defeat the Soviet Union, Americans would have to embrace far-reaching cultural changes that elevated minorities and women to a status of equality in society. Despite such idealism, however, *Star Trek* in general, and "The Omega Glory" in particular, all too often relied on traditional and heavily stereotyped views of minority groups and women that marginalized and disempowered them. Roddenberry's muddled solution arose quite naturally from two decades of Cold War experiences and ideas, suggesting just how complicated and contested Cold War culture and society had become.

Roddenberry's solution pleased some but not all Americans. Many embraced what they saw as an optimistic view of a better world. Such sentiment later prompted NASA's decision to honor the *Star Trek* creator posthumously with a Distinguished Public Service Medal in 1993, citing his "service to the Nation and the human race in presenting the exploration of space as an exciting frontier and a hope for the future."[7] Others, however, expressed unhappiness with the marked shortcomings inherent in Roddenberry's view of the future. In particular, some African Americans and women noted the limitations of *Star Trek*'s vision. Despite Roddenberry's heartfelt belief in the need for change, his solutions unconsciously reflected the limits of liberal reform in the late 1960s. These constraints, apparent throughout American life, angered many minorities and women, who saw too little change and too much compromise in the solutions being offered by the white liberal establishment. Feeling betrayed even by white liberals who honestly wanted to help, both the civil rights and the women's movement radicalized in response to an unresponsive power structure.

Close examination of "The Omega Glory," then, reveals how Cold War anxieties foregrounded the issues of race and gender. Many American could understand, if only grudgingly in some cases, the need to reevaluate race, a key issue as the U.S. and Soviet Union competed for influence in the Third World. Similarly, many could also see gender inequalities that suggested that the U.S. had not lived up to its founders' lofty ideals of equality. But while some Americans undoubtedly wanted to change attitudes about race and gender, many too often simply retreated to the past and long-held stereotypes in only superficially reevaluating cultural norms. These solutions displeased some activists, and many not surprisingly turned to increasingly radical solutions. Understanding this complicated response, as highlighted by "The Omega Glory," thus helps us to better understand the cultural conflicts of the U.S. in the late 1960s. In particular it helps to showcase Chafe's fundamental questions about the Great Society: Could President Johnson's liberal programs embodied in the Great Society provide effective and realistic solutions to the nation's myriad problems? Were liberal values and methods consistent with liberal objectives?

Gene Roddenberry, Star Trek, and "The Omega Glory"

Although the show was clearly a collaborative effort, Gene Roddenberry represented the driving force behind *Star Trek*. Born in 1921, Roddenberry inherited his father's political outlook, which included a "hatred of Republicans."[8] While Roddenberry admired his father's love for his family, he struggled to reconcile that admirable quality with his father's deep intolerance for blacks and Jews. Rejecting his father's racism, Roddenberry voiced consistently progressive attitudes about race despite having been raised in a household devoted "to the values of the 'old' South."[9]

A fan of pulp magazines and the radio shows modeled on them, Roddenberry began to write stories that he sold to flying magazines while piloting a B-17 bomber during World War II. After a brief stint as a commercial pilot after the war, during which he continued to study writing, Roddenberry returned to Los Angeles in hopes of finding employment as a writer in the fledgling television industry. Unable to secure steady writing work, he joined the police department and spent much of his free time writing story treatments based on his colleagues' experiences for *Dragnet*. Through his affiliation with the Los Angeles Police Department (LAPD), Roddenberry also became first a technical advisor and then a full-time writer for *Mr. District Attorney*. Roddenberry resigned from the LAPD in 1956 to write full-time, and he eventually created and produced *The Lieutenant* (1963–1964), a short-lived series. As that show neared its conclusion, Roddenberry began to look for a new series and eventually came upon the idea of creating a "Wagon Train to the Stars," the concept which eventually led to *Star Trek*.[10]

By this stage in his career, Roddenberry knew that he wanted to use television to explore pressing social and political issues. Science fiction allowed him to do so and to bypass network censors, he explained in 1968, with "tales about important and meaningful things [including] politics, sex, economics, the stupidity of war, and half a hundred other vital subjects usually prohibited on television."[11] While Roddenberry clearly believed that one could only move ahead on "any ... controversial issue ... a little at a time," his liberal-humanist outlook decisively shaped his agenda.[12] Stressing political, social, racial, and gender equality based on individual worth and the capacity of human reason to solve problems, Roddenberry looked to a brighter future, although not without inconsistencies in his own thinking that he did not always clearly perceive or understand. Thus, Daniel Bernardi cogently argues, *Star Trek* was "inconsistent and contradictory," at times promoting the racism that it sought to denounce.[13] Still, whatever his shortcomings, it seems clear that Roddenberry honestly hoped that his epitaph would read, "He loved humanity."[14]

Roddenberry struggled to find network support for *Star Trek*. NBC eventually agreed to a pilot, but was both uneasy and interested enough to make the unusual request for a second pilot, after which it agreed to air *Star Trek*.[15] And so Roddenberry went to work, exploiting a western format that represented "the only indigenous mythic narrative of the white American" to produce a series that would help viewers imagine and ultimately, he hoped, build a better future.[16] The resulting show produced contradictory results that allow Joel Engel to praise *Star Trek* for envisioning "a future in which … racism and sexism do not exist" and yet also to criticize Roddenberry for betraying these ideals in his private life.[17]

"The Omega Glory" aired midway through *Star Trek*'s third and final year.[18] Originally written by Roddenberry as a potential second pilot for NBC, the show had been rewritten several times in attempts to overcome, according to one critic, being an implausible, "clumsy," and "heavy-handed parable."[19] Despite such criticism, Roddenberry clearly valued "The Omega Glory." In addition to writing it originally to sell the series to NBC, he later promoted it heavily to the network and even suggested that it be used to kick off a (never ordered) fourth season because it was "a smasheroo of an opening episode."[20]

Despite Roddenberry's enthusiasm, "The Omega Glory" offered a farfetched and relatively complicated story that began with the discovery of an abandoned starship, the *Exeter*, with only the dehydrated remains of its crew members in orbit around Omega IV. The landing party, including Kirk, Spock, and McCoy, soon discover that a deadly disease, with which they are now infected, has caused the carnage, and that they can survive only by beaming down immediately to Omega IV. On Omega IV, the landing party meets Ron Tracy, commander of the *Exeter*, who has sided with a group called the Khoms, clearly Asian in origin, against the savage Yangs, who Tracy notes are white. Tracy, who has violated the Prime Directive in helping the Khoms kill hundreds of attacking Yangs, soon takes the crew captive, throwing Kirk in jail with two primitive Yangs and forcing McCoy to work on a formula for a fountain of youth (as Khoms live impossibly long lives). After a long fight in jail with the Yang inmate, leader Cloud William, Kirk connects to him when he uses the word "freedom," which the Yang leader refers to as a "worship word."

The crew eventually discovers that bacteriological warfare had occurred on Omega IV, wiping out most of the population, and McCoy explains that the long lifespans of the Khoms resulted from the survival of the fittest principle kicking in after the war; he points out the folly of Tracy's attempt to find a fountain of youth, which would require destroying the world and hoping for the best in the aftermath. Kirk eventually pieces the mystery together, figuring out that the Khoms and Yangs had waged the total war that had been avoided on his earth. After winning a duel with Tracy to determine who is good and who is evil, Kirk educates the Yangs about where their "worship words" come from — the U.S. Constitution. He explains that the Yangs do not understand the meaning of the words and that the ideals contained in their holy document "must apply to everyone or they mean nothing." Although the Yangs do not fully understand, they promise to live by the words, at which point the crew leaves to let the Yangs (re)discover their history and, ultimately, liberty.[21]

Cold War Anxieties, Television Industry Realities, and "The Omega Glory"

A close reading of "The Omega Glory" highlights a number of deep-seated anxieties that had been developing in the U.S. since the end of World War II. Facing rapid and seemingly radical changes locally, nationally, and internationally, some Americans embraced *Star Trek* as a solution to their worries about nuclear catastrophe. Like most science fiction, *Star Trek* addressed contemporary social and cultural issues, and one fan even suggested in 1991 that the show had helped to prevent Armageddon. The fan, who had grown up "during the cold war, with the relentless dread of nuclear holocaust, ... believed that *Star Trek*'s vision of the future — at the time virtually unique in its optimism — had contributed to the world's survival."[22] Indeed, as the Cold War took shape and nuclear war threatened, Roddenberry had seen a similar connection between his series and a world riven with atomic anxieties, describing the basic message of *Star Trek* bluntly: "we must learn to live together or most certainly we will soon all die together."[23]

Roddenberry in fact always emphasized an optimism that underlay his exploration of American culture. While *Star Trek* clearly reflected Cold War tensions, it also suggested, according to M. Keith Booker, "a new sense of excitement and possibility linked to the oppositional political movements of [the 1960s]."[24] Indeed, believing that positive, exciting adventures lay ahead in a future where people ethically marshaled science to improve instead of threaten mankind's existence, *Star Trek* imagined a benevolent Federation based on the Prime Directive — never to interfere in the development of societies not as sophisticated as their own — instead of a colonizing power.²⁵

Roddenberry had to work in the television industry of the late 1960s, of course, and this reality limited what he might do with his series, his optimism notwithstanding. Prior to the mid–1960s, McCarthyism had affected the American media in far-reaching ways as its proponents sought to head off any message that they defined as subversive. The crusaders, historian Ellen Schrecker notes, convinced Hollywood to end its "brief flirtation with the real world and ensured that the fledgling television industry would never even begin one." Instead of socially conscious motion pictures, Hollywood sold dumbed-down films with "conservative, though less obviously political" messages that painted a simplistic world of good guys battling bad in westerns as well as an unthinking patriotism that did not have room for "blacks, workers, and uppity women."²⁶

Television, not surprisingly, was even more timid, having good reason to fear J. Edgar Hoover and his potential influence with the FCC. Furthermore, sponsors worried almost obsessively about avoiding any and all controversy. In this context, television programs "supported the status quo" with quiz shows that featured monetary success, westerns and cop shows that presented simple morality tales, and sitcoms that reinforced traditional gender roles. "Moreover," Schrecker concludes, "the conviviality that suffused [1950s television] programs trivialized the issues they dealt with and reinforced the notion that Americans had nothing to disagree about." These trends would carry over well beyond the era of McCarthy.²⁷

Television only began to consider addressing real social issues in the 1960s, when the threat of blacklisting and overly sensitive worries about viewer response began to decline.²⁸ Indeed, as blacklisting ended in the mid–1960s and at least some opening to address contemporary issues appeared, Roddenberry found himself, by chance, at a point when he could make the socially conscious shows that he wanted. He would become a pioneer of sorts, in fact, with his work on *Star Trek*.

In this context, "The Omega Glory" both consciously and unconsciously reflected a number of deep American anxieties that grew out of more than two decades of the Cold War. By the mid–1960s, some Americans began to critique what they saw as mindless nationalism. This unthinking patriotism had coalesced as part of a liberal consensus grounded in confidence in the essential soundness of American society as well as the assumption of a pervasive communist threat to the U.S. and its allies. Many supporters of the liberal consensus believed that economic growth and development would solve any remaining social inequalities while damping class conflict.[29]

The plot of "The Omega Glory" suggested that such a mindless nationalism had driven the U.S. far from its founding ideals. The episode insinuated, in fact, that McCarthyism had bastardized American ideals. As Kirk explains to Cloud William, he and his Yang tribesmen recite the words of the Constitution "badly, ... without meaning." The document, he explains, was not written for the elite, pointing to the "tall words" that introduce it: "We the People." He warns the Yangs that, although the Constitution had been written for "all the people," they had slurred its meaning over time. Importantly, given Roddenberry's call for a multicultural solution to Cold War anxieties, Kirk also stresses that the words must apply to the Khoms as well as the Yangs; if they do not, he argues, the words mean nothing.

In addition to concerns about mindless nationalism, overconfidence, and corruption, Americans worried about technology run amok. Such worries had emerged earlier in *Dr. Strangelove*, which contested the popular notion of science and technology as benevolent and progressive forces. Stanley Kubrick satirized the growing expert literature that analyzed U.S. nuclear policy and media reports that presented nuclear warfare as "acceptable, even tolerable" at the same time that one study estimated that 80 percent would die in an all-out nuclear exchange. Further, Kubrick examined the difficulties of men maintaining control over increasingly lethal technology, showing that they lacked the social, political, and moral capabilities to handle nuclear arsenals. Worrying that policymakers had failed to understand how nuclear weapons fundamentally changed that nature of warfare, Kubrick questioned "the 'progress' inherent in technology."[30]

Much like Kubrick, Roddenberry sensed a direct and ominous connection between mindless nationalism and the increasing dangers of technology. Indeed, the planet Omega IV stands as a symbol of the destructive capacity of science, the victim of a bacteriological war that could have, the crew notes, happened "foolish[ly]" on earth in the 1990s. Omega IV's war literally destroyed its civilization, and the tribes that survived had lost any sense of the high ideals that had shaped the U.S. and, in Roddenberry's science fiction vision, eventually the world and beyond.

In addressing such pressing anxieties, "The Omega Glory" suggested what Roddenberry believed to be a clear and equitable solution, although his presentation was in fact problematic. Many *Star Trek* fans, in the late

1960s and after, embraced what they saw as *Star Trek*'s vision of world without racism and sexism, which represented Roddenberry's basic solution to Cold War anxieties. Those who celebrate Roddenberry's vision of building a better country and world often go to extremes, one even arguing that *Star Trek*, "indirectly, has done more for civil rights and the space program than Martin Luther King, Jr. and John F. Kennedy."[31] While such praise overstates the case, Roddenberry clearly saw *Star Trek* as presenting a progressive liberal vision to win the Cold War: the U.S. could triumph by building a society free of racism and sexism.

"The Omega Glory" and Race

Many Americans by the late 1960s were promoting a similar message. Frightened by the Cold War and the intensifying battle for allies in the Third World, liberals increasingly considered civil rights an integral part of U.S. foreign policy. Government policy makers, in fact, had viewed civil rights as an important component of foreign policy for almost two decades by 1968. Historian Mary L. Dudziak has demonstrated that from 1946 to the mid–1960s key policy makers had "worried about the impact of race discrimination on U.S. prestige abroad," especially in Asia and Africa where negative perceptions could undermine American efforts to rally Cold War support. Thus, the government attempted to tell "a particular story about race and American democracy" that emphasized progress by showcasing how the American system made social justice possible. While change might come slowly in the U.S., government propaganda suggested, it still represented a better alternative than dictatorship.[32]

Dudziak persuasively demonstrates the continuity of such concerns for presidents, both Republican and Democrat, who served between 1946 and the mid–1960s. Aware of international outrage at racial discrimination in the U.S., Harry Truman directly connected civil rights to national security, most tellingly perhaps in his administration's arguments before the Supreme Court to overturn school segregation. Although presidents Eisenhower and Kennedy would have preferred to postpone civil rights action for various reasons, Dudziak contends, both found themselves pushed by events to act. In contrast, Johnson managed to pass important civil rights legislation that his predecessors had not, and this success, as well as the growing opposition to the Vietnam War, lessened the salience of civil rights for American foreign policy. Thus, Dudziak concludes, the United States Information

Agency reported in the mid–1960s that concerns over racial discrimination had "comparatively little effect on general opinion of the U.S."[33]

This clear sense of the direct connection between civil rights and foreign policy did not immediately disappear, however, when the government abandoned its effort to link the two. Instead, the linkage, established subtly over almost twenty years, continued to exist in U.S. popular culture. Perhaps not surprisingly, liberals like Roddenberry continued to support a similar message — that the U.S. could win the Cold War only by advancing civil rights at home — even after government officials had abandoned such an argument.

Roddenberry's attitude toward race, indeed, grew quite naturally out of these currents in American life, although he expressed it in even broader terms. "If there was one theme in all of *Star Trek*," he explained, "it was that the glory of our universe is its infinite combinations of diversity.... [A]ll beauty comes from diversity."[34] Roddenberry repeated such sentiments frequently when discussing *Star Trek*, often connecting his celebration of diversity with the desire to end the Cold War, arguing that intolerance could not exist in the 23rd century. "If man survives that long," he asserted, "he will have learned to take delight in the essential differences ... between cultures.... This infinite variation and delight, this is part of the optimism we built into *Star Trek*."[35] Roddenberry's liberal emphasis on the merits of diversity clearly influenced the series. As M. Keith Booker has argued, *Star Trek* showed that civilization meant "acceptance of racial difference" at the height of the civil rights movement.[36]

Star Trek, however, did not always achieve its creator's lofty ideals. In his 1968 book co-written with Stephen Whitfield, Roddenberry devoted one entire chapter to each of the lead characters, all played by white men. The remaining characters, all marked as racially different, merited only one chapter. Such evidence clearly supports Daniel Bernardi's conclusions that whites dominated the series. As he correctly notes, while Roddenberry wanted diversity in his series, it actually appeared mostly in the background of both shots and stories. While asserting that Roddenberry intended to use science fiction to avoid network censors while calling for a multicultural future, Bernardi points out that *Star Trek* typically depicted racism as an alien problem, not a human one. Roddenberry probably did so, it is worth noting, to make two interrelated points: the future could be harmonious, but to achieve it Americans would have to solve race issues. Although the show always remained connected to real life race relations of the 1960s, this approach muted Roddenberry's call for change.[37]

Still, the accomplishments of *Star Trek* should not be overlooked, and *Star Trek* did in fact make important steps in a "white" television industry dominated by a "segregationist tone."[38] While attempts had been made to capture the unfolding social drama of the mid–1960s, efforts specifically to address ethnicity were usually packaged as "race" programs. *Star Trek* broke an important barrier, then, with its multicultural cast, a conscious decision hailed by Jan Johnson-Smith as "forward-thinking."[39] Backed by NBC, which wanted to start integrating some of its casts, Roddenberry moved slowly, explaining that "[i]n lesser roles, a mixture of types was featured."[40] Such pragmatic circumspection resulted in part from network concerns that some viewers would object to an integrated Star Fleet and that some Southern stations would refuse to air the series.[41] At any rate, cultural constraints clearly limited *Star Trek*'s ambitions and agenda.

The complicated relationship between historical context and individual intent resulted in a mixed message that has been read quite differently by various observers. Scholar Elyce Rae Helford, for example, offers a nuanced assessment of *Star Trek* that credits the series with at least suggesting that African Americans could participate in the "American Dream." Martin Luther King, Jr., saw a similar potential much earlier, telling Roddenberry, "Because of you and the way you portray [Uhura], people will see us. The world will see us as we should be seen — men and women on an equal basis going where no one has gone before."[42] Likewise, actress Whoopi Goldberg recalled explaining her desire to appear in *The Next Generation* to Roddenberry by relating to the producer "that his was the only vision that had black people in the future."[43]

Despite the fact that some viewers and critics have found positive messages concerning race in *Star Trek*, the limits of liberal concern for African Americans have also been documented. Bernardi points out, for example, that the good guys were white while the Klingon villains were darker. Furthermore, even the famous first interracial kiss on television between Kirk and Uhura was only implied off-screen.[44] Stereotypes, in fact, burdened Uhura in ways both blatant and subtle. For example, according to the character description of Uhura written by Roddenberry and Whitfield, the crew always wanted her to sing, pushing her into the stereotypical role of black entertainer. Furthermore, while Uhura was technologically adept, the show's notes stressed that she represented Africa's blending of technology "with a naturalistic agrarian philosophy."[45]

Such limits were also evident in the portrayal of Asian characters that were influenced by the "model minority" stereotype that arose in the late

1960s. In doing so, the series polished up both reality and fiction. For example, in describing Japanese American actor George Takei's background, Whitfield and Roddenberry simply note that he "was born ... in Los Angeles and lived there until World War II, when his family moved to Arkansas."[46] Such an explanation consciously ignored the reason for the family's move — the exile and incarceration of all Japanese Americans living on the west coast during the war — in trying to forget an unpleasant episode in American history that did not fit with Roddenberry's vision of what the U.S. was and should be. Furthermore, the character description of Sulu drew considerably from ideas inherent in the model minority concept. In initiating their description of Sulu, Roddenberry and Whitfield accept stereotypes while attempting to combat racism by noting that "Sulu, despite mixed Asian ancestry, is definitely not an inscrutable Oriental." They go on to describe an assimilated Sulu who, while "drawn to the samurai concept as a philosophy," is "a rather 'hip' character [with] an excellent sense of humor." When an Asian American civil rights group complained that a white character always got the girl in *Star Trek* episodes, Roddenberry demonstrated the limits of his vision by flippantly brushing off their concerns by replying that Takei's contract was "based on the Kellogg-Briand Treaty of 1925 [and provided that Sulu] would receive three girls for every five that Kirk and McCoy got."[47]

While most scholars would now agree that *Star Trek* was "(at best) naïve or (at worst) racist [in presenting] a 'white' and American-led future," Johnson-Smith correctly points out that the series still made important points about racial attitudes.[48] Still, most scholars have presented strongly negative critiques of "The Omega Glory." Bernardi, for example, argues that the patriotic and mythic symbols in the episode buttress white superiority. While the early scenes suggest a seemingly counter-hegemonic message that whites can be uncivilized and yellows can be civilized, he argues that such a superficial interpretation fails to account for the fact that the yellow Khoms have established an oppressive empire that the white Yangs, portrayed as noble savages, resist while battling to regain what is rightfully theirs, especially the land. Thus, Bernardi concludes, "The Omega Glory" in reality "ultimately celebrates nationalism."[49]

While Bernardi and others have clearly identified racist elements in the purportedly multicultural series, a closer look at the connections between "The Omega Glory" and its era suggests that more can be gleaned from the show. In particular, by slightly refocusing the examination of "The Omega Glory" to explore the episode as part of a larger dialogue within the mass media, the state of race relations in 1968 is illuminated. Instead of focusing on the Yangs as noble savages, the Yangs can now be seen as an example of the result of mindless nationalism run amok, albeit still salvageable in Roddenberry's ever-optimistic view of the future. From this perspective, the "glimmers of hope" detected by Johnson-Smith in other episodes of the original series appear in "The Omega Glory," too.[50] Thus, the mass media simultaneously supported existing restrictive racial constructs and encouraged viewers to move beyond them.[51]

Read this way, "The Omega Glory" suggests that whites could be savages just as easily as others, especially if divorced from key democratic principles. Many of the qualities ascribed to the Yangs mirrored terms used to describe the "yellow peril" at an earlier time in U.S. history. For example, Tracy, after noting directly that the Yangs are white, describes them as vicious and deceptive enemies who cannot communicate intelligently. An almost insane race that attacks anything that moves, the Yangs are contemptuous of life. Tracy's conclusion dehumanizes the Yangs: they are animals "who happen to look like us." Kirk's initial encounter with Cloud William, the Yang leader, and a Yang girl in prison reinforces Tracy's conclusion. Any attempt at reasoning with the non-verbal Yangs fails, and the female fights, too.

Ultimately, in fact, the "yellow" and "white" civilizations that Kirk identifies on Omega IV seem to live in a world where the white Yangs have become the Asian "other" of Roddenberry's own earth. Cloud William later explains succinctly — if unintelligently — that he did not initially talk because Yangs do not "speak to Khoms. They only for killing." The Yangs, it would seem, have literally become the "yellow horde" of the twentieth-century world. Tracy describes his battle with them with horror. In one bloody showdown, he relates, the Yangs "came and came," sacrificing lives to draw the Khoms into the open, not giving up even as their losses mounted into the thousands.

Kirk's lesson on the Constitution also speaks directly to race when Spock is identified as evil because he looks different. Faced with such discriminatory preconceptions, Kirk explains that you cannot tell if someone is good or bad based on how they look. This lesson reinforces McCoy's observation at the beginning of the show as the landing party discovers the dehydrated remains of the *Exeter*'s crew: without water, all human beings are an identical 3–4 pounds of chemicals.

"The Omega Glory" and Gender

While many Americans saw racial progress at home as essential to winning the Cold War, the mainstream message on gender was just as complicated and more often reactionary. "For in the early years of the cold war," historian Elaine Tyler May contends, "amid a world of uncertainty brought about by World War II and its aftermath, the home seemed to offer a secure private nest removed from the dangers of the outside world." Because many contemporary observers feared radical changes in gender roles, the traditional roles of male breadwinners and female homemakers were actually reinforced. As women were pushed back into traditional roles as the result of Cold War anxieties, the media drove this point home by portraying Soviet women as overworked and unfeminine.[52]

American women took note of the implications of such thought, although the contradictions inherent in such thinking became apparent only later. Susan Douglas, for example, recalls how women understood their dual roles in the post–*Sputnik* era. "The Russians had lots of women engineers, doctors, too," she writes, "and we all knew what they looked like: Broderick Crawford in drag. It was because all their women were dead ringers for Mr. Potato Head that we knew their society was, at its heart, joyless, regimented, and bankrupt. No one was going to let that happen here. But it might if they took over. Our girls were going to stay feminine, but they were also going to roll up their sleeves and make America number one again."[53] Uhura, as we will see, realized the painful and ultimately self-defeating results of trying to remain feminine and go to work in a man's world.

Domestic containment established a "powerful political consensus" that prevailed until the early 1960s as baby boomers came of age and began to challenge it. By the end of the decade, in fact, a burgeoning women's movement would be waging a broad war against sexism.[54] Roddenberry thus found himself and *Star Trek* caught in the midst of a momentous transition from Cold War domestic containment to women's liberation. His response, perhaps not surprisingly, was uncertain and ambiguous. While he strove to promote a kind of feminism as a part of his larger multicultural view of the future, he failed to make the jump completely. As a result, his efforts to portray women as equal to men were often undermined by old assumptions about a woman's proper place that Roddenberry continued to hold.

Much like race, Roddenberry and *Star Trek* ultimately presented a mixed message. On the one hand, Roddenberry was tuned in enough to women's issues to promote secretary Dorothy Fontana to story editor, a position rarely held by women at this time. On the other hand, despite whatever good intentions he may have harbored, Helford notes bluntly that the notion that "the original *Star Trek* ... is sexist hardly needs articulation" as stereotypes and exoticization prevail.[55] Many critics, she notes, see Kirk as an "oppressive patriarch" overseeing a universe full of women who appear only as "recognisable stereotypes."[56] As others have concluded, in *Star Trek* "[t]he men are men, and the women are endowed. (Though set in the 23rd century, sexual roles are those of the 50's.)"[57]

Roddenberry's initial proposal for a female Number One highlights *Star Trek*'s basic attitude toward gender, grounded as it was in a liberal desire to do good but limited ultimately by that perspective as well. While making the second in command a woman was in part visionary, the character was described by Roddenberry as "a glacierlike, efficient female."[58] Thus, empowered females existed in the 23rd century, but only at the price of sacrificing their "feminine" qualities to succeed in what was very clearly still a man's world. The network and test audiences seemed threatened by such a female character, expressing both resentment and disbelief. Faced with such negative reactions, Roddenberry cut the character out of the show, demonstrating in a very direct way how American culture imposed constraints on *Star Trek*'s message.[59]

A second female character description in Roddenberry's series proposal suggests clear limits on his liberal outlook on feminism. J.M. Colt, unlike the masculine Number One cut from the series, was "uncomfortably lovely.... With a strip-queen figure even a uniform cannot hide, Colt serves as Captain's secretary, reporter, and bookkeeper — and with surprising efficiency. She undoubtedly dreams of serving [the Captain] with equal efficiency in more personal departments."[60] Thus, while Roddenberry could write memos ordering scenes in which women hide in their cabins in times of danger cut because "'[w]e're playing women crewmen as equal to men,'" the end result on screen still depicted men acting and women being observed.[61]

Uhura's character, the most prominent female in the series, also embodied mixed messages that ultimately supported sexism. While in some ways Uhura represented an "'empowered' womanhood beyond the boundaries of domesticity [that found] meaningful work outside of marriage and family," she also "served primarily as a receptionist" who was meant to be observed.[62] The character description provided by Roddenberry clearly, just as with Number One, stressed that women could not be both mothers and successful professionals. A sense of adventure had led Uhura to join Star Fleet as "a highly proficient communications professional," but she found herself "torn between the idea of someday becoming a wife and mother, and a desire to remain in the service as a career officer. Her life at present is a battle with her female need for the pleasant routine of Earthbound home and family versus the personal challenge of starship life and continued new worlds to conquer."[63] Clearly Uhura's choice lay between professional success as a defeminized ice queen or her "female need" for family.

Although Uhura is largely absent from "The Omega Glory," as might be expected given her typical role in the background of the series, other characters in the episode embody some of her key qualities. After taking McCoy captive, Tracy and the Khoms force him to work on discovering the formula of Tracy's illusive fountain of youth. An Asian women serves McCoy dutifully, expressing absolutely no sense of individualism or empowerment. She clearly lives only to serve men. Cloud William's girl is similarly primarily an object to be observed, scantily clad and unable to protect herself. Even when she does act, she seems to be swayed either by Kirk's sexual attractiveness or Spock's intellectual superiority. The absence of female roles beyond those used to create an attractive background in "The Omega Glory" suggests just how far *Star Trek* had to go in achieving any real vision of gender equality.

Conclusion

While much of what has been written on *Star Trek* takes an extreme position, either celebrating its visionary qualities or condemning its shortcomings inspired by racism and sexism, a more nuanced view of "The Omega Glory" in the context of the late 1960s helps fashion a better understanding of both the series and the era. *Star Trek* provides important insights into the 1960s and the increasingly radical activism at work by the end of that decade. Produced during the passage of "an array of progressive legislation unmatched in the annals of congressional history," *Star Trek* aired just as a growing number of Americans began to feel that "the achievement was not enough, and society's capacity to contain and ameliorate tension burst under the combined pressure of those who insisted on challenging the very premises of liberalism...."[64]

Arriving at an opportune time when developments in the television industry and in attitudes toward race and gender created the potential for *Star Trek* to present a truly multicultural future, "The Omega Glory" and the series as a whole strove to embody a "positive message of hope for a better tomorrow," but too often fell short of such a goal, largely because its creators subscribed to the prevailing limited liberal outlook of the day.[65] Some scholars attribute these limits to simple but misleading notions of "ethnic and gender diversity (what we might call *liberal chic*) [that] superficially validate[d] liberal perspectives on multiculturalism and feminism."[66] Such a perspective, however, obscures the point that *Star Trek* and "The Omega Glory" actually represented all too well the superficial nature of the liberal thought, a shortcoming that led many minorities and women to adopt more radical approaches because even those in power who were sympathetic could not clearly see the need for more far-reaching reform. It was not ultimately that *Star Trek* presented a superficial view of liberalism; instead, the series stands as a testament to the ways in which liberalism undermined itself in pursuing what were in reality all too often superficial goals.

Notes

1. The overview of U.S. history that follows relies upon William H. Chafe, *The Unfinished Journey: America Since World War II* (New York: Oxford University Press, 2003), 333–368.

2. Stephen E. Whitfield and Gene Roddenberry, *The Making of* Star Trek (New York: Del Rey, 1968), 22–23; Susan Gibberman, "Gene Roddenberry," http://www.museum.tv/archives/etv/R/htmlR/roddenberry/roddenberry.htm.

3. *Ibid.*, 216.

4. *Ibid.*, 333.

5. Walter LaFeber, *The Deadly Bet: LBJ, Vietnam, and the 1968 Election* (Lanham, MD: Rowman and Littlefield, 2005), 179.

6. Wm. Blake Tyrell, "*Star Trek* as Myth and Television as Mythmaker," *Journal of Popular Culture* 10.4 (Spring 1977): 712.

7. Gibberman.

8. David J. Alexander, Star Trek *Creator: The Authorized Biography of Gene Roddenberry* (New York: Roc, 1994), 11; David Alexander, "A Brief Biography of Gene Roddenberry," http://www.philosophysphere.com/bio.html; Andrew Tong, "Eugene Wesley 'Gene' Roddenberry," http://www.pathcom.com/~boby/gene.htm.

9. Alexander, Star Trek *Creator*, 23–26, 180.

10. Tong; Gibberman; Alexander, "A Brief Biography"; Alexander, Star Trek *Creator*, 185–186; Joel Engel, *Gene Roddenberry: The Myth and the Man Behind* Star Trek (New York: Hyperion, 1994), 39; Whitfield and Roddenberry, 22–23.

11. Whitfield and Roddenberry, 21–22; Gibberman.

12. Yvonne Fern, *Gene Roddenberry: The Last Conversation* (Berkeley: University of California Press, 1994), 164; Daniel Bernardi, Star Trek *and History: Race-ing Toward a White Future* (New Brunswick, NJ: Rutgers University Press, 1998), 28.

13. Bernardi, 30–31.

14. Fern, 210.

15. Alexander, "A Brief Biography of Gene Roddenberry"; Gibberman.
16. Tyrell, 711.
17. Engel, bookjacket.
18. Gibberman; Engel, 126; Alexander, Star Trek *Creator*, 262. *Star Trek* premiered on September 8, 1966, and suffered low ratings from the start. Indeed, fearing cancellation as the first season wrapped, Roddenberry secretly initiated a fan campaign to renew the series for a second season. The series struggled on for two more seasons after the first, but was finally canceled after its third year.
19. Engel, 63, 116; Alexander, "A Brief Biography of Gene Roddenberry." Many fans likewise seem to view "The Omega Glory" as one of the series' worst shows.
20. Engel, 116.
21. "The Omega Glory," March 1, 1968 (written by Gene Roddenberry, directed by Vincent McEveety).
22. Engel, 5; Fried, 9; Jan Johnson-Smith, *American Science Fiction TV: Star Trek, Stargate, and Beyond* (Middletown, CT: Wesleyan University Press, 2005), 79.
23. Whitfield and Roddenberry, 112; Richard M. Fried, *Nightmare in Red: The McCarthy Era in Perspective* (New York: Oxford University, 1990), 6.
24. M. Keith Booker, *Science Fiction Television: A History* (Westport, CT: Praeger, 2004), 16.
25. Johnson-Smith, 58; Booker, 55.
26. Ellen Schrecker, *Many Are the Crimes: McCarthyism in America* (Boston: Little, Brown, 1998), 396–399.
27. *Ibid.*, 399–400.
28. *Ibid.*, 364, 369.
29. Charles Maland, "Dr. Strangelove: Nightmare Comedy and the Ideology of Liberal Consensus," in Peter C. Rollins, ed., *Hollywood as Historian: American Film in a Cultural Context* (Lexington: University of Kentucky Press, 1983) (revised edition, 1998), 190. A revolt against such mindless nationalism had already appeared in popular culture, perhaps most strikingly with the film *Dr. Strangelove* in 1964. As Charles Maland has noted, *Dr. Strangelove* presented a "moral protest of revulsion against the dominant cultural paradigm in America — what Godfrey Hodgson has termed the Ideology of Liberal Consensus."
30. Maland, 192–194, 198–201, 203–205.
31. Tong; Bernardi, 5.
32. Dudziak, 6, 13.
33. *Ibid.*, 13–17, 240.
34. Fern, 212.
35. Whitfield and Roddenberry, 40.
36. Whitfield and Roddenberry, 40; Booker, 53. Roddenberry also wrote a public service ad that stressed the same message, although it was never produced. See Alexander, 180–182.
37. Whitfield and Roddenberry; Bernardi, 11, 28, 34–37, 39.
38. Bernardi, 32.
39. Johnson-Smith, 59; Bernardi, 33; Gibberman.
40. Whitfield and Roddenberry, 111–112; Engel, 107.
41 Whitfield and Roddenberry, 111–112, 127; Engel, 98.
42. Fern, 213; Elyce Rae Helford, ed., *Fantasy Girls: Gender in the New Universe of Science Fiction and Fantasy Television* (Lanham, MD: Rowman & Littlefield, 2000, 3.
43. Engel, 8.
44. "Plato's Stepchildren," November 22, 1968 (written by Meyer Dolinsky, directed by David Alexander).
45. Bernardi, 43, 56; Whitfield and Roddenberry, 253.

46. Whitfield and Roddenberry, 247.
47. *Ibid.*, 247–249.
48. Johnson-Smith, 82.
49. Bernardi, 57–59.
50. Johnson-Smith, 89.
51. Bernardi, 19.
52. Elaine Tyler May, *Homeward Bound: American Families in the Cold War Era* (New York: Basic Books, 1988), 3, 5, 16–19.
53. Douglas, 22.
54. May, 208, 220.
55. Helford, 11–12; Harrison, 11–12; Engel, 107.
56. Helford, 11–12; Harrison, 11–12; Johnson-Smith, 80.
57. Tyrell, 712.
58. Whitfield and Roddenberry, 24.
59. Engel, 66; Johnson-Smith, 80; Whitfield and Roddenberry, 127. Interestingly, the militaristic Romulans practiced gender equality, even in leadership positions, in stark contrast to Star Fleet's strong patriarchy. See Whitfield and Roddenberry, 256.
60. Whitfield and Roddenberry, 24, 30.
61. Engel, 90.
62. Helford, 3.
63. Whitfield and Roddenberry, 252.
64. Chafe, 216.
65. Gibberman.
66. Taylor Harrison, Sarah Projansky, Kent A. Ono, and Elyce Rae Helford, eds., *Enterprise Zones: Critical Positions on Star Trek* (Boulder, CO: Westview Press, 1996), 1.

BIBLIOGRAPHY

Alexander, David. "A Brief Biography of Gene Roddenberry." http://www.philosophy-sphere.com/bio.html
_____. *Star Trek Creator: The Authorized Biography of Gene Roddenberry*. New York: Roc, 1994.
Bernardi, Daniel. *Star Trek and History: Race-ing Toward a White Future*. New Brunswick, NJ: Rutgers University Press, 1998.
Booker, M. Keith. *Science Fiction Television: A History*. Westport, CT: Praeger, 2004.
Chafe, William H. *The Unfinished Journey: America Since World War II*. New York: Oxford University Press, 2003.
Douglas, Susan J. *Where the Girls Are: Growing Up Female with the Mass Media*. New York: Three Rivers Press, 1995.
Dudziak, Mary L. *Cold War Civil Rights: Race and the Image of American Democracy*. Princeton: Princeton University Press, 2000.
Engel, Joel. *Gene Roddenberry: The Myth and the Man Behind Star Trek*. New York: Hyperion, 1994.
Fern, Yvonne. *Gene Roddenberry: The Last Conversation*. Berkeley: University of California Press, 1994.
Fried, Richard M. *Nightmare in Red: The McCarthy Era in Perspective*. New York: Oxford University, 1990.
Susan Gibberman. "Gene Roddenberry." http://www.museum.tv/archives/etv/R/htmlR/roddenberry/roddenberry.htm.
Harrison, Taylor, Sarah Projansky, Kent A. Ono, and Elyce Rae Helford, eds. *Enterprise Zones: Critical Positions on Star Trek*. Boulder, CO: Westview Press, 1996.

Helford, Elyce Rae, editor. *Fantasy Girls: Gender in the New Universe of Science Fiction and Fantasy Television.* Lanham, MD: Rowman & Littlefield, 2000.
Johnson-Smith, Jan. *American Science Fiction TV: Star Trek, Stargate, and Beyond.* Middletown, CT: Wesleyan University Press, 2005.
LaFeber, Walter. *The Deadly Bet: LBJ, Vietnam, and the 1968 Election.* Lanham, MD: Rowman & Littlefield, 2005.
Maland, Charles. "*Dr. Strangelove*: Nightmare Comedy and the Ideology of Liberal Consensus." In Peter C. Rollins, ed., *Hollywood as Historian: American Film in a Cultural Context.* Lexington: University of Kentucky Press, 1983 (revised edition, 1998).
May, Elaine Tyler. *Homeward Bound: American Families in the Cold War Era.* New York: Basic Books, 1988.
"The Omega Glory." http://www.tv.com/star-trek/the-omega-glory/episode/24935/summary.html.
Schrecker, Ellen. *Many Are the Crimes: McCarthyism in America.* Boston: Little, Brown, 1998.
Tong, Andrew. "Eugene Wesley 'Gene' Roddenberry." http://www.pathcom.com/~boby/gene.htm.
Tyrell, Wm. Blake. "*Star Trek* as Myth and Television as Mythmaker." *Journal of Popular Culture* 10.4 (Spring 1977), 711–719.
Whitfield, Stephen E., and Gene Roddenberry. *The Making of* Star Trek. New York: Del Rey, 1968.

Filmography

"The Omega Glory," March 1, 1968 (written by Gene Roddenberry, directed by Vincent McEveety).

5

Lost in Translation
Autonomy, Agency, and Cybernetic Anxiety from Apollo to The Six Million Dollar Man

DARYL LEE

"Better, stronger, faster": Narratives of Technology at the Apogee of the Space Age

When Apollo 17 splashed down in the south Pacific on December 19, 1972, it brought to a close a seminal chapter in American technological and cultural history. Conceived in the early 1960s as an audacious demonstration of Cold War supremacy, the Apollo program represented a remarkable technocratic achievement, the product of an intricate and concerted mobilization of technological capabilities, engineering ingenuity, and bureaucratic organization, not to mention public resources. But for all the triumphant celebration of both technological prowess and human achievement, the manned space program also heightened unsettling questions about the future of the human being and its place within an increasingly complex technological society. It is thus telling that just months after the final moon landing was broadcast live another image appeared on American television screens: astronaut and test pilot Steve Austin, strapped into the cockpit of an experimental aircraft, falling uncontrollably out of the sky.

As much a political and cultural project as it was a technological endeavor, the Apollo space program was ready-made to fit familiar humanist narratives extolling the promises of technology in securing humanity's future and enhancing human freedom and autonomy.[1] The exploration of space renewed the Enlightenment promise of technological science as a means for furthering human advancement, offering a peaceful vision of the future that had been shaken by the threat of nuclear annihilation. Moreover, the carefully crafted "aura of competence" projected by NASA helped to restore Americans' confidence that complex technological undertakings and the immense powers that they channeled could be effectively managed and controlled through technocratic administration and directed towards peaceful purposes.[2] The endeavor to land men on the moon resonated powerfully with the deeply engrained American myth about the utopian promises implicit in the expanding frontier, mapping these hopes onto the boundlessness of the extra-terrestrial sphere. Taken together, the notion of manned space exploration affirmed human mastery over its technologies at a time when such guarantees seemed anything but certain. The philosopher William Irwin Thompson, reflecting on the final moon shot in the pages of *The New York Times*, wrote, "Had we merely sent out efficient instruments of measurement, we would have expanded our technology while constricting our culture. The machines would literally encircle man and inevitably tighten the space around us." But by opting for manned spaceflight, he continued, "America has taken one giant step toward humanizing its technology."[3]

No one reading Thompson in 1973 needed reminding of the more ominous payloads that these rockets that had hurled men into space were devised to carry, and as William Atwill suggestively argues in *Fire and Power: The American Space Program as Postmodern Narrative*, the decision to send men to the moon was a conscious effort to forge a cohesive story about technology, human progress, and American destiny in an uncertain world fractured by other, less comforting narratives propelled by the experiences of the Cold War, Vietnam, and domestic social unrest. Yet if the United States' venture to the moon was, at the cultural level, an effort to restore its Enlightenment legacy, this era of manned space travel also marks the moment when this narrative of human progress encountered its own limits, in large part because of how the unprecedentedly complex technological configurations of man and machine demanded by the Apollo space program problematized the ideals of autonomy and human mastery of technology that laid at the imaginative origins of the endeavor.[4]

Nowhere was this tension more evident than in the pressure placed upon the human figure at the center of this narrative: the astronaut. As the face of the nation's most complex technological endeavor, the astronaut embodied the human being's place within an increasingly technologized future, the heroic bearer of its promises but also its most fragile and vulnerable component. Within the cultural economy of the space program, the astronaut functioned as a crucial symbolic pivot, a subject that represented both the individual and humanity, and which converted the narrative of space exploration into a story of technologically realized humanism. In doing so, this heroic subject lent its value to this narrative, legitimating its costs, risks, and dangers. It is worth noting that while NASA officials were initially taken by surprise by the fervent public interest in the men who volunteered to ride atop of its rockets, they quickly recognized the pivotal role played by these astronauts in soliciting public identification and support for the space program and its exorbitant budgetary expenditures.[5] But if the meaningfulness of the humanist narrative is predicated upon the value conferred upon it through man and mankind, space exploration, as Megan Stern reminds us, exposes the contradiction implicit within this narrative by rendering the human subject who elevates itself out of its world and into the vastness of space as simultaneously "omnipotent and ... insignificant."[6]

The sense of transcendence and pride that Thompson expressed in the wake of the Apollo project, while hyperbolic, was not especially uncommon; watching the launch of the Saturn V rocket was a sublime experience perfectly attuned to the technological era, as David Nye has pointed out, and thousands of Americans made the pilgrimage to Cape Canaveral to witness this awe-inspiring display of power improbably harnessed to launch men toward the heavens.[7] However, the hopes that Apollo would renew and reinvigorate the Enlightenment promise of beneficent technology and help chart a new and more humane direction for modern society proved to be fleeting. Apollo did not usher in a new age of humanistic endeavor, and the years following the last moon mission were characterized by a distinct lack of enthusiasm for further ventures. In one respect, this failure to inspire anything new is not surprising; as Howard McCurdy has suggested, the realization of spaceflight has exhausted the imaginative energies that inspired the enterprise, and this dynamic is perhaps especially true in the wake of the lunar missions where the empty monotony of space travel, punctuated but briefly by moments of exhilaration and wonder, was televised live.[8]

Within the context of this cultural exhaustion, science fiction film and television of this era underwent a similar period of imaginative malaise. Joan Dean observed that the years between 1968 and 1977 — a period framed by *2001: A Space Odyssey* and *Star Wars*— was a period of drought, producing few science fiction films and even fewer that were greeted with any commercial success. Thematically, the relatively small number of films of this time period often reflected this exhaustion, turning away from the uncharted frontiers of space and toward decidedly terrestrial problems. The dominant theme for films of these years, Dean noted, revolved around the looming concern over "overpopulation and its concomitant problems of food shortage and old age."[9] Science fiction television reflected the creative exhaustion afflicting its cinematic counterpart, with few shows of any lasting significance appearing on American airwaves between *Star Trek* (1966–1969) and *Battlestar Galactica* (1978–1979). Within this cultural vacuum, only one notable and enduring figure stood out: Steve Austin, the former astronaut and "the world's first bionic man," and science fiction television's first cyborg.

"A man barely alive": Remembering The Six Million Dollar Man

Today, cyborgs have become ubiquitous. Realized through the myriad couplings of the technological and the human that characterize the past quarter-century, cyborgs have multiplied exponentially and are now encountered in fields as disparate as information sciences and medical engineering to popular culture and social theory. This proliferation is a measure of the ability of cybernetic theory to reconceptualize the world of discrete objects, reconfiguring and rewriting their boundaries, while dissolving and assimilating the world of bounded entities into cybernetic systems. But it is also a testament to the imaginative potential unlocked by the image of this human-machine hybrid, and as Donna Haraway's celebrated cyborg manifesto attests, this image offers a powerful metaphor for thinking and rethinking the relationships between and among human beings and their machines at this moment in humanity's social and technological history.[10] At the same time, the proliferation of cyborgs threatens to blunt both the imaginative potential and the critical incisiveness of this concept, obscuring the complex problematics that they attempt to interpret and understand. If the cyborg is to continue to have value as a critical metaphor for thinking about the relationships between human beings and technology, it is necessary to relocate it within the cultural, technological, and historical contexts from which it has developed. Given this, revisiting *The Six Million Dollar Man*, one of the original sites of the cyborg, allows a close examination of the cultural logics and cybernetic anxieties that helped to launch the first cyborg into popular consciousness.

First aired as a 90-minute made-for-television movie in March 1973, *The Six Million Dollar Man* is principally responsible for introducing the figure of the cyborg to television audiences.[11] Based upon the 1972 novel *Cyborg* by the prolific aeronautics and science fiction writer Martin Caidin, the series, measured by any commercial standard, was a success: it was ABC's highest-rated program in the year it debuted, ran for five seasons, and at its height in 1976–77 rated as the seventh most-viewed program on network television.[12] The series also launched a successful spinoff series, *The Bionic Woman*, which ran for three seasons between 1976 and 1978, as well as spawning three made-for-television movies that reunited Steve Austin and bionic woman Jaime Sommers on the small screen. *The Six Million Dollar Man* also generated a merchandising phenomenon, inspiring products ranging from lunch boxes to a Steve Austin action figure with interchangeable bionic arms.

Despite the popular success enjoyed by the series, *The Six Million Dollar Man*'s significance, both as a cultural phenomenon and for its place within the genealogy of the cyborg, has been largely overlooked. This dearth of attention may be explained by the fact that *The Six Million Dollar Man* is often remembered as a frequently hapless series characterized by more than its fair share of B-movie moments, the most memorable of which included the slow-motion bionic action, the cheesy sound effects, and Steve Austin's showdown with an alien Bigfoot. Arthur Berger, in one of the few serious considerations of the series, described it as "frequently corny and melodramatic" with acting that was "flat and mechanical, as if the technological premise of the program affected the actors." However, Berger (who wrote these words in 1976) suggested that it was for precisely these reasons that the show needed to be taken seriously, for the popularity of *The Six Million Dollar Man* in spite of its shortcomings suggested that it had struck a deeply meaningful chord among its viewers. "The relation between man and machines has become today's critical issue," Berger noted, and the heroic figure of Steve Austin — a man made powerful through technology — offered its viewers a humane and hopeful vision of how this increasingly pressing tension could be resolved.[13]

In its broad outlines, Berger's analysis remains a convincing one; taken as a whole, the narrative drive of *The Six Million Dollar Man* is towards resolving the man-machine dialectic in comfortably humanist terms, emphasizing Steve Austin's mastery of his bionic components and presenting a heroic protagonist whose unwavering moral compass assures viewers that the technological components to which he is so intimately bound have been thoroughly humanized. Moreover, the prodigious feats of strength that Austin displayed speak to the implicit if contradictory promise that new technological developments might restore some proportion to the widening imbalance between the fragile and increasingly impotent individual and the impersonal and powerful forces that give shape to modern existence. The memorable title sequence of the series recounting Austin's rebirth at the hands of modern techno-science, which Berger presciently described as the most significant thirty seconds of each episode, provides, at least on the surface, a case in point:

> Steve Austin, astronaut. A man barely alive. Gentlemen, we can rebuild him. We have the technology. We have the capability to make the world's first bionic man. Steve Austin will be that man. Better than he was before. Better, stronger, faster.[14]

The voiceover, delivered over a sequence of computer-generated models outlining the cybernetic remapping of the protagonist's body, resounds with a progressivist faith in technology to both restore and improve the human being. But the more telling aspect of this new creation story is the rhythmic incantation of the object-subject of this narrative: "Steve Austin ... Astronaut ... Man." If the purpose of this incantation is to reassure the viewer of just *who* or *what* will emerge out of this bionic experiment, the need for such assurances betrays the underlying anxiety that the new cyborg subject fashioned by cybernetics would not be so easily contained within the older humanist framework.

A Genealogy for Cyborgs

The brief history of cybernetics is pregnant with these tensions between humanist and cybernetic ideals and the anxieties that they provoke. Its father, the American mathematician Norbert Wiener, described this new science as one born out of the "essential unity of the set of problems centering about communication, control, and statistical mechanics, whether in the machine or in living tissue."[15] By establishing a language of communication and control common to both machines and animals, cybernetics dissolves any essential difference between the technological and the organic. And by recognizing that boundaries are impermanent, permeable, and rewriteable, cybernetics made it possible to disperse, transfer, and reintegrate various functions into integrated systems without regard to the "natural" boundaries of individual objects. This allows the capacities of the human body to be translated and transferred to machines, but just as equally it enables machines to absorb the human being as a function within a larger system.

However, even as he described the revolutionary implications of cybernetics in reshaping the way we think about machines and organisms, Wiener resisted the more radical implications for western ideas of identity and individuality that his ideas suggested. In *How We Became Posthuman*, Katherine Hayles shows how throughout his work Wiener sought to frame the science of cybernetics as a humanist project, producing interpretations of self-regulating systems that served to sustain and reinforce the autonomy and agency of the human being. He thus struggled to forge an uneasy coexistence between his cybernetic ideas and the subject of liberal humanism, a conception of the individual that Hayles draws from the influential formulation of the political theorist C.B. Macpherson. Macpherson conceptualizes the western tradition of individualism in terms of possessive individualism, tracing an idea of the human being in which *self-possession*— a "conception of the individual as essentially the proprietor of his own person or capacities, owing nothing to society for them"— forms the underlying condition for the individual's freedom and autonomy.[16] Cybernetics, by dissolving and reconstituting the boundaries of the individual, radically undermines the foundations of the possessive individual by rendering the natural integrity of the human being and the concomitant notion of self-possession problematic. To put it simply, how can a cyborg possess itself when "it" is inextricably part of an "other"? And if it does not possess itself, then how can its actions be the sole product of its own will?

The questions raised by cyborg existence are implicit within the science of cybernetics that Wiener and his contemporaries pioneered. The cyborg, however, is more immediately the imaginative progeny (and prodigy) of the space program, its existence announced by Manfred Clynes and Nathan Kline in a 1960 article titled "Cyborgs and Space" and published in the journal *Astronautics*. Taking as their starting point the challenges posed by manned space exploration, Clynes and Kline proposed that the future of space travel would depend not on the unwieldy and inefficient recreation of the fragile environments that support human life in space, but on modifying the human being to enable it to survive in the extraterrestrial environments it would encounter in the course of space exploration. Such adaptations, they explained, were made possible by the new understanding of self-regulating, homeostatic mechanisms offered by cybernetic science, thus allowing for the development of an "exogenously extended organizational complex functioning as an integrated homeostasis system," or, as they proposed to call it, "'Cyborg.'"[17]

The resulting cybernetic being Clynes and Kline envisaged constituted a radical remapping and redesign of the physiological and psychological functioning of the human being in order to adapt it to the hostile environments, physical rigors, and psychological demands encountered in space, from exposure to radiation, temperature extremes, and weightlessness to the experience of prolonged periods of wakefulness and sensory deprivation, potentially resulting in psychosis. For example, the most basic challenge of providing astronauts with a breathable atmosphere could be circumvented by developing an "inverse fuel cell" to convert carbon dioxide into oxygen; such a system "would replace the lung, making breathing, as we know it, unnecessary." They proposed that a similar closed system, designed to shunt waste from the "ureters to the venous circulation" after running through a purification system, could be devised to take care of the "[f]luid balance in the astronaut." Meanwhile, the functioning of the cardiovascular system could be altered and adapted to specific environments both by drugs administered by automatic systems and by "[a]lteration of the specific homeostatic references within or outside the brain."[18] The extended distances of space travel would require adjusting the natural rhythms of consciousness; for extended periods of wakefulness (up to several months), they anticipated the use of automatically-administered pharmacological stimulants, while for the long periods of inactivity they suggested placing the body in a state of hibernation to lower its metabolic rate and conserve limited resources.

As radical as these proposed modifications appear even today, their significance here lies not in the technological feasibility of these possibilities, but in the underlying ideals and fantasies that the resulting cyborg-astronaut expressed. As the authors explained, modifying and extending the natural homeostatic mechanisms of the human body and integrating them with external cybernetic systems was necessary in order to retrofit human beings for the increasingly complex technological systems that space exploration would require. "If man in space," they noted, "in addition to flying his vehicle, must continuously be checking on things and making adjustments merely in order to keep himself alive, he becomes a slave to the machine."[19] Extending the self-regulating mechanisms of the human body to encompass similar self-regulating technological systems would thus free the astronaut from the responsibility for all of these critical but routine tasks, allowing him or her to focus on more important goals. For this reason, they celebrated the cybernetic fusion of man and machine as a mechanism for human self-realization. "The purpose of the Cyborg," they declared, "is to provide an organizational system in which such robot-like problems are taken care of automatically and unconsciously, leaving man free to explore, to create, to think, and to feel."[20]

In this manner, Clynes and Kline fashioned the cyborg-astronaut as the technological embodiment of liberal humanism. Liberated not just from routine tasks but from its very environment, the cyborg is imagined as a self-enclosed, self-contained, monadic thinking being whose autonomy is guaranteed by its cybernetic enhancement. Yet just as Wiener retreated from the manner in which his cybernetic vision undermined the foundations of liberal individualism and the autonomy of the individual, so too did Clynes and Kline avoid the more troubling questions that their radically technologized cyborg raised. It is telling that they framed the possibilities of cyborg existence as a *spiritual* challenge, a question of humanity's willingness to direct its own evolution; positing the cyborg as a vehicle for self-realization allowed them to elide the tangible and more unsettling material relationships that such a cybernetic future might raise. Indeed, in an interview published in 1995, Clynes decried the depiction of cyborgs in popular culture, evincing outrage at how his idea has been appropriated by films such as *The Terminator* (1984) and expressing horror at how these representations "dehumanized the concept completely."[21]

This brief genealogy demonstrates how the figure of the cyborg emerged out of the intersection of humanist and cybernetic narratives, with the tensions between these two possibilities inscribed upon its technologized body. The cyborg's journey from Clynes and Kline's formulation in 1960 to its weekly appearance on American televisions throughout much of the 1970s suggests that the figure of the cyborg is certainly capable of providing purchase for humanist narratives and interpretations of technology. But at the same time, the currency of the cyborg as the bearer of more revolutionary cybernetic ideas also demonstrates that these traditional narratives were no longer adequate vehicles for making sense of its viewers' experiences of their technological world and the anxieties that living within this world provoked — anxieties about the increasingly intimate connections between technology and the individual, about the increasingly complex technocratic apparatuses that sustained American society's investment in these technologies, and about the implications that these developments held for the identity, autonomy, and agency of the individual navigating the bewildering cybernetic landscape.

"Something like that": Man, Machine, and Cybernetic Compromise

The humanist narrative offered by the manned space program proved to be obsolete, failing to offer a convincing account about the future of the human being within the technocratic world that the Apollo project both epitomized and heralded. In contrast, the popular success of *The Six Million Dollar Man* suggests that its introduction of the cyborg spoke to these experiences and anxieties in a more compelling manner. From its beginning, the imaginative terrain of *The Six Million Dollar Man* was framed by the intersection of the space program and cybernetics: the pilot movie introduces Austin as a former astronaut, and the experimental aircraft that he pilots on his ill-fated test flight prominently bears the emblem of NASA.[22] But from these origins, the series opens onto a bewildering technological landscape characterized not only by rockets and bionics but also by massive arrays of computers, information and biomedical sciences, robots, cryogenics, and super-weapons of all imaginable types. The various spaces and settings of the series represent a society both captivated by and yet oddly disconnected from its technological future, with the settings of individual episodes often alternating in jarring fashion between a high-tech world bound together by an imposing bureaucratic, governmental, and military infrastructure and an everyday life impacted by but not comfortably part of this technological world.

Similarly, the series regularly capitalized upon the symbolic value of Austin's identity as a former astronaut, with star-struck strangers recognizing him as a national hero (and sometimes regarding him with suspicion, as when a Soviet official questioned if he was really to believe that Austin was just an "astronaut-playboy on holiday").[23] In either case, Austin's celebrity makes him an unlikely secret agent, but this serves to underscore the more problematic issues of identity posed by his cybernetic nature. Austin is neither who nor what he appears to be, and the pilot opens by foregrounding these confusions, introducing viewers to its unfamiliar and ontologically compromised subject with a computer readout of the following definition: "Cy'borg 'A human being whose original human parts have had to be replaced to one extent or another by machines that perform the same functions.'"[24]

Steve Austin's reconstruction as the world's first cyborg, however, obscures the crucial point that he was, even before his accident, a cybernetic being. The viewer is introduced to him as an irrepressibly roguish test pilot, one whose civilian status outside the rigid command structure of the military affords him a degree of freedom to antagonize the high-ranking officers around him. This characterization of Austin is fraught with significance for it highlights the fundamental tension at the origins of cybernetics. Timothy Leary, in his rereading of the etymological origins of the term "cybernetics" recounted by Norbert Wiener, incisively exploits the tension between the Greek *kubernetes* ("steersman") and its Latin variant *gubernetes* ("governor"). Whereas Wiener equates the two meanings as examples of feedback mechanisms, Leary points out that *kubernetes* also refers to a pilot, and resonates with the "Greek traditions of independence and individual self-reliance" in contrast to the Roman governor which emphasizes the exercise of authority and regulation.[25] But if in the Hellenic tradition the pilot embodies the ideals of freedom, self-reliance, and autonomy, this representation is immediately thrown into question in *The Six Million Dollar Man*. Romantically figured as rugged individualists with "the right stuff," test pilots are in fact part of a cybernetic feedback mechanism, and the moment Austin steps into the cockpit he is enmeshed in a complex network of command and control consisting not just of the pilot-aircraft coupling, but also of ground controllers, the B-52 launch aircraft, chase planes, tracking and monitoring stations, and communications systems, together with all their own personnel, that effectively disperses control throughout the network, rendering the autonomy and agency that Leary celebrated as the birthright of the pilot as impossible to locate and isolate. Ironically, it is only when the system fails — "Flight Com, I can't hold it, she's breaking up, she's break..." — that Austin's autonomy as a pilot, manifested negatively as his lack of control, reappears.[26]

Whereas the complex cybernetic network of the test flight renders the agency of the human pilot problematic, the cyborg project conceived under the auspices of the government's clandestine Office of Strategic Operations (OSO) seeks to eradicate this autonomy entirely. From the outset, the cyborg prototype proposed by OSO director Oliver Spencer is figured as a physical extension of the calculative rationality of the intelligence agency, a precision-guided weapon designed to carry out delicate operations where the use of blunt force risks causing the situation to spiral dangerously out of control. When asked whether he intended to seek out volunteers to participate in the experimental cyborg program, Spencer cavalierly responds, "No, no, accidents happen all the time. We'll just start with scrap."[27] Scrap material or not, though, the resulting human-machine entity reveals a paradox in the cybernetic rationality of the OSO: whereas the cyborg's ability to carry out its assigned mission depends on its capacity to "reprogram itself in the field, on the basis of new information and altered circumstances," this specification highlights the underlying tension between command and control and self-regulation, between the cyborg's "utter dependability" and autonomy in the field. As Spencer laconically explains to a leery and recalcitrant Austin, "Actually, we would have preferred a robot. A robot doesn't have emotional needs and responses. You do. We have you because you are the optimum compromise in the present state of technology, Mr. Austin. A cybernetic organism. Part machine, part human being. The cyborg. Yes, we had to settle for that."[28]

Austin's emotional responses do, indeed, throw his viability as a cybernetic being into question. Coupled to the life-support systems that sustain his damaged body, Austin is faced with a more troubling cybernetic future. It is an emasculated existence that leads Austin to attempt to end his own life, imploring the nurse who rushes to his room to allow him to die. (As Rudy Wells, Austin's flight surgeon and friend, as well as the biomedical engineer who will rebuild him knowingly confides, "Steve Austin isn't anyone. Of all the men I know, he's the last that would want to live the way he is now.")[29] Austin's failed suicide attempt resigns him to his situation, but Wells' promise of bionic reconstruction is scarcely more appealing. Rather, the bionic arm — an uncanny metal skeleton, stuffed with electronic components and servomechanisms, and partially covered with plastic skin — that Wells removes from its wooden box and proudly displays to Austin at his bedside provokes reactions of horror.

Wells, aware of how such radical technological reconstruction could subvert his subject's sense of self, promises Austin that his new bionic prostheses will restore him to the man that he once was, not only replacing their function but also their appearance. "This is your arm, Steve. It will be covered with skin that will match your skin in color, texture, the number of hairs on your forearm. The skin on the fingertips will have your fingerprints on them. Look at it, Steve. Steve, this is not something *alien*. This is your arm." While the uncanny quality of this nuclear-powered arm is heightened by its lifelikeness, Wells assures Austin that in no way will its bionic potency compromise his human identity or autonomy; quite the opposite, this arm, he tells Austin, "will take orders from your brain. It will be alive to do what you want it to do."[30] Austin's bionic components do lend him an expanded degree of freedom and agency, but this new mode of existence comes at a cost. Sporting his newly-attached arm, Austin examines his hands, from all appearances indistinguishable from one another. "Two hands, both mine, right down to the fingerprints," he muses to his nurse and love interest Jean Manners. "Which one do I touch you with?" Austin wonders how the sensory circuits in his bionic hand function; will he be able to feel? Manners can only reply with the equivocal truth: "Something like that." The cybernetic translation of capabilities from the human to the machine may be functionally equivalent, but this does not mean they are the same; something is lost in translation. Such is also true with cybernetic agency: it is not identical to human autonomy, but instead is "something like that."[31]

Wells' promise that cybernetics can restore him to the man he was, Austin quickly realizes, is at best compromised and at worst illusionary. As the title of the series highlights, building a bionic man out of human scrap comes at an exorbitant cost, and Austin is all too aware that there is a price to be paid. Repeatedly he asks: "You all have given me a gift, and I thank you very much, but what is the price tag?"; "I want to know is who's paying the freight?"; and "Now why am I worth a few million dollars, and what will I have to do for it?"[32] He receives, of course, no answer because no amount can cover the true extent of the debt that he owes. While he may control his bionic components, he does not own them nor, by extension, himself. The underlying problem is that Austin's cybernetic nature undermines his claims of self-possession and self-ownership, notions that Hayles reminds us are the foundations of the liberal humanist subject and its autonomy. Austin, whose cyborg being is constituted by technology, can never pay his debt in full because his very existence and the cybernetic agency he exercises is predicated upon those technological elements from which he can never separate himself. As Spencer pointedly reminds him, "There is no end to obligation."[33] Ironically, in the end it is the same emotional needs that Spencer had identified as the source of Austin's unreliability that enable him to reconcile his place within the cybernetic order of which he is a part. For while Austin is initially suspicious of the intentions of the OSO and particularly of its designs for him, his overriding sense of duty, obligation, and patriotism eventually aligns his will—his self-regulating, goal-seeking autonomy—with the goals of the government.

Grounded in a disorienting technological and technocratic landscape, the pilot for *The Six Million Dollar Man* offers a sober exploration of the cyborg and the anxieties it provokes. Significantly, the television series that followed adjusted a number of elements from the original movie in ways that alleviated some of the cybernetic anxieties that the pilot generated. Steve Austin's position was shifted from that of a civilian astronaut to a colonel in the Air Force; meanwhile, the government organization in charge of the secret Cyborg Program was transformed from the shadowy "Office of Strategic Operations" (with its whispered expertise in covert operations and assassination) to the more benignly identified "Office of Scientific Intelligence" (OSI) tasked with dealing with an assortment of mad scientists, techno-savvy master criminals, and international arms dealers. The character of Oliver Spencer, whose robotic heartlessness was punctuated by his own rudimentary prosthetic (a walking cane), was replaced by the more humane Oscar Goldman, whose responsibility for making difficult decisions was tempered by his concern for Austin's well-being. The result of these adjustments is to more closely orient Austin's own sense of purpose and duty with the teleology of the larger cybernetic system, thus minimizing (but not eliminating) conflicts, and making it easier to narratively reconcile Austin's anxiety over his own status as a purposeful agent within the labyrinthine machinations of the secret organization.

Thus, even when Austin acts independently and of own free will (and sometimes in explicit opposition to the directives of his superiors), his actions and judgment ultimately end up according with the interests of his government, a teleological outcome that the cybernetic rationality of the agency that built and employs him counts on. For instance, in the two-part episode "Wine, Women and War" an insubordinate Austin, angered by the "need-to-know" secrecy of the OSI that keeps him operating in the dark while he carries out his missions, escapes from his sequestered supervision and travels to the island vacation home of an acquaintance.[34] He is, however, unaware that his unauthorized tropical vacation is in fact an elaborate ploy concocted by Goldman to send Austin to the headquarters of a notorious arms dealer suspected of trading in nuclear missiles and that his actions have been calculated and planned for in advance and are being monitored by Goldman's functionaries. Thus even when Austin operates thinking he is an autonomous agent, he is nevertheless a known quantity, his actions governed by a logic that renders him a predictable element within the cybernetic operations of the OSI.

Eventually, Austin earns the confidence of Goldman, his reliability paradoxically affording him the freedom to exercise more autonomous judgment during his missions. Thus, Steve Austin comes to epitomize the well-adjusted cyborg citizen, with his anxiety over both his machine identity and his problematic self-possession reduced to providing fodder for his self-deprecating wisecracks. Annoyed at constantly being treated as an object of scientific curiosity, in one instance Austin deflects a doctor's unwelcome fascination with his cybernetic experience ("Steve, how has it affected you?

What does it *feel* like?" to which Austin snaps, "It feels just peachy, doctor!") by later quipping that he would think about her proposal by running it "through my computer."[35] And in another episode, Austin pokes fun at Goldman's awkwardly self-conscious declaration that what makes Austin irreplaceable is not his bionic capabilities but his uniquely human qualities by reminding his superior of the real measure of his value: "You know, Oscar, that's very flattering. How about a raise?"[36]

Not everyone, however, was so successful in coming to terms with the compromises of cybernetic existence. In the episode titled "The Seven Million Dollar Man," a second cyborg prototype, race car driver Barney Miller, is unable to resolve the contradictions of his bionic hybridization, his superhuman abilities causing his self-worth to oscillate uncontrollably. At one moment he is intoxicated by his ability to do anything he imagines; with the next he plummets into despair because what lends his achievements meaning is that they are the actions of "normal Barney Miller, flesh and blood." But now, he explains, "It's not me, just a bunch of wires and nuclear muscles."[37] Accordingly, he swings between self-aggrandizement and self-destruction, his sense of worth both constituted though and undermined by his cyborg being. He, thus, expresses the conundrum of cybernetic culture: the impossibility of calculating the value — that is to say, the significance or meaning — of the human being so inextricably bound to its technological existence.

Introduced to television viewers just weeks after the nation celebrated the achievements of the last men to walk on the moon, *The Six Million Dollar Man* posed timely questions about the human being's autonomy, agency, and identity at the moment when the American public was confronting the increasingly complex and intimidating technological world that the Apollo program presaged. Steve Austin's bionic man thus stands at a pivotal point in American cultural history, marking the transition from the comforting narratives of technological humanism to more unsettling explorations of cybernetic culture. While Austin's successive roles as astronaut, test pilot, and heroic agent reprise the humanist promise of an autonomous human actor in control of technology, his bionic being is inescapably enmeshed in an intricate cybernetic system in which human autonomy and agency is compromised by the increasingly intimate and bewildering interconnections between man and machine, both technological and social. The result is a conflicted portrayal of human agency within a cybernetic world, one in which the subject's self-possession and autonomy can never be fully realized. As Austin, frustrated by the limitations of his role as an agent of the

OSI defiantly asserts to Wells, the scientist who built him, "I owe you everything.... But I'm nobody's robot."[38]

NOTES

1. The cultural contexts and narratives of the American space program have been the subject of a number of recent studies. See, for example, William D. Atwill, *Fire and Power: The American Space Program as Postmodern Narrative* (Athens: University of Georgia Press, 1994); Roger D. Launius, "Perceptions of Apollo: Myth, Nostalgia, Memory or All of the Above?" *Space Policy* 21 (2005): 129–139; and Howard E. McCurdy, *Space and the American Imagination* (Washington, D.C.: Smithsonian Institution Press, 1997).
2. McCurdy, 83–107.
3. William Irwin Thompson, "The Deeper Meaning of Apollo 17," *New York Times*, January 1, 1973, 13.
4. On this point, see David Mindell's excellent analysis of the various configurations of man and machine articulated by the American manned space program culminating with the Apollo missions. As Mindell shows, the different methods of integrating man and machine, pilot and automated system, were the result of complex negotiations between various constituencies and expressed compromises between engineering demands, human expectations (particularly those of the astronauts), and technical philosophies regarding the appropriate role of the flight crew in spaceflight. David A. Mindell, *Digital Apollo: Human and Machine in Spaceflight* (Cambridge, MA: MIT Press, 2008).
5. Roger D. Launius, "Heroes in a Vacuum: The Apollo Astronaut as Cultural Icon" (paper presented at the 43rd AIAA Aerospace Sciences Meeting and Exhibit, Reno, Nevada, January 10–13, 2005), 2–3.
6. Megan Stern, "Imaging Space through the Inhuman Gaze," *Inhuman Reflections: Thinking the Limits of the Human*, eds. Scott Brewster, et al. (Manchester: Manchester University Press, 2000), 203.
7. David E. Nye, *American Technological Sublime* (Cambridge, MA: MIT Press, 1994), 241–251.
8. McCurdy, 233–243.
9. Joan F. Dean, "Between 2001 and Star Wars," *Journal of Popular Film and Television* 7.1 (1978): 37.
10. Donna J. Haraway, "A Cyborg Manifesto: Science, Technology, and Socialist-Feminism in the Late Twentieth Century," *Simians, Cyborgs, and Women: The Reinvention of Nature* (New York: Routledge, 1991), 149–181.
11. Of course, representations of man-machine assemblies of various types pre-date *The Six Million Dollar Man*. However, the series offers one of the first cyborgs *per se* (evidently the only earlier identification of the cyborg in either film or television is the 1966 film *Cyborg 2087*). Films explicitly organized around cybernetic themes did appear earlier, e.g., *Fail-safe* (1964) and *Colossus: The Forbin Project* (1970).
12. Tim Brooks and Earle Marsh, *The Complete Directory to Prime Time Network and Cable TV Shows 1946–Present*, 8th ed. (New York: Ballantine, 2003), 1463–64.
13. Arthur Asa Berger, "The Six Million Dollar Man," *Society* 13.5 (1976): 78, 80.
14. "The Moon and the Desert — Part I," The Six Million Dollar Man: *The Complete Season One*, DVD, directed by Richard Irving (1973; Universal Studios, 2005). In fact, the opening sequence and its accompanying narrative was edited for various lengths, with the longest version running approximately 105 seconds.
15. Norbert Wiener, *Cybernetics: Or Control and Communication in the Animal and the Machine*, 2d ed. (Cambridge, MA: MIT Press, 1961), 11.

16. C.B. Macpherson, *The Political Theory of Possessive Individualism: Hobbes to Locke* (Oxford: Oxford University Press, 1962), 3, quoted in N. Katherine Hayles, *How We Became Posthuman: Virtual Bodies in Cybernetics, Literature, and Informatics* (Chicago: University of Chicago Press, 1999), 3.

17. Manfred E. Clynes and Nathan S. Kline, "Cyborgs and Space," *Astronautics* 74 (1960), *The Cyborg Handbook*, ed. Chris Hables Gray (New York: Routledge, 1995), 30–31.

18. Ibid., 32.

19. Ibid., 31.

20. Ibid.

21. Chris Hables Gray, "An Interview with Manfred Clynes," *The Cyborg Handbook*, ed. Chris Hables Gray (New York: Routledge, 1995), 47.

22. Austin's role as an astronaut is made even more explicit in the adaptations made to the original television movie to expand it into a two-part pilot for the series, opening with six minutes of footage recounting Austin's place on the fictional Apollo 19 lunar mission. Throughout the five-year life of the series, space-related themes figured prominently in a number of the episodes.

23. "Wine, Women and War — Part 1," The Six Million Dollar Man: *The Complete Season One*, DVD, directed by Russ Mayberry (1973; Universal Studios, 2005).

24. *The Six Million Dollar Man*, VHS, directed by Richard Irving (1973; Universal Studios, 1999).

25. Timothy Leary, "The Cyberpunk: The Individual as Reality Pilot," *Storming the Reality Studio*, ed. Larry McCaffery (Durham: Duke University Press, 1991), 247. On Wiener's discussion of the term "cybernetics" see Wiener, *Cybernetics*, 11–12.

26. "The Moon and the Desert — Part I." While the title sequence attributes the cause of Austin's crash to engine failure, the actual scene identifies the cause as a control failure; as Austin reports, "She's really oscillating now." This is of some significance because oscillation — an error in the feedback loop of a self-regulating system — is a primary problem of cybernetics.

27. *The Six Million Dollar Man*.

28. Ibid.

29. Ibid.

30. Ibid.

31. Ibid.

32. Ibid.

33. Ibid.

34. "Wine, Women and War" was originally aired as a 90-minute television movie prior to the debut of the series and later edited into a two-part episode for the first season.

35. "Population Zero," The Six Million Dollar Man: *The Complete Season One*, DVD, directed by Jeannot Szwarc (1974; Universal Studios, 2005).

36. "The Seven Million Dollar Man," The Six Million Dollar Man: *The Complete Season Two*, DVD (1974; Universal Studios, 2006).

37. Ibid.

38. "Wine, Women and War — Part I."

Bibliography

Atwill, William D. *Fire and Power: The American Space Program as Postmodern Narrative*. Athens: University of Georgia Press, 1994.

Berger, Arthur A. "The Six Million Dollar Man." *Society* 13:5 (1976)

Brooks, Tim, and Earle Marsh. *The Complete Directory to Prime Time Network and Cable TV Shows 1946–Present*, 8th ed. New York: Ballantine, 2003.
Clynes, Manfred E., and Nathan S. Kline. "Cyborgs and Space." *The Cyborg Handbook*, ed. Chris Hables Gray. New York: Routledge, 1995.
Dean, Joan F. "Between 2001 and *Star Wars*." *Journal of Popular Film and Television* 7.1 (1978): 37.
Gray, Chris Hables. "An Interview with Manfred Clynes." *The Cyborg Handbook*, ed. Chris Hables Gray. New York: Routledge, 1995.
Haraway, Donna J. "A Cyborg Manifesto: Science, Technology, and Socialist-Feminism in the Late Twentieth Century." *Simians, Cyborgs, and Women: The Reinvention of Nature*. New York: Routledge, 1991.
Hayles, N.K. *How We Became Posthuman: Virtual Bodies in Cybernetics, Literature, and Informatics*. Chicago: University of Chicago Press, 1999.
Launius, Roger D. "Heroes in a Vacuum: The Apollo Astronaut as Cultural Icon." Paper presented at the 43rd AIAA Aerospace Sciences Meeting and Exhibit, Reno, Nevada, January 10–13, 2005.
_____. "Perceptions of Apollo: Myth, Nostalgia, Memory or All of the Above?" *Space Policy* 21, 2005.
Leary, Timothy. "The Cyberpunk: The Individual as Reality Pilot." *Storming the Reality Studio*, ed. Larry McCaffery. Durham: Duke University Press, 1991.
Macpherson, C.B. *The Political Theory of Possessive Individualism: Hobbes to Locke*. Oxford: Oxford University Press, 1962.
McCurdy, Howard E. *Space and the American Imagination*. Washington, D.C.: Smithsonian Institution Press, 1997.
Mindell, David A. *Digital Apollo: Human and Machine in Spaceflight*. Cambridge, MA: MIT Press, 2008.
"The Moon and the Desert — Part I." The Six Million Dollar Man: *The Complete Season One*. DVD. Directed by Richard Irving. 1973, Universal City, CA: Universal Studios, 2005.
Nye, David E. *American Technological Sublime*. Cambridge, MA: MIT Press, 1994.
"Population Zero." The Six Million Dollar Man: *The Complete Season One*. DVD. Directed by Jeannot Szwarc. 1974, Universal City, CA: Universal Studios, 2005.
"The Seven Million Dollar Man." The Six Million Dollar Man: *The Complete Season Two*. DVD. Directed by Richard Irving. 1974, Universal City, CA: Universal Studios, 2006.
The Six Million Dollar Man. VHS. Directed by Richard Irving. 1973, Universal City, CA: Universal Studios, 1999.
Stern, Megan. "Imaging Space through the Inhuman Gaze." *Inhuman Reflections: Thinking the Limits of the Human*, ed. Scott Brewster, et al. Manchester: Manchester University Press, 2000.
Thompson, William Irwin. "The Deeper Meaning of Apollo 17." *New York Times*, January 1, 1973.
Wiener, Norbert. *Cybernetics: Or Control and Communication in the Animal and the Machine*, 2d ed. Cambridge, MA: MIT Press, 1961.
"Wine, Women and War — Part 1." The Six Million Dollar Man: *The Complete Season One*. DVD. Directed by Russ Mayberry. 1973, Universal City, CA: Universal Studios, 2005.

6

It's about Tempus
Greece and Rome in "Classic" Doctor Who[1]

ANTONY KEEN

The British science fiction (sf) series *Doctor Who*, directed initially at children, ran from 1963 to 1989, making an icon out of the mysterious time-traveler known only as "the Doctor"[2] (initially played by William Hartnell, later by other actors). The show successfully returned to television screens in 2005. As time travel is a fundamental element in the show, history has featured prominently through the years. To tackle all the ways that the series used history is beyond the scope of a single essay. Instead, a close examination of five key stories[3] involving ancient Greece and Rome (*The Romans*, *The Myth Makers*, *The Time Monster*, *Underworld* and *The Horns of Nimon*) demonstrates a changing approach to history in the 1960s and 1970s.

When *Doctor Who* began, it had a twofold purpose: to introduce children to science and history and to entertain them. The creators envisaged "past," "future," and "sideways" (trips to alien planets) stories.[4] "Future" and "sideways" stories were in a science fiction style, while travel to the "past" resulted in stories where the only sf element was the presence of the Doctor and his companions.

Early trips into the past tackled, amongst other periods, the Stone Age, Mongol China, and the Aztec empire. Roman history was in the 1960s commonly taught in British schools (as it still is), and most of the population would have had some familiarity with the period. Therefore, a story drawing upon Rome was an obvious choice, and one set in Roman Britain, with the working title *Britain 408 AD*, was planned for the first season in 1963–64, and commissioned from writer Malcolm Hulke. The story dealt with the withdrawal of the Roman legions and the resulting clash between those attempting to maintain Roman civilization and those willing to ally themselves with Saxons for personal gain.[5] This subject had been featured in Rosemary Sutcliff's 1959 children's novel *The Lantern Bearers* and was therefore familiar to a large part of *Who*'s original target audience.[6]

This story was never produced,[7] but would probably have been a typical early *Who* historical, similar to *Marco Polo* (1964), placing the Doctor and his companions into a familiar period of history, or at least the popular version of it. But the choice of 408 as the date, rather than the more traditional 410, may be significant. Though at the time (and indeed still, to a degree) popular imagination supposed that troops packed up and left for the continent at the end of Roman Britain, no evidence exists to suggest that a single person relocated in 410; the Emperor Honorius only declined to fund the apparatus of Roman government and military in Britain. But three years earlier, troops *had* left, in support of Constantine III's bid for the imperial throne, and not come back.[8] Was *Who* fulfilling its educational remit by planning to show what actually happened, rather than what people imagined?

The idea of a Roman story did not go away. *Doctor Who*'s creators planned another for the second season, which did get made, broadcast in January 1965. *The Romans*[9] was written by Dennis Spooner, newly-appointed script editor. Instead of Roman Britain, the setting was Italy at the time of the Emperor Nero.

Who fan publications have witnessed considerable debate over the historical accuracy of this story; some castigate it for its hostility to Nero, while others defend its approach.[10] Arguably, this misses the point. Though the Doctor's companion Ian quotes from both Shakespeare and Cicero,[11] there is little evidence of intense research. There are only four historical characters: Nero, his wife Poppaea, Tigellinus (misspelled as Tigilinus, and fictionalized as a mute slave rather than the Praetorian Prefect), and Locusta, whom Nero's mother allegedly hired to poison the Emperor Claudius.[12] Locusta is here elevated to a position as court poisoner.[13] Historical inaccuracies abound, such as the continual repetition of the popular confusion between the circus and the amphitheatre. Unlike previous historicals, such as *Marco Polo* or *The Aztecs* (both 1964), the creators' intentions were not to produce an accurate impression of life in first-century A.D. Italy.

Rather, it is something that *Who* would do much more frequently in later decades, telling a story in the style of some well-recognized genre, in this case the Hollywood historical epic. As Spooner himself admitted, the intention was to parody *Quo Vadis* (1951).[14] Derek Francis' performance (at forty-one, rather too middle-aged to play the twenty-six-year-old Nero), which he seems to have enjoyed,[15] owes much more to Peter Ustinov in *Quo Vadis* and Charles Laughton in *The Sign of The Cross* (1932) — and indeed to British comic character actors and *Carry On* film stars Sid James and Kenneth Williams — than to Suetonius or Tacitus. Several scenes, such as the final shot of Nero playing the lyre as Rome burns, or the end of the second episode, when the Doctor's companion Ian rushes to the bars of his cell to see the lions to which he is about to be thrown, directly imitate those of Mervyn LeRoy's epic. Other clichés of the historical epic appear — two regular cast members sold into slavery, one ending up as a galley-slave (as in *Ben-Hur*), a scheming woman in the imperial household (shades of *I, Claudius* and many others), a gladiatorial fight, and, as noted, characters told that they will be thrown to the lions. Stock footage of Italo Gismondi's model of Rome is employed for scene-setting. Only a chariot scene is missing, presumably for budgetary reasons. The same restricted budget undercuts the satire of epic; the lions, for instance, are rather placid examples from stock footage of London Zoo, and the gladiatorial battle occurs in a very small arena, just about the size of a (small) television studio.

Romans marked a significant change in the format of the historical. Though (contrary to later understanding) historicals were as popular with audiences as science fiction stories, BBC Head of Serials Donald Wilson admitted that historicals were seen by the creators as makeweights between sf stories.[16] Producer Verity Lambert, keen to push the boundaries of the series by doing a comedy story, saw historicals as the obvious venue for this experiment. Spooner had previously written for comedians Harry Worth and Tony Hancock (as well as the Gerry Anderson series *Stingray*, a more lighthearted show than early *Who*). As a result, the emphasis in *Romans* shifted to humor instead of historical education. Spooner envisioned a *Who* version of the Burt Shevelove/Larry Gelbart/Stephen Sondheim musical comedy *A Funny Thing Happened on the Way to the Forum*, still enjoying its highly successful first London run.[17] Any direct influence, beyond doing a Roman comedy, is not easy to spot; but the general influence of British music-hall and stage farce is visible in the third episode; there Nero, displaying the sort of sexual enthusiasm out of which Sid James made a career, chases the Doctor's companion Barbara through his palace, and she constantly just misses running into the Doctor and Vicki, who are also in the palace, as unaware of her presence as she is of theirs.

The story was further influenced by *Carry On Cleo* (1964), the tenth in a long-running series of British comedy films.[18] It is probably misleading to say that the *Who* story was wholly inspired by *Cleo*[19]; previous script editor David Whitaker had sent a memo on April 14, 1964, suggesting a Roman story[20] three months before *Cleo* began filming. Nevertheless, Spooner was a neighbor of *Carry On* actor Jim Dale, both productions used the same researcher, and Spooner had visited the set of *Cleo*. Spooner has confessed that all these factors influenced how he wrote *Romans*.[21] A number of scenes resemble ones in the film, most notably a slave market scene, though *Who* plays it a little less for laughs. Both *Who* story and film also quote Shakespeare's line "Friends, Romans, countrymen…"[22] to comic effect.

Despite its partial Hollywood model, *Romans* maintains a British attitude (i.e., an Anglo-Saxon British attitude, the only sort likely to be reflected in sixties *Who*) towards the Roman empire,[23] regarding the empire as a whole as a good thing, while disapproving of individual emperors. In this story, although much of the focus is on the madness at Nero's court, the earlier scenes show the empire working relatively well in rural Italy, though there are dangers on the roads from the likes of slave traders happy to kidnap people from their houses.

This imposition of British cultural values over an essentially American genre causes a few oddities. For instance, Nero's slave-buyer, Tavius, is revealed to be secretly a Christian, in a brief wordless sequence where he holds a small cross.[24] But the story takes Christianity no further than explaining why Tavius helps Ian and Barbara.[25] This contrasts with most Hollywood epics, where the coming dominance of the Roman world by Christianity usually provided a prominent theme.[26]

Romans was not well-received, either at the time, as indicated by the BBC's audience responses,[27] or subsequently in fan publications. In later years, fan writer Paul Mount[28] thought the excessive use of humor undermined *Romans*. The most overtly humorous episode, the third, "Conspiracy," features the farce-influenced chase through Nero's palace, and a scene where the Doctor plays a lyre completely silently and fools his audience into thinking they are hearing beautiful music, in homage (as the Doctor explains to Vicki) to Hans Christian Andersen's "The Emperor's New Clothes," where the emperor is persuaded that he is wearing elaborate robes when he is in fact naked, and all his courtiers go along with the idea. This episode had the misfortune of being broadcast on the day of Winston Churchill's funeral, when it was generally felt the nation should be in mourning.[29] The repeat of the comic experiment, in *The Myth Makers* (discussed below) and *The Gunfighters* (the gunfight at the O.K. Corral) could be argued to have undermined the historicals in general.

Perhaps partly because of this reception, *Romans* is the only broadcast story prior to 2008 to have a principally Roman background, though displaced Romans appear in *The War Games* (1969).[30] *Who*'s subsequent interaction with the Classical world focused much more on the Greeks. This represented a change in the way *Who* dealt with the classical past, drawing upon it for myth rather than history.

This is encapsulated in the title of the next story to draw on classical sources. Now missing from the BBC's archives, *The Myth Makers* (1965) was another historical, written by Donald Cotton. But rather than using historical accounts, Cotton turns to literature for his tale of the Doctor landing on the plain of Troy in the tenth year of the Trojan War. His main sources are Homer's *Iliad* and the rest of the corpus of Greek literature dealing with the Trojan War and its immediate aftermath, but he is also influenced by Shakespeare's *Troilus and Cressida* (and Chaucer's earlier version), from which he borrows the love triangle of Troilus, Cressida, and Diomede (placing companions of the Doctor in the last two roles, with Vicki as Cressida and Steven as Diomede). Cotton does not compete with Homer by retelling the *Iliad*; instead he begins at the killing of Hector by Achilles, close to where Homer ends.

As with *Romans*, comedy comes to the fore. A working title for the third episode (rejected as too humorous) was "Is there a Doctor in the Horse?" The approach can be seen particularly in the rather camp portrayal of Paris. Comedy is, however, abandoned in the final scenes, when most of the Trojan characters are killed in a Greek massacre. This is quite harrowing after the viewer has been led to build up affection for some of the Trojan characters, especially Priam. The Greeks are presented in a less sympathetic fashion, yet win, while the characters that die are those with whom the viewer has been encouraged to empathize.

Unlike Spooner in *Romans*, however, Cotton's writing is well-versed in Greek mythology. He had previously adapted a number of Greek tales for the BBC's Third Programme (on radio), in the early 1960s.[31] This familiarity with other interpretations probably influenced Cotton's noteworthy treatment of Helen of Troy. Casting Helen is very difficult for a naturalistic (i.e., non-masked) stage, film, or television production. Helen represents an ideal, the most beautiful woman in the world. Experienced through the written word, readers can construct her appearance according to their own subjective taste in female beauty. But once the ideal becomes concrete and real, a conflict is almost inevitably set up with audience expectations.[32] Cotton solved this problem by never bringing Helen on screen, though others often speak of her; thus, her appearance always remains solely in the viewers' imaginations. Hector Berlioz similarly omitted Helen from the onstage cast of his opera *Les Troyens*, and this may have given Cotton the idea.

Cotton's scripts include references that now seem obscure to anyone without a detailed knowledge of the mythology. For instance, in an exchange from the first episode, "Temple of Secrets," the story of Agamemnon and Clytemnestra, and the latter's infidelity, familiar from the Greek playwright Aeschylus, is presented in an allusive manner—Clytemnestra's name is never mentioned. This is far more subtle than the overt homage to Hans Christian Andersen in *Romans*.

A further allusion comes at the end of *Myth Makers*, when Trojan survivors depart to found a new Troy. Only if the viewer knows the Aeneas legend, as retold by Virgil, will they realize that this new Troy will be Rome. *Myth Makers* assumes a considerable knowledge of Greek mythology, more than one might now expect in a children's show. However, it stands as a monument to the education of 1950s and 1960s Britain, where a much greater familiarity with Homer, Aeschylus, Virgil, and Shakespeare could be assumed. In any case, such knowledge is not essential to enjoying the story.

The traditional legends are, of course, slightly changed in order to accommodate the Doctor and his companions.[33] For example, the Doctor himself supplies Odysseus with the idea of the Trojan Horse, which he got from reading Homer—a classic time paradox. Vicki becoming Cressida is identified by critic Kim Newman as a rare moment where one of the Doctor's companions becomes fully involved in history.[34] To accommodate this, Cotton changes the end of this myth to have Troilus kill Achilles, and survive the sack of Troy. He does, however, play with audience expectations set up by a knowledge of earlier versions; Troilus believes himself betrayed by Cressida for Diomede (the name assumed by the Doctor's other companion Steven), as he does in Shakespeare, but at almost the last minute, Cressida returns to him, and the lovers are reunited, to escape with Aeneas' refugees.[35]

By all accounts, the production design matched the attention to detail in the script (John Wood's sets have been especially praised).[36] Unfortunately, *Myth Makers* is today visually very poorly documented. Not only have the episodes been lost, but there is no good still photographic record, as for many lost stories. Only eight photos exist, as well as sixty-one seconds of off-air clips.[37] What survives (including the original model of the Trojan

Horse, now in the hands of a private collector) suggests that the BBC Costume department maintained its usual standards.

Both *Myth Makers* and *Romans* illustrate what Newman has identified as a problem with the historicals, and a possible reason why they fell from favor; the bad guys win.[38] In Earth's history, the Doctor is bound by the audience's knowledge of what actually happened. He cannot prevent Nero setting the fire of Rome. Nor can he save the Trojans from the Greeks, though the Trojans have been portrayed throughout as, in general, the more personable.

At the conclusion of *Myth Makers*, the Doctor gains a new companion, a Trojan handmaiden called Katarina. This development was intriguing, but difficult to make work. The companion's primary role is someone to whom the Doctor can explain what's going on (and thus explain the plot to the viewers). The character, therefore, cannot be either too far behind or too far ahead of the audience's knowledge. A companion who has to have what the audience takes for granted explained to them can significantly slow down the storytelling. This is not to say that a companion from technologically backward background cannot work in *Who*. Jamie, a Jacobite from eighteenth-century Scotland, lasted from 1966 to 1969 as companion to Patrick Troughton's Doctor, and is still fondly remembered, while Leela, from a tribe of human colonists that had fallen into savagery, was the companion through all of 1977 and early 1978. But Jamie rapidly came up to a twentieth-century level of understanding. And neither Jamie nor Leela revered the Doctor. Katarina treats him as a god, always referring to him as "Great One."

The limitations of Katarina are obvious in the early episodes of the next story, *The Daleks' Masterplan*. She is killed four episodes into that story. The death scene, a pre-filmed insert, was the first work actress Adrienne Hill had done in the role, before the video recording of the last episode of *Myth Makers*. Producer John Wiles and script editor Donald Tosh had rapidly come to understand the problems the character created,[39] but were unable to remove her from the scripts already commissioned for the end of *Myth Makers* and the beginning of *Masterplan*.

As the show moved into the late 1960s and Hartnell was replaced by Patrick Troughton, *Who* further changed its relation to history. "Straight" historical stories ceased with *The Highlanders* (1966–67), though there were "pseudo-historicals," set in Earth's past, but including sf elements (beyond the Doctor and his companions), usually an alien invasion of some kind.[40] Even these were rare, with only two in the Troughton era.

The era of Jon Pertwee's Doctor saw *Who* change again, becoming oriented towards a slightly older audience (with the Doctor based on twentieth-century Earth), and more prone to satire and allegory.[41] In 1972 *The Time Monster* saw the first major use of a Greek background in eight years, as well as the first visit to Earth's past since *The Abominable Snowmen* in 1967 (not counting *The War Games*, where eras from Earth's past are recreated on an alien world).[42] Barry Letts and Robert Sloman[43] wrote a story in which the destruction of Atlantis takes centre stage, choosing to ignore 1967's *The Underwater Menace*, a near-future story set in Atlantis, and indeed the claim of Azal the Daemon to have destroyed Atlantis in 1971's *The Daemons* (which Letts and Sloman had also written).[44] The writers focused upon then-fashionable theories seeking the origins of the Atlantis legend in the Bronze Age eruption of a volcano at Thera and the fall of the Minoan civilization. The theory was first proposed by K.T. Frost, and J.V. Luce had recently popularized it.[45] As a result of the Minoan association in *Time Monster*, the Minotaur is inserted into the story (ignoring its appearance as an entirely fictional character in 1968's *The Mind Robber*).

The creators evidently undertook a lot of research. The production designers took much of their inspiration for sets and costumes from Minoan artifacts. Plato is mentioned at the beginning of the story, when the Doctor's current assistant Jo Grant is explaining theories on Atlantis to a disinterested Doctor. Familiarity with Plato presumably explains the naming of minor characters Hippias and Crito, the titles of two Platonic dialogues. There may even be a brief allusion to the Platonic Theory of Forms, when the Crystal of Kronos and the Doctor's own TARDIS are said to be outside time, with only their appearances being in the universe of time and space.[46]

The eponymous Time Monster is called Kronos, a name not picked randomly. The Titan of Greek myth embodies strong contradictions; in some tales he presides over a golden age, in others he is a tyrannical figure who castrated his father and swallowed his children.[47] Kronos the Time Monster has a similarly dual nature, explaining some characters' motivations. The High Priest Krasis believes that the return of Kronos will restore Atlantis' glory, while King Dalios fears (rightly) that it will bring destruction. Kronos' duality is explicitly stated in a line of dialogue given to Kronos: "I can be all things. A destroyer, a healer, a creator. I am beyond good and evil as you know it."[48]

Time Monster shares many parallels with the 1970 story *The Daemons*, not all of which are relevant to this essay. In both stories the Doctor's archenemy, The Master, disguises himself through a classical version of his name:

the Rev. Magister in *Daemons* and Professor Thascalos in *Time Monster*.[49] And in both the Doctor berates other characters (Jo Grant in *Daemons*, his nominal superior Brigadier Lethbridge-Stewart in *Time Monster*) for their lack of a classical education and consequent failure to see through the Master's subterfuge.

The Tom Baker era of the late seventies saw a return to the Doctor as a wanderer through the universe (in the Pertwee era, the Doctor did sometimes travel though time and space, but these were trips from his base on Earth). In this period, the series was characterized by taking familiar genres and stories, such as Sherlock Holmes or *Frankenstein*, and recasting them as *Who* stories. Greek mythology was not immune. Leaving aside the use of Greek art, filtered through an Art Deco lens, in *The Robots of Death* (1977), three stories directly appropriate Greek myth for a *Who* serial.

In 1978, script editor Anthony Read suggested to writers Bob Baker and Dave Martin that they use the story of Jason and the Argonauts as the basis for a story; this resulted in *Underworld*. Andrew Martin writes that *Underworld*

> is one of a long line ... with an uncredited extra author. In this case it is not the script editor or another trusted, experienced writer but the generations of Greek storytellers who created and refined the myth of Jason and the Argonauts. While stories such as *The Brain of Morbius* are reworkings of classic tales of literature under greater or lesser disguise, *Underworld* is an instance of a story owing so much to its roots that the authors feel obliged to acknowledge the fact in its closing moments: "I called Jackson 'Jason'? ... Jason was another captain on a long quest."[50]

The story practices a knowing form of quasi-anagram. There are a group of Minyans,[51] on a ship called the *RIC* (= *Argosy*). They are on a Quest for race banks (= the Golden Fleece), which are hanging on "a tree at the end of the world"— in the *Who* story the tree is a schematic way of describing a network of tunnels in a planet on the edge of the known universe. This tree is in Heidis (= Hades). The Minyans are called Jackson (= Jason), Herick (= Hercules), Orfe (= Orpheus), and Tala (= Atalanta). Other Classical elements in this story include an Oracle (turned into a super-computer), Persephone (the name of the ship the race banks were on is called *P7E*), and the sword of Damocles. Just in case anyone had not yet got the point, the writers give the Doctor a final scene musing on whether ancient myths and legends are not in fact echoes of the future.[52] The viewer may well sympathize with the Doctor's robotic companion K-9, who, asked to comment on the Doctor's theorizing, simply says, "Negative."

There were two different views on this approach. Graham Williams, producer at the time, felt that the names were a bonus feature for anyone who knew the original story, layered on to a *Who* story that stood up in its own right. John Nathan-Turner, who was production unit manager, and went on to succeed Williams as producer, objected to what he saw as in-jokes, which would allow a certain part of the audience to feel smarter than others.[53]

In the following season, *The Armageddon Factor* (1979), the last story in the "Key to Time" arc, and again written by Baker and Martin, used the Trojan War in a less heavy-handed fashion. Two planets called Atrios and Zeos are locked in a never-ending war, the key to which is a Princess. Yet the mythological elements are mostly window dressing for a story more interested in commenting on the Cold War.[54]

After he became a freelance writer, Read himself wrote another story along similar lines to *Underworld* in the next season (1979). This time he used the myth of Theseus and the Minotaur. In *The Horns of Nimon*, the Minotaur becomes the Nimon, Knossos is Skonnos, Athens is Aneth, Theseus is Seth, Daedalus is Soldeed, and Corinth becomes Crinoth. At the end of the story, the Doctor notes that at least he remembered to get Seth to paint his ship white, unlike the last time—a reference to the part of the Minotaur legend where Theseus forgets to raise a white sail to signal his victory and survival to his father Aegeus. Thus, the Doctor implies his presence at the time of Theseus' adventure in Crete, which contradicts the version of the Minotaur shown in *Time Monster* and the fictional Minotaur from *Mind Robber*.[55]

As John Tulloch and Manuel Alvarado note,[56] *Nimon* relies on a certain degree of privileged information for its full effect, as does *Underworld*. Done well, adapting a Greek myth into another setting can produce significant works of art, such as James Joyce's novel *Ulysses* (1922) or the Coen brothers' film *O Brother Where Art Thou?* (2000), both of which use the *Odyssey* as a stepping-off point, but then go in different directions. Done badly, it becomes an excuse for lazy writing, and this is the case with these *Who* stories. Naming characters by quasi-anagram is both too knowing and clumsy, and both stories lack imagination. *Underworld* has some novelty, though it really only does what *Who* had done before with other prototypes with more subtlety and flair, such as Mary Shelley's *Frankenstein*, reworked as *The Brain of Morbius* (1976). *Nimon* is even more obvious about its sources than *Underworld* and is consequently less interesting. Both require a degree of knowledge of the original legends to work fully, as *Myth Makers* did. But *Myth Makers* has an extra layer of meaning for those who know that will pass unnoticed for those who do not. *Underworld* and *Nimon* explicitly tell the audience that there is an extra layer of meaning that some of them might not get.

Yet, one wonders whether many current children's productions would even bother with this level of extra meaning. A comparison with the modern children-orientated *Who* spin-off, *The Sarah Jane Adventures*, is instructive. In a two-part story, "Eye of the Gorgon" (2007), Greek mythological elements are used, but all the information needed to understand them is provided in the script. There is no assumption of further knowledge.

The use of classical mythology seen in *Underworld* and *Nimon* would not be repeated. Indeed, the closest the program came to drawing again on Greece and Rome before its cancellation is 1989's *Battlefield* (when the Doctor was Sylvester McCoy), based on Arthurian mythos.[57] But the 2005 relaunch saw a different show once again. Deliberately tying itself to Earth, the series is forced to re-engage with the planet's history, and Christopher Eccleston and David Tennant have gone into the past more often than any Doctor since Hartnell, though all these stories have actually been pseudo-historicals. It was almost inevitable that the Classical world should be featured eventually; so in 2008 the second episode was "The Fires of Pompeii," a pseudo-historical involving the eruption of Vesuvius. This story lies outside the scope of this essay, but shows the series returning almost full circle, back to engaging with actual Roman history, rather than Greek myth.

Notes

1. This chapter is based on papers delivered to Open University seminars and the science fiction conventions SecconD (May 2001) and Helicon 2 (March 2002). I thank all the organizers and audiences, and particularly Mark Slater and Graham Sleight for generous provision of research materials, and SMS (pen name for an artist and *Doctor Who* fan) for a helpful written response.

2. This essay follows the convention that the show is called *Doctor Who*, but the character is simply "the Doctor."

3. Between 1963 and 1989, *Doctor Who* was made in 25-minute episodes (apart from a brief experiment with 45-minute episodes in 1986). These were grouped into stories, running from two to fourteen episodes. Up until 1966, *Who* used individual episode titles; overall story titles, not shown on screen, were purely for production purposes, and tended to be simple and self-explanatory. From 1966, overall story titles were used on screen, with the individual episodes being numbered within the story. Since the 2005 return, the show has adopted the 45-minute format, and reverted to individual episode titles. Overall story titles are not used. In this essay, italics are used to indicate story titles (e.g., *The Romans*), and quotation marks for episode titles (e.g., "The Slave Traders").

4. David J. Howe and Stephen James Walker, Doctor Who: *The Television Companion* (London: BBC, 1998), 3.

5. See the memorandum from script editor David Whitaker quoted in Matthew Kilburn, "Bargains of Necessity? *Doctor Who, Culloden* and Fictionalising History at the BBC in the 1960s," *Time and Relative Dissertations in Space*, ed. David Butler (Manchester: Manchester University Press, 2007), 77, and cited in James Chapman, *Inside the TARDIS: The Worlds of* Doctor Who. *A Cultural History* (London & New York: I.B Tauris, 2006), 225.

6. Sutcliff's novel actually begins *c.* A.D. 450, but includes many elements commonly associated with the traditional end of Roman Britain in A.D. 410.

7. Hulke resubmitted the idea in 1965, but it was rejected because in the intervening period *The Romans* had been produced.

8. This is stated explicitly in Sheppard Frere, *Britannia: A History of Roman Britain* (London: Routledge, 1967), 365, and is implicit in R.G. Collingwood and J.N.L. Myres, *Roman Britain and the English Settlements* (Oxford: Oxford University Press, 1945), 290–3. The popular view is shown in *The Lantern Bearers*.

9. The episode titles for *Romans* are "The Slave Traders," "All Roads Lead to Rome," "Conspiracy," and "Inferno."

10. See a summary in Howe and Walker, 47. The debate does not appear very sophisticated, each writer seemingly reflecting whichever Roman history book they have borrowed from their local library.

11. *First Catiline* 1.2: *O tempora, O mores!* (Albert Curtis Clark, ed., *M. Tulli Ciceronis Orationes* [Oxford: Oxford University Press, 1908]; Michael Grant, trans., *Cicero: Selected Political Speeches* [London: Penguin Books, 1989], 76).

12. Tacitus, *Annals* 12.66 (Michael Grant, trans., *Tacitus: The Annals of Imperial Rome* [London: Penguin Books, 1996], 282).

13. Tacitus does say that she had "a long career of imperial service."

14. Sean Patrick Sullivan, "Serial M: *The Romans*," A Brief History of Time (Travel), http://www.shannonsullivan.com/drwho/serials/m.html, claims that the *original* intention was to parody *Quo Vadis*, but this was abandoned in favor of the Great Fire of Rome when it was discovered that *Carry On Cleo* would be poking fun at the Hollywood movie. There is clearly some confusion here, as the Great Fire is a central part of *Quo Vadis*, and *Romans* is far closer to *Quo Vadis* than *Cleo*, whose prime target is the notorious 1963 *Cleopatra*.

15. See the interview cited by Peter Haining, Doctor Who—*25 Glorious Years* (London: W.H. Allen, 1988), 135. Francis had specifically requested a part in *Who*, and director Christopher Barry thought the part had been written for him (see Tat Wood and Lawrence Miles, *About Time 1: The Unauthorized Guide to* Doctor Who *1963–1966: Seasons 1 to 3* (Des Moines: Mad Norwegian Press, 2006), 129).

16. Chapman, 31–32.

17. Wood and Miles 2006, *About Time 1*, 127.

18. On the *Carry On*s, see Mark Campbell, *The Pocket Essential Carry On Films* (London: Pocket Essentials, 2002), with 36–38 on *Cleo*.

19. As suggested by Mark Campbell, *Doctor Who* (London: Pocket Essentials, 2007), 23.

20. Sullivan.

21. Spooner, quoted in Doctor Who*: An Adventure in Space and Time. Serial M: The Romans* (n.d.), 10. Spooner says that his set visit was while writing *Romans*, but he was not actually commissioned until August 31, 1964, and filming on *Cleo* ended on July 28.

22. *Julius Caesar*, Act III, Scene II.

23. On British identification with Rome, see Christopher Kelly, *The Roman Empire: A Very Short Introduction* (Oxford: Oxford University Press, 2006), 114–22. On *Who* as a reflection of a post-imperialist British viewpoint, see Nicholas Cull, "'Bigger on the inside...' *Doctor Who* as British Cultural History," *The Historian, Television and Television History*, eds. Graham Roberts and Philip M. Taylor (Luton: The Historian, Television and

Television History, 2001), 95–111, and, somewhat stretching the point, Alec Charles, "The Ideology of Anachronism: Television, History and the Nature of Time," *Time and Relative Dissertations in Space*, ed. David Butler (Manchester: Manchester University Press, 2007), 108–22.

24. This is anachronistic, as Christians had yet to adopt the cross in A.D. 64, but the correct symbol, the fish, would not have been recognized by the audience, and in any case is not found in the mise-en-scène of the Hollywood Roman epic.

25. There are hints, though nothing explicit, that Tavius helps Barbara because her kindness to another slave suggests to him that she is also a Christian.

26. A possible reference is a similar moment in Anthony Mann's *The Fall of the Roman Empire* (1964), in which James Mason's Timonides is revealed on his death to be a Christian solely by a crucifix falling out of his clothing.

27. Howe and Walker, 48.

28. Paul Mount, "Story Review," Doctor Who: *An Adventure in Space and Time. Serial M: The Romans* (n.d.): 5–6. See also John Tulloch and Manuel Alvarado, Doctor Who: *The Unfolding Text* (London: Palgrave Macmillan, 1983), 156.

29. Wood and Miles, 129.

30. In 1967 Roger Dixon submitted a story idea called *Bar Kochbar*, involving the Doctor in the second century A.D. Jewish revolt that resulted in the change of the province name from Judaea to Syria Palestina. This was rejected, perhaps because in the context of contemporary Arab-Israeli conflict it was too controversial. Romans also appear in the novelizations of two later stories, Terrance Dicks, Doctor Who—*The Time Monster* (1985, original story 1972) and Malcolm Hulke, Doctor Who *and the Dinosaur Invasion* (1976, original story 1974), but not in the actual broadcast versions.

31. Cotton wrote "Echo and Narcissus" (broadcast August 15, 1959), "The Golden Fleece" (May 2, 1962), and "The Tragedy of Phaethon" (February 10, 1965—this was a comedy). Humphrey Searle, who provided the incidental music for *Myth Makers*, had done the same for "The Golden Fleece." Max Adrian, who appears as Priam, had also starred in at least one of these.

32. Bettany Hughes, *Helen of Troy: Goddess, Princess, Whore* (London: 2006), 307.

33. But far fewer liberties are taken with Homer and other Greek accounts than in Wolfgang Petersen's film *Troy* (2004). See Antony G. Keen, "*Troy*: A Reflection," *Troy*: Views and Reviews, The Open University, Department of Classical Studies, http://www.open.ac.uk/Arts/classtud/troy/keen-troy.htm, for the argument that altering myths from the traditional canon is not *per se* a bad idea.

34. Kim Newman, *Doctor Who* (London: BFI, 2005), 46. For more discussion of Vicki becoming Cressida, see Wood and Miles, 2006, *About Time 1*, 205–7.

35. Further classical allusions are to be found in Cotton's novelization (Doctor Who—*The Myth Makers*, 1985), which expands considerably on the televised story. Cotton includes Homer himself (usually placed four centuries after the war he describes) as a character and first-person narrator. Cotton also novelized *The Romans* (1987), as an epistolary novel, in the form of letters from various characters.

36. Howe and Walker, 72. Outside location filming was done in Frensham Ponds, Surrey, and a glass shot was used for the city of Troy; see Campbell, *Doctor Who*, 4th ed., 30.

37. This footage can be viewed on the Doctor Who: *Lost in Time* DVD. The soundtrack also survives, and is available on CD.

38. Newman, 26.

39. See Tosh's remarks, quoted in Patrick Mulkern, "Adrienne Hill Interviewed," Doctor Who *Magazine Summer Special* (1986): 5.

40. On these as a genre, see Gary Russell, "Making History!" Doctor Who *Magazine Summer Special* (1986): 40–45.

41. Newman, 74.

42. The return to Earth's history was party driven by fan requests; see Jeremy Bentham, "Production Office," Doctor Who: *An Adventure in Time and Space* 15 (n.d.): 8.

43. Letts was at the time the show's producer. Since a BBC staff producer was not supposed to write for his own series, the story was credited to Sloman alone; see David J. Howe, Mark Stammers and Stephen James Walker, Doctor Who—*The Seventies* (London: Doctor Who Books, 1994), 51.

44. Tat Wood and Lawrence Miles, *About Time 2: The Unauthorized Guide to* Doctor Who *1966–1969: Seasons 4 to 6* (Des Moines: Mad Norwegian Press, 2006), 57–61, try to reconcile all the different versions of Atlantis, but in truth production teams in the 1970s were not that bothered about continuity at this level of detail.

45. K.T. Frost, "The *Critias* and Minoan Crete," *Journal of Hellenic Studies* 33 (1913): 189–206; J.V. Luce, *The End of Atlantis: New Light on an Old Legend* (London: Thames & Hudson, 1969). Modern scholarship now tends to seek Atlantis's origins in the thought-processes and philosophy of Plato (i.e., he made it up), though popular books continue to assume some reality behind the legend.

46. David Rafer, "Mythic Identity in *Doctor Who*," *Time and Relative Dissertations in Space*, ed. David Butler (Manchester: Manchester University Press, 2007), 128.

47. Kronos and the golden age: Hesiod, *Works and Days* 111; Kronos as tyrant: Hesiod, *Theogony* 137–38, 154–69, 453–95 (see Dorothy Wender, trans., *Hesiod and Theognis* [London: Penguin Books, 1973], 62, 27, 28, 38–9).

48. I am grateful to Dr. Naoko Yamagata of the Open University, who helped me recognize the importance of this particular reference.

49. The name often appears in secondary literature as "Thasca*les*." However, the cast can clearly be heard saying "Thasca*los*," the correct pronunciation of the Greek δασκαλός, and this is the spelling in Terrance Dicks' novelization. The error seems to go back to Terrance Dicks and Malcolm Hulke, *The Making of* Doctor Who (London: Target, 1976), 84.

50. Andrew Martin, "Playing the Blues," *In-Vision* 28 (November 1990): 8.

51. This is usually taken as being derived from "Minoans" (e.g., Martin, 8; Howe and Walker, 337), but the Minyans were a heroic race of mythological Greece, from whom most of the Argonauts were descended. Hence the term is often used in Greek literature as an alternate description for the Argonauts, and that is surely why it is in *Underworld*.

52. See Rafer, 129.

53. Both are quoted in Tulloch and Alvarado, 146.

54. Lawrence Miles and Tat Wood, *About Time 4: The Unauthorized Guide to* Doctor Who *1975–1979: Seasons 12 to 17* (Des Moines: Mad Norwegian Press, 2004), 264–5. Baker and Martin had previously written *The Mutants* (1972), where the planet was called Solos and the inhabitants Solonians, and *The Three Doctors* (1972–1973), featuring a character called "Omega," so Greek-derived names were something they had done before.

55. In the preceding story but one, *The Creature from the Pit*, there is a throwaway joke about a ball of wool found in the TARDIS, with a note of thanks from Ariadne and Theseus. This story was written by Bob Baker, and features a character called Erato, who in no other way resembled the Muse of lyric poetry. Terrance Dicks clearly did not care for the comment about painting the ship, and in his novelization (Doctor Who *and the Horns of Nimon*, 1980) replaces it with theorizing about the nature of myth lifted from the end of *Underworld*.

56. Tulloch and Alvarado, 145.

57. Though, there are plenty of examples in spin-off novels and audio productions, which cannot be discussed here.

Bibliography

Bentham, Jeremy. "Production Office." *Doctor Who: An Adventure in Space and Time* 15 (n.d.): 8.

Campbell, Mark. *Doctor Who*, 4th ed. London: Pocket Essentials, 2007 (first edition, 2000).

_____. *The Pocket Essential Carry On Films*. London: Pocket Essentials, 2002.

Chapman, James. *Inside the TARDIS: The Worlds of Doctor Who. A Cultural History*. London & New York: I.B. Tauris, 2006.

Charles, Alec. "The Ideology of Anachronism: Television, History and the Nature of Time." *Time and Relative Dissertations in Space*, ed. David Butler, 108–22. Manchester: Manchester University Press, 2007.

Clark, Albert Curtis, ed. *M. Tulli Ciceronis Orationes*. Oxford: Oxford University Press, 1908.

Collingwood, R.G., and J.N.L. Myres. *Roman Britain and the English Settlements*. Oxford: Oxford University Press, 1945 (first edition, 1937).

Cull, Nicholas. "'Bigger on the inside...' *Doctor Who* as British Cultural History." *The Historian, Television and Television History*, eds. Graham Roberts and Philip M. Taylor, 95–111. Luton: University of Luton Press, 2001.

Dicks, Terrance, and Malcolm Hulke. *The Making of Doctor Who*. London: Target, 1976 (first edition, 1972).

Frere, Sheppard. *Britannia: A History of Roman Britain*. London: Routledge, 1967.

Frost, K.T. "The *Critias* and Minoan Crete." *Journal of Hellenic Studies* 33 (1913): 189–206.

Grant, Michael, trans. *Cicero: Selected Political Speeches*. London: Penguin Books, 1989 (first published, 1969; revised edition, 1973; reprinted with a new bibliography, 1989).

_____, trans. *Tacitus: The Annals of Imperial Rome*. London: Penguin Books, 1996 (first published, 1956; revised edition, 1971; reprinted with a new bibliography, 1996).

Haining, Peter. Doctor Who—*25 Glorious Years*. London: W.H. Allen, 1988.

Howe, David J., and Stephen James Walker. *Doctor Who: The Television Companion*. London: BBC, 1998.

Howe, David J., Mark Stammers and Stephen James Walker. *Doctor Who—The Seventies*. London: Doctor Who Books, 1994.

Hughes, Bettany. *Helen of Troy: Goddess, Princess, Whore*. London: Pimlico, 2006 (first published by Jonathan Cape, 2005).

Keen, Antony G. "*Troy*: A Reflection." *Troy*: Views and Reviews. The Open University, Department of Classical Studies, 2005. http://www.open.ac.uk/Arts/classtud/troy/keen-troy.htm (accessed September 7, 2008).

Kelly, Christopher. *The Roman Empire: A Very Short Introduction*. Oxford: Oxford University Press, 2006.

Kilburn, Matthew. "Bargains of Necessity? *Doctor Who, Culloden* and Fictionalising History at the BBC in the 1960s." *Time and Relative Dissertations in Space*, ed. David Butler, 68–85. Manchester: Manchester University Press, 2007.

Luce, J.V. *The End of Atlantis: New Light on an Old Legend*. London: Thames & Hudson, 1969.

Martin, Andrew. "Playing the Blues." *In-Vision* 28 (November 1990): 8–9.

Miles, Lawrence, and Tat Wood. *About Time 4: The Unauthorized Guide to Doctor Who 1975–1979: Seasons 12 to 17*. Des Moines: Mad Norwegian Press, 2004.

Mount, Paul. "Story Review." *Doctor Who: An Adventure in Space and Time. Serial M: The Romans* (n.d.): 5–6.

Mulkern, Patrick. "Adrienne Hill Interviewed." *Doctor Who Magazine Summer Special* (1986): 4–7.

Newman, Kim. *Doctor Who*. London: BFI, 2005.

Rafer, David. "Mythic Identity in *Doctor Who.*" *Time and Relative Dissertations in Space*, ed. David Butler, 123–37. Manchester: Manchester University Press, 2007.
Russell, Gary. "Making History!" Doctor Who *Magazine Summer Special* (1986): 40–45.
Sullivan, Sean Patrick. "Serial M: *The Romans.*" A Brief History of Time (Travel). http://www.shannonsullivan.com/drwho/serials/m.html (last updated 2007, first published online 1995) (accessed September 7, 2008).
Tulloch, John, and Manuel Alvarado. Doctor Who*: The Unfolding Text*. London: Palgrave Macmillan, 1983.
Wender, Dorothy, trans. *Hesiod and Theognis*. London: Penguin Books, 1973.
Wood, Tat, and Lawrence Miles. *About Time 1: The Unauthorized Guide to* Doctor Who *1963–1966: Seasons 1 to 3*. Des Moines: Mad Norwegian Press, 2006.
_____, and _____. *About Time 2: The Unauthorized Guide to* Doctor Who *1966–1969: Seasons 4 to 6*. Des Moines: Mad Norwegian Press, 2006.

7

Constructing a Grand Historical Narrative
Struggles through Time on Highlander: The Series

DAVID C. WRIGHT, JR.

Highlander: The Series was first shown from 1992 to 1998; during those years, and in subsequent years, due to reruns and delayed broadcasts worldwide, the series built a cult following. Yet, in contrast to other cult favorites, such as *Xena: Warrior Princess*, *Buffy the Vampire Slayer*, and *Farscape*, *Highlander* has attracted little scholarly attention.[1] Like these television series, *Highlander* episodes could be either farcical, earnest, or even reaching for grandeur, on occasion; similarly the acting could be quite effective, and the story arcs complex. However, unlike these other fantasy or science fiction cult shows, *Highlander* has a traditional male romantic action hero, as well as little transgression of gender norms.[2] The series' relatively conventional deployment of gender roles, typical of much historical romance and action fiction, might be one reason for the relative critical neglect of *Highlander*, since many recent popular culture readings have utilized feminist or queer theory.[3] The one scholarly publication devoted to *Highlander* is the exception that proves the rule since the author, Shawn Shimpach, criticizes the series as a celebration of "explicitly retrograde white masculinity" and its protagonist as having an identity that is based upon "violent, white, heterosexual masculinity."[4] Thus, he studies *Highlander* for the shortcomings he sees in it, just as others have undoubtedly avoided studying the series for its failure to subvert traditional gender and sexuality norms.

However, *Highlander* is an ideal popular culture text for exploring recent concerns, or even, one might say, obsessions in the theory of history,

7. *Constructing a Grand Historical Narrative* (Wright) 117

such as memory, narrative, and identity. The series merits analysis especially due to one aspect of the show that is unusual and notable: the frequent use of flashbacks (relived memories) to convey substantial amounts of historical narrative. Since it is a fantasy series, some of its characters, including the protagonist Duncan MacLeod, are immortal, and their flashbacks can go back decades, centuries, and, in some instances, millennia. Thus, over the course of six seasons, scores of historical locations are visited, which, if stitched together through the regular viewing characteristic of cult television fans, can provide a grand historical narrative, one with a global reach.[5]

When grand historical narratives are presented in popular culture, they are usually revealing of ideology, and more generally of cultural mood. The historical narrative constructed by *Highlander* is one of struggle, by the oppressed, the well-intentioned, and the caring against the powerful, the cruel, and the selfish. Although Duncan MacLeod has some doubts and self-recriminations, as does any romantic hero with any complexity, he appears in the series' numerous historical vignettes always in defense of the innocent and the good, combating tyranny in its myriad forms, and its various agents. By closely examining the historical flashbacks in *Highlander*, a progressive, if not radically feminist, interpretation of history is revealed, and a guardedly optimistic cultural outlook is evident.

The *Highlander* series visits many crucial moments in early modern and modern history. Duncan MacLeod fights alongside his fellow Scots against the English in the early eighteenth century. *Highlander* also has episodes with MacLeod in the Napoleonic Wars, World War I, the Spanish Civil War, and World War II. MacLeod opposes twentieth-century totalitarian governments by smuggling Jews from Fascist Germany and endangered refugees from Communist Russia. American historical settings include the Civil War, the nineteenth-century Pacific Northwest, and the beginnings of the Civil Rights Movement. This chapter will examine these and other historical vignettes in order to discern the historical pattern woven by the series. Thus, while not as daring as other cult series in some ways, *Highlander* will be shown to have constructed in remarkable detail a comprehensive view of human history; a grand narrative with a good heart, a heart beating with populist sympathy. Ignoring the critiques of "master narratives" by postmodernism, the show is able to affirm the importance of the historically-informed individual in acting to shape the future of humanity.[6]

Jean-Francois Lyotard, the French theorist of postmodernism who, in *The Postmodern Condition*, equated postmodernism with "incredulity toward metanarratives,"[7] wrote elsewhere that "in remembering we do want too much: we want to take hold of the past; we want to grasp what is gone; we want to master and reveal the lost initial [event]...."[8] Although Lyotard claimed that to achieve this recuperation is to "want too much," in *Highlander*, Duncan MacLeod does exactly what Lyotard doubts can be done. MacLeod is repeatedly subjected to flashbacks of events long since past; "remembering," in Lyotard's words, in order "to take hold of the past." MacLeod desires to "grasp," that is, to both understand and to hold, the past. By doing this, he attempts to use this "now" that is gone to create a narrative with an end (a teleology), that is, create a life with a meaning. This rearview way of living is noted in the first episode of the series when MacLeod, commenting on his life, says that "you always live in the past."[9] By, in Lyotard's terms, "mastering" and revealing the "lost initial event," MacLeod tries to infuse existence (the present) with meaning, by making it part of a narrative arc originating in the past. In short, life's gift of the now and the existing, the present, is continually found wanting, lacking in meaning, so memories of past, often traumatic, events are revisited in order to "master" them, creating a "master narrative" that creates meaning for MacLeod, and by his proxy, the loyal viewer. The master narrative constructed from the series of flashbacks serves a double purpose, to give a shape to historical events and to underline the trajectory MacLeod himself has undergone.

Duncan MacLeod's life history, pieced together through dozens of flashbacks, shows an action hero with a strict, though evolving ethical code. He must defend friends, compatriots, and the victimized, and he must oppose evil, that is, those who use power for personal gain and to oppress others. Thus, his personal history, and by implication the world's history, is constructed as a narrative of struggle between good versus evil, although some ambiguity is shown at points. MacLeod asserts this Manichean view, equating beauty with good, while lecturing to a class on art history: "Throughout history we see two human traits continually showing up, even though they are completely opposed: one is the need for destruction, the other is the urge to create beauty...."[10]

MacLeod's actions demonstrate that an individual can make a difference, that history (and humanity) requires action. As he simply states, when asked why he is an ambulance driver for the Red Cross in World War I, "I chose this duty."[11] Whether providing humanitarian relief or going into battle for a just cause, MacLeod shows that he, and therefore, perhaps fans of the show, must take a stand. By this code of conduct, withdrawal from engagement is only justified when one is grieving, needing time apart for personal renewal.[12] MacLeod's life embodies a basic tenet of Hinduism annunciated in the *Bhagavad Gita*: "right action" is preferable to "renunciation of action."[13] If, however, there is no clear moral distinction between the two sides in a conflict, then a different, non-interventionist form of engagement might be sought.

The grand historical narrative created by MacLeod's actions and experiences through the centuries starts in the early modern period. The lower classes of this pre-industrial era are presented with sympathy and the aristocracy with some skepticism; nobles are often shown to be vain, arrogant, and oppressive. Although originating from humble origins, Duncan became literate and more culturally sophisticated during this time. Yet, he never acquired the attitudes of the aristocracy, remaining in sympathy with the poor and downtrodden.

The episode in which MacLeod became notably more sophisticated is also an instance in which he rejected joining the dominant elite of the time, preferring to hold on to his identity as a Highland warrior. Under the tutelage of his fellow Immortal and lover Kristen Travis, who lived in a chateau on an extensive estate, MacLeod became "presentable" to the aristocratic society of 1660. Although he was successful in learning her lessons and could assume a new, more refined persona, he soon decided, "The gentlemen I've known I care not imitate.... All this ... the wine, the clothes ... 'tis all appearance. It has no meaning to it ... 'tis not me, 'tis not right." With these words MacLeod asserted that remaining rooted in the authenticity of a marginalized, indigenous warlike people is preferable to joining the effete, "civilized" class that dominated western society during the early modern period. Declaring that "Duncan MacLeod is who I am, not some silken fop," MacLeod retained his core identity as a roughhewn hero who believes in a stout heart and a strong sword arm. Kristen then sent for material made of his clan's tartan in order to clothe him for a portrait on her estate. In this way, while seeming to concede his identity, she tried to recoup him for her civilized memory, as a sanitized and domesticated version of a "Highland barbarian." This effort also failed; MacLeod would not be domesticated.[14]

Duncan MacLeod's identity as a Scottish Highlander plays an important role in the series' anti-imperialist thread of its historical narrative. Not only did Duncan oppose the English oppression of the Scots, but he is also presented as sympathizing with the people of Ireland and India. However, after learning his lesson in the aftermath of the Battle of Culloden, he limited his actions, condemning the more extreme acts of anti-colonial nationalism, such as carrying on fighting and seeking revenge after a cause is lost, killing civilians, or terrorism.

In 1746, after the English defeated the Scots at Culloden, Duncan MacLeod, with the help of Immortal Ceirdwyn, originally a Celtic woman who had fought the Romans, but known now as Flora MacDonald, helped Bonnie Prince Charlie, the Scottish claimant to the throne, escape to France. MacLeod wanted vengeance for atrocities committed by the English, but Ceirdwyn, based on her own experience of loss and vengeance-taking, told him that "more blood does not make it better." In her struggle against the Romans, she had believed that "if there's a cause worth dying for, it's this one. A troubled people must stand when they can."[15] However, even this justified resistance of a people to conquest by an imperial power ended unhappily, with all (but the immortal) dying.[16] Similarly, centuries later, after killing many English, MacLeod learned that she was right: vengeance achieves nothing. He then left the British Isles to wander Europe and Asia. Thus, a double lesson is taught: viewers learn of the history of struggle by the colonized, but also that killing carried out in order to obtain revenge leads only to emptiness and guilt, not contentment and satisfaction over justice achieved.

Critique of English imperialism is also leveled in contexts other than Scotland by the series. Given his visceral understanding of English imperialism, it is not surprising that Duncan MacLeod would sympathize with the people of other oppressed countries, such as Ireland and India. However, his sympathy for them, or hostility to their common foe, English imperialism, would never extend to support for assassination, killing of civilians, or terrorism in general.

For instance, in 1919 Ireland, Immortal Annie Devlin and her mortal Irish husband tried to convince Duncan to join the Irish revolt against the English. He refused and Annie's husband is killed in an ambush. Duncan escapes but Annie will not go with him, preferring to continue the struggle for decades, becoming a terrorist, someone who recruits new generations of young men to her cause. In the present, during the waning years of conflict in the mid–1990s, MacLeod confronts her, asking: "How many boys have you sent to their death?" This question does not cause her to reconsider because she wants revenge. He says, "Annie, you can't get them all." She replies, "I can try ... this will never end." Although her cause is presented sympathetically, her use of a just cause to justify endless bloodshed is shown to be wrong.[17]

Similarly, in "The Wrath of Kali," when MacLeod traveled to colonial

India in 1764, he found himself in sympathy with the indigenous people, and repelled by the British who complained about their lot while benefiting from their imperial positions. In this episode, Duncan prevented an Indian widow from dying in a suttee. Then he repulsed the advances of a bored English woman who saw him as a new, interesting plaything. He instead preferred the Indian woman, whose life he had saved, who wanted one night of happiness with him before she killed herself, which by the logic of her people's customs, she must. Years later, in the late twentieth-century, MacLeod confronts the Indian Immortal Kamir, a priest for the god Kali, who kills in order to recover India's sacred artifacts. Thus, the show suggests that post-colonial depredation (by money) is as bad as the former colonial oppression (by gun). Further, Kamir and MacLeod debate whether one can one judge someone from a different culture and religion. However, after some hesitancy, MacLeod rejects this use of cultural relativism to justify murder.[18] Or put another way, he reaffirms that certain human values are universal, even if this seems to reinforce the master narrative of Western moral superiority over "barbaric" non–European customs.[19]

By the beginning of the modern era, MacLeod had become able to live with his memories of the aftermath of the Battle of Culloden, and returned to Europe from Asia to fight alongside the English. But the horrible slaughter of the Napoleonic Wars and his new friendship with Darius, an immortal pacifist monk, soon caused him to start over in the New World. In June 1815, on the Waterloo battlefield, MacLeod met Darius, who was tending to the wounded. He questioned why MacLeod was fighting, and was told, "I was raised a warrior, I choose battles I believe to be just." Darius replied: "Oh, I'm sure you're quite loyal to your convictions and compatriots. But I wonder what these men (dead and wounded) think about that, about convictions and compatriotism now?" Although impressed with the outlook of his new friend, MacLeod was not ready to embrace non-violence yet. So, a year later, in Paris, when victorious English soldiers move to plunder Darius' church, MacLeod set himself in opposition to them. Darius asked MacLeod to desist, but he refused, saying, "What else can I do? I cannot just stand by."[20]

MacLeod's commitment to stopping injustice does not extend to vigilantism, however. When living with a group of gypsies in mid-nineteenth-century Central Europe, he appealed to local authorities when his Immortal gypsy friend Irena is raped. Dismissal of the accusations and insults by local villagers then led Duncan's other Immortal gypsy friend Jacob to kill the rapist, claiming "blood for blood." MacLeod responded that vengeance is pursued for one's own pride, not justice for the wronged person.[21]

Wanting to leave the conflicts of Europe behind him, Duncan MacLeod left for the United States, seeking a fresh start in a new nation. Nevertheless, he would find conflicts once again, and take action to help the oppressed, constructing an American thread in the show's grand historical narrative. For instance, in 1862, Macleod went to Virginia as an Abolitionist helping former slaves escape to freedom and safety in the North. To accomplish this, he must bring them to an Underground Railroad station through a battle.[22] He undertook this dangerous work because he believed that it was the right thing to do. In another episode, MacLeod succinctly revealed his moral assessment of the Confederate "cause," by telling Captain Lucas Désirée, a confederate officer who happened to be a fellow Immortal, "You know you're on the wrong side."[23]

A few years later, after the end of the war, like many others, Duncan MacLeod traveled westward. But unlike the settlers who brought their civilization with them as much as possible, in 1872, MacLeod had found peace, love, and serenity dwelling with the Lakota Sioux. He was happily living with a native woman named Little Deer and helping her raise her son Kahani; her husband, MacLeod's friend, had died. MacLeod had adopted the tribe's ways, but he was not able to leave western civilization behind for long. The "Blue Coats" were expanding the territory to be used by white settlers and an Immortal army scout, identified only as Kearn, then led the troops to massacre the encamped Sioux.[24] MacLeod, who was not there at the time, returned to discover amidst the carnage the bodies of Little Deer and Kahani. Filled with rage, he vowed vengeance.[25] As shown in another episode, a Native American holy man, Coltec, would soon after heal MacLeod's soul, so that violence did not beget violence.[26] MacLeod then retreated to (Native American) holy ground for a decade to grieve and withdraw from the conflicts of the world.[27]

After returning to "civilized" American society, MacLeod would time and again encounter injustice, such as the economic oppression he found in a Pennsylvania coal mining community. The coal baron, whose company dominated the town, refused to respond to the workers' demands for livable wages. His son Jesse, a decent compassionate young man, was MacLeod's friend. The coal company's use of security guards against the striking workers ensured there would be violence if the strikers followed those urging militant action. Although sensitive to the miners' plight, Macleod advised them to avoid bloodshed and certain defeat by the company's well-armed men. His plea went unheeded and the company owner's son, saying "some things are worth dying for," joined the insurgent strikers, only to be killed. While clearly sympathetic to the workers, this episode indicates the futility and even foolishness of militant class struggle, particularly when incited by demagoguery.[28]

In the twentieth century Duncan MacLeod returned repeatedly to Europe. While MacLeod would once again fight for "the right side," for good against evil, not all conflicts in Europe would have clear moral sides. The most prominent case in point was the Great War, where trench warfare seemed to be just pointless slaughter. Therefore, as noted before, MacLeod served in the Red Cross, transporting the wounded to safety and care.[29] However, he did not renounce taking action, but in order to avoid committing wrongful deeds, he acted only to save lives, not end them.

MacLeod did not always eschew choosing a side in twentieth-century European conflicts; for instance, he helped those who are fleeing victimization by totalitarianism. In Berlin, Germany, in 1936, MacLeod helped a presumably Jewish scientist escape the Nazis, making sure they did not obtain his discoveries by helping him burn his papers. MacLeod commented about the Nazis: "The madmen are running the asylum."[30] Shortly afterwards, in late 1930s Russia, MacLeod helped people escape Stalin, asserting that "Stalin is madman." Trying to help a group of Russians, who were about to become victims of Stalin's insanity, escape, MacLeod gained them passage on a ship. However, Alexis Voshin, the ship's Immortal captain, betrayed them, saying: "Deal Comrade Stalin offered was just too good." The episode suggests that Voshin is perhaps one of many who participated in Stalin's oppressive system out of self-interest, not ideological agreement. In fact, it is he who many years later delivers the more telling judgment of Stalin: "He had a talent for brutality."[31] MacLeod, and the series, links Nazism and Stalinism together as totalitarian ideologies that enable those without sane, humane values to forcibly govern and control society.

During World War II, Duncan fought with the French Resistance, taking a more interventionist stance than in World War I. In the episode titled "Mortal Sins," he is shown in Paris in 1943, working with a Resistance group, using a hidden radio to keep in touch with London. When members of the group ambushed the Nazis on a road, Bernard, a boy who later became a priest, believed he had killed the Nazi Major, the Immortal Ernest Daimler. In the present, Daimler has reappeared as a neo–Nazi leader who kills Father Bernard. In turn, MacLeod fights and kills Daimler. During this episode, when asked how many men he has killed, MacLeod replied, "Too many." Yet, he justifies having taken action against Daimler and the Nazis by saying words that have been attributed to Edmund Burke: "For Evil to triumph it takes but the failure of a few good men to act."[32]

After the war, back in America, Macleod is shown in the South on May 17, 1954, visiting the Immortal Carl Robinson, a former slave, and then sharecropper, who MacLeod had helped to escape from a lynch mob in 1929. Now a baseball player about to go north, Robinson and his friend MacLeod went to a crowded local restaurant and tried to order a meal. When they were denied service, MacLeod protested, and was then threatened by the town's sheriff. After MacLeod knocked him out, they quickly leave. Seeing a newspaper announcing the Supreme Court's desegregation ruling, Carl decided to go to college, considering a career in politics. Thus, this episode brings to more recent times the anti-racist thread of *Highlander*'s grand historical narrative.[33]

Using flashbacks from early modern Europe to twentieth-century America, *Highlander: The Series* created a social memory for viewers through a weekly fragmented narrative, that when put together weaves a multi-threaded grand narrative. This grand narrative is a staunchly progressive view, one critical of imperialism, racism, and the twin evils of Stalinism and Fascism. But MacLeod, and thus the show, does not embrace radical action. Whether in the past or the present, MacLeod repeatedly speaks and acts against terrorism or symbolic violence, even when in the name of Scottish and Irish nationalism, causes close to his heart. He favors racial uplift over separatism, and improvement in the lot of the poor is usually depicted as something only a determined individual can do on his or her own, like MacLeod's friends Charlie DeSalvo (a half–Italian, half–Black veteran who had experienced hardship due to his mixed-race background) and Richie (an orphan and former petty thief).

Highlander is an example of how cultural production, such as a television series, can construct collective memory. Most studies of television series that have constructed narratives of the past have mostly focused on docudramas or documentaries, such as the late–1970s mini-series *Roots* and *Holocaust* or the many documentaries by Ken Burns.[34] However, a multi-season, episodic, and fictional television series, like *Highlander*, allows character development and lengthy story arcs so that characters, especially the protagonist, can have a variety of events to which to respond.[35] With a central character that has lived over four hundred years, *Highlander*, through the use of extensive flashbacks, can, in the course of six television seasons, provide hours and hours of historical material. Thus, the cumulative time devoted to recreating historical developments far exceeds most docudramas or documentaries.

Highlander's use of flashbacks is not just a narrative technique, but also a psychological reality, as the growing body of work on Post-Traumatic Stress Syndrome indicates.[36] Flashbacks occur when the past, in the form of memory, is forced upon a person ("triggered") by events or objects in the present.[37] Thus, these vignettes connect the past with the present, so those past moral choices, and consequences, frame present deliberations. This framing of present alternatives by past events provides the means to make a moral choice, for Duncan MacLeod, and for the viewers.[38] Or as Michael Lambek has put it: "Memory is a form of moral practice."[39]

Although at first several of MacLeod's friends resist the call to action based upon knowledge of the past, they sooner or later come under his moral influence, striving to "make a difference," as he has.[40] For instance, MacLeod's actions show the cynical, middle-aged Joe Dawson, a Watcher, that is, a member of an organization which has observed the Immortals for centuries without intervention, that he should take action. Dawson initially only observed events, but he does eventually violate his vow of non-interference in order to help MacLeod.[41] If the Watchers, with their mission of creating an archive based upon detached, scientifically-constituted historical narratives, represent positivist historians, then Dawson's rejection of this ideal conveys to viewers that historians, and the historically-minded, should take a more activist stance or at least follow the anthropologist's participant-observer approach.

Another of MacLeod's friends, the Immortal Methos avoided action for millennia, even concealing his identity by assuming a role in the Watchers' organization in order to minimize his involvement in conflict. Like many postmodernists, Methos suspects that historical narratives are malleable, shaped to fit the needs of those writing them: "We rewrite history so that we can live with it." Therefore, Methos is wary of using history as a guide to action. MacLeod responds that "the truth's what matters," indicating his faith that historical truth can be discovered and serve as a guide to action.[42] By the end of the series he does eventually convince Methos that one must not abstain from action, but take social action based on one's historical understanding of what is morally right.

Similarly, MacLeod's ethical stance affected his other friends, the Immortals Richie Ryan and Amanda Donahue. On more than one occasion, Richie merited MacLeod's disapproval for causing unnecessary bloodshed, and Amanda has her tendency to dishonesty and theft repeatedly curbed by MacLeod's consistent moral example.[43] He shows that one should be active and engaged with others in the world, but within strict moral limits.

In *Highlander*, Duncan MacLeod's personal memory creates American, and indeed international, social memory. His fictional memory, and thus the social memory of the show's viewers, frame moral choices, just as, dialectically, his (and humanity's) past moral choices form present identity (his and that of the viewers). Therefore, this television show's historical narrative, that is, its construction of a past, gives meaning to the present, in particular, the viewers' present. As Maureen Turim has asserted, with regard to flashbacks in film, this narrative device can "often merge the two levels of remembering the past, giving large-scale social and political history the subjective mode of a single, fictional individual's remembered experience." The flashback renders history through the "subjective experience of a character in the fiction, and [creates] ... the Subject in history" by means of viewer identification with the protagonist.[44]

A grand historical narrative provides meaning not only to MacLeod, thus forging his identity as a moral individual who can make a difference, but provides viewers with a meaningful social and political world, and a way for them to situate themselves within it. Or put another way, *Highlander* charges viewers to examine the past, specifically the past the series creates, to determine who they are, and what they should do. This charge is exactly what series creator Bill Panzer intended according to one of the show's directors, Dennis Berry. In an interview Berry claimed that Panzer "was looking for a way to raise the audience's moral standards, ethical standards, a sense of civilization, a sense of culture, a memory of the world that is more than what is brought normally to American television...."[45]

Probably few, beyond some dedicated *Highlander* fans, have realized there was, for over half a decade in the 1990s, a television show that addressed history, memory, and morality through the creation of a grand historical narrative of anti-imperialist efforts, resistance to racism, humanitarian aid to those in need, and desperate action against totalitarianism. Perhaps now, more will recognize that this action-fantasy-historical romance television series with a limited budget deserves a place in the canon of significant science fiction and fantasy television shows, as well as the canon of notable television shows about history. While *Highlander* does not subvert gender roles as much as some cult series, and does not urge collective struggle against economic oppression, it does portray a moral universe, one in which a person, even without immortality, can make a difference in history. This study suggests that not only documentaries and docudramas should be analyzed to see how collective memory is being shaped by television. *Highlander: The Series* shows that a hybrid-genre television show, in particular, a fantasy/romance adventure story with relatively traditional sexual politics, can also play a significant role in the construction of the public's collective memory, and by extension the formation of a shared moral identity.

Notes

1. For examples, see Sara Gwenllian Jones, "Histories, Fictions, and *Xena: Warrior Princess*," *Television & New Media* 1.4 (Nov. 2000): 403–418; Rhonda V. Wilcox and David Lavery, eds., *Fighting the Forces: What's at Stake in* Buffy the Vampire Slayer (Lanham, MD: Rowman & Littlefield, 2002); Renny Christopher, "Little Miss Tough Chick of the Universe: Farscape's Inverted Sexual Dynamics," *Action Chicks: New Images of Tough Women in Popular Culture* (New York: Palgrave Macmillan, 2004).

2. See Bill Osgerby and Anna Gough-Yates, eds., *Action TV: Tough-Guys, Smooth Operators and Foxy Chicks* (London: Routledge, 2001) for extensive analysis of gender norms associated with "action TV."

3. However, like the original *Star Trek* series whose gender norms also were relatively conventional, the *Highlander* television series spawned "slash" fan fiction, which depicts same gender characters as having romantic relationships not show in the actual series. Anne Kustritz, "Slashing the Romance Narrative," *The Journal of American Culture* 26.3 (Sept. 2003): 379.

4. Shawn Shimpach, "The Immortal Cosmopolitan: The International Co-production and Global Circulation of *Highlander: The Series*," *Cultural Studies*, 19.3 (2005): 357 and 362. Also, twice in his article, Shimpach compares *Highlander* unfavorably with *Buffy the Vampire Slayer*. Thus, it is not surprising that he devotes more attention to production of the series than to a reading of specific episodes, and even mistakes MacLeod's role in World War I (358).

5. This study is based on a study of all 119 episodes (the European versions) of the six-year television series in the DVD boxed set. *Highlander* stories in feature films and other media, such as novels and comics, were not considered, in effect, placed outside the *Highlander* "canon," in order to focus on representations of history in a television series.

6. For more on the critiques of "master narratives" or "grand narratives" by theorists of postmodernism, see F.R. Ankersmit, "Historiography and Postmodernism," *History and Theory* 28.2 (1989): 137-153; Allan Megill, "'Grand Narrative' and the Discipline of History," *A New Philosophy of History*, eds. Frank Ankersmit and Hans Kellner (Chicago: University of Chicago Press, 1995), 151–73, 263–71; Keith Jenkins, ed., *The Postmodern History Reader* (London: Routledge, 1997); Richard J. Evans, *In Defense of History* (New York and London: W.W. Norton, 1999); Ernst Breisach, *On the Future of History: The Postmodernist Challenge and Its Aftermath* (Chicago: University of Chicago Press, 2003).

7. Jean-François Lyotard, *The Postmodern Condition: A Report on Knowledge* (Minneapolis: University of Minnesota Press, 1984; 13th reprinting, 2002), xiv.

8. J.-F. Lyotard, "Rewriting Modernity," *Substance* 54.3 (1987): 6.

9. *Highlander: The Series*, Episode #1.

10. *Highlander*, Episode #70.

11. *Highlander*, Episode #73.

12. For example, as noted later in this chapter, MacLeod retreated to Holy Ground after the murder of his Lakota wife and stepson in 1872. See *Highlander*, episodes #46 and #79.

13. Shri Purohit and Kendra Crossen Burroughs (trans. and ann.), *Bhagavad Gita: Annotated and Explained* (Woodstock: Skylight Paths, 2001), 43.

14. *Highlander*, Episode #76.
15. *Highlander*, Episode #61.
16. Note that this episode seems to substantiate, but actually just reiterates, a key element in the Scottish invention of a national tradition identified by Hugh Trevor-Roper: "The claim that the Celtic, Irish-speaking Highlanders of Scotland were not merely invaders from Ireland in the fifth century a.d., but had an ancient history in Scotland and were in fact the Caledonians who had resisted the Roman armies...." Hugh Trevor-Roper, "The Highland Tradition of Scotland," *The Invention of Tradition*, eds. Eric Hobsbawm and Terence Range (Cambridge: Cambridge University Press, 1983), 16–17.
17. *Highlander*, Episode #28.
18. *Highlander*, Episode #75.
19. For more on this dilemma, especially as it pertains to writing history, see Barbara Weinstein, "History Without a Cause? Grand Narratives, World History and the Postcolonial Dilemma," *International Review of Social History* 50.1 (Apr. 2005): 71–93.
20. *Highlander*, Episode #13.
21. *Highlander*, Episode #87.
22. *Highlander*, Episode #51.
23. *Highlander*, Episode #4.
24. MacLeod's integration into the Lakota culture and subsequent massacre committed by the U.S. cavalry strongly echoes *Dances with Wolves*, which had won wide attention and awards only a few years prior. See Robert Baird, "'Going Indian': *Dances with Wolves*," Peter C. Rollins and John E. O'Connor, eds., *Hollywood's Indian: The Portrayal of the Native American in Film* (Lexington: The University Press of Kentucky, 1998), 153–169.
25. *Highlander*, Episode #46.
26. *Highlander*, Episode #79.
27. *Highlander*, Episode #1. The portrayal of Coltec, especially in a later episode, can be seen as a continuation of the American literary tradition in which Native Americans are characterized as "demons, apparitions, shapes, specters, phantoms, or ghosts." Renee L. Bergland, *The National Uncanny: Indian Ghosts and American Subjects* (Hanover, NH: University Press of New England, 2000), 1.
28. *Highlander*, Episode #28.
29. *Highlander*, episodes #15 and #80.
30. *Highlander*, Episode #29.
31. *Highlander*, Episode #9.
32. *Highlander*, Episode # 63.
33. *Highlander*, Episode #31.
34. For example, see Leslie Fishbein, "Roots: Docudrama and the Interpretation of History," *Why Docudrama?: Fact-Fiction on Film and TV*, ed. Alan Rosenthal (Carbondale: Southern Illinois University Press, 1999), 271–295; Thomas Elsaesser, "Subject Positions, Speaking Positions: from *Holocaust*, *Our Hitler*, and *Heimat* to *Shoah* and *Schindler's List*," *The Persistence of History: Cinema, Television, and the Modern Event*, ed. Vivian Sobchak (New York and London: Routledge, 1996) 145–185; Gary Edgerton, "Ken Burns's Rebirth of a Nation: Television, Narrative, and Popular History," *The Historical Film: History and Memory in Media*, ed. Marcia Landy (New Brunswick, NJ: Rutgers University Press, 2001), 303–315.
35. Michael J. Porter, et al., note that "[o]ne of the most striking components of television programs is that many of the same characters reappear each week. We not only get a glimpse of the characters' worlds, but we remember their past experiences." The authors use narrative theory to analysis how the narratives of television dramas differ from the "linear, finite narratives" of "novels or films." Michael J. Porter, et al., "Re(de)fining Narrative Events: Examining Television Narrative Structure," *Journal of Popular Film and*

Television 30.1 (Spring 2002): 23. This article, however, does not consider the implications of a television narrative in which some of the characters live for centuries.

36. For overviews of recent work on Post-Traumatic Stress Disorder, see Richard J. McNally, "Progress and Controversy in the Study of Posttraumatic Stress Disorder," *Annual Review of Psychology*, 54 (2003): 229–252; Anthony Charuvastra and Marylene Cloitre, "Social Bonds and Posttraumatic Stress Disorder," *Annual Review of Psychology*, 59 (2008): 301–328; Glenn R. Schiraldi, *The Post-Traumatic Stress Disorder Sourcebook: A Guide to Healing, Recovery, and Growth*, 2d ed. (New York: McGraw-Hill, 2009).

37. Michael G. Kenny, "Trauma, Time, Illness, and Culture: An Anthropological Approach to Traumatic Memory," *Tense Past: Cultural Essays in Trauma and Memory*, eds. Paul Antze and Michael Lambek (New York: Routledge, 1996), 156. For more on the connections between trauma, memory, and history, see the rest of the essay by Kenny, as well as other essays in Paul Antze and Michael Lambek, eds., *Tense Past: Cultural Essays in Trauma and Memory* (New York: Routledge, 1996).

38. Similarly, Ernst Breisach argues that traditional historians, in contrast to postmodernists, have sought to illuminate the "historical nexus" linking the past to the present. As a result of these efforts, "insights gained have been used as guidance for people's lives..." Breisach, 18–19.

39. Michael Lambek, "The Past Imperfect: Remembering as Moral Practice," *Tense Past: Cultural Essays in Trauma and Memory*, eds. Paul Antze and Michael Lambek (New York: Routledge, 1996), 235.

40. The series concludes with a two-part story drawing upon the central concept in Frank Capra's film *It's a Wonderful Life*. In these episodes MacLeod is shown what the world would have been like without him, and like Capra's character George Bailey, MacLeod (and viewers) realize the tremendous difference an individual can make in the lives of others. *Highlander*, episodes # 118 and 119.

41. Dawson became so involved in supporting MacLeod's actions that he was tried for betraying his organization's commitment to non-interference. *Highlander*, Episode #86.

42. *Highlander*, Episode # 82.

43. Richie's readiness to take other lives without justification is shown in *Highlander*, episodes #35 and #89. Amanda's thieving ways are in evident in a number of episodes.

44. Maureen Turim, *Flashbacks in Film: Memory and History* (New York: Routledge, 1989), 2.

45. From the DVD extras for *Highlander*, Episode #88.

BIBLIOGRAPHY

Ankersmit, F.R. "Historiography and Postmodernism." *History and Theory* 28.2 (1989): 137–153.

Antze, Paul, and Michael Lambek, eds. *Tense Past: Cultural Essays in Trauma and Memory*. New York: Routledge, 1996.

Baird, Robert. "'Going Indian': *Dances with Wolves*." In *Hollywood's Indian: The Portrayal of the Native American in Film*, eds. Peter C. Rollins and John E. O'Connor, 153–169. Lexington: University Press of Kentucky, 1998. 1–11.

Bergland, Renee L. *The National Uncanny: Indian Ghosts and American Subjects*. Hanover, NH: University Press of New England, 2000.

Breisach, Ernst. *On the Future of History: The Postmodernist Challenge and Its Aftermath*. Chicago: University of Chicago Press, 2003.

Charuvastra, Anthony, and Marylene Cloitre. "Social Bonds and Posttraumatic Stress Disorder." *Annual Review of Psychology* 59 (2008): 301–328.

Christopher, Renny. "Little Miss Tough Chick of the Universe: *Farscape*'s Inverted Sexual Dynamics." In *Action Chicks: New Images of Tough Women in Popular Culture*, ed. Sherrie. A. Inness, 257–281. New York: Palgrave Macmillan, 2004.

Edgerton, Gary, "Ken Burns's Rebirth of a Nation: Television, Narrative, and Popular History." *The Historical Film: History and Memory in Media*, ed. Marcia Landy, 303–315. New Brunswick, NJ: Rutgers University Press, 2001.

Elsaesser, Thomas. "Subject Positions, Speaking Positions: from *Holocaust, Our Hitler*, and *Heimat* to *Shoah* and *Schindler's List*." *The Persistence of History: Cinema, Television, and the Modern Event*, ed. Vivian Sobchak, 145–185. New York: Routledge, 1996.

Evans, Richard J. *In Defense of History*. New York and London: W.W. Norton, 1999.

Fishbein, Leslie. "Roots: Docudrama and the Interpretation of History." In *Why Docudrama? Fact-Fiction on Film and TV*, ed. Alan Rosenthal, 271–295. Carbondale: Southern Illinois University Press, 1999.

Highlander: The Complete Series (Seasons 1–6). DVD. Ray Austin, et al., 1992–1998, Anchor Bay Entertainment, 2005.

Jenkins, Keith, ed. *The Postmodern History Reader*. London: Routledge, 1997.

Jones, Sara Gwenllian. "Histories, Fictions, and *Xena: Warrior Princess*." *Television & New Media* 1.4 (Nov. 2000): 403–418.

Kenny, Michael G. "Trauma, Time, Illness, and Culture: An Anthropological Approach to Traumatic Memory." *Tense Past: Cultural Essays in Trauma and Memory*, eds. Paul Antze and Michael Lambek, 151–171. New York: Routledge, 1996.

Kustritz, Anne. "Slashing the Romance Narrative." *The Journal of American Culture* 26.3 (Sept. 2003): 371–384.

Lambek, Michael. "The Past Imperfect: Remembering as Moral Practice." *Tense Past: Cultural Essays in Trauma and Memory*, eds. Paul Antze and Michael Lambek, 235–254. New York: Routledge, 1996.

Lyotard, Jean-Francois. *The Postmodern Condition: A Report on Knowledge*. Minneapolis: University of Minnesota Press, 1984 (13th printing, 2002).

_____. "Re-writing Modernity." *Substance* 16.3 (1987): 3–9.

Magill, Allan. "'Grand Narrative' and the Discipline of History." *A New Philosophy of History*, eds. Frank Ankersmit and Hans Kellner, 151–73, 263–71. Chicago: University of Chicago Press, 1995.

McNally, Richard J. "Progress and Controversy in the Study of Posttraumatic Stress Disorder." *Annual Review of Psychology* 54 (2003): 229–252.

Porter, Michael J., et al. "Re(de)fining Narrative Events: Examining Television Narrative Structure." *Journal of Popular Film and Television* 30.1 (Spring 2002): 23–30.

Purohit, Shri, and Kendra Crossen Burroughs (trans. and ann.). *Bhagavad Gita: Annotated & Explained*. Woodstock, VT: Skylight Paths, 2001.

Schiraldi, Glenn R. *The Post-Traumatic Stress Disorder Sourcebook: A Guide to Healing, Recovery, and Growth*, 2d ed. New York: McGraw-Hill, 2009.

Shimpach, Shawn. "The Immortal Cosmopolitan: The International Co-production and Global Circulation of *Highlander: The Series*." *Cultural Studies* 19.3 (May 2005): 338–371.

Trevor-Roper, Hugh. "The Invention of Tradition: The Highland Tradition of Scotland." In *The Invention of Tradition*, eds. Eric Hobsbawm and Terence Ranger, 15–41, Cambridge: Cambridge University Press, 1983.

Turim, Maureen. *Flashbacks in Film: Memory and History*. New York: Routledge, 1989.

Weinstein, Barbara. "History Without a Cause? Grand Narratives, World History and the Postcolonial Dilemma." *International Review of Social History* 50.1 (Apr. 2005): 71–93.

Wilcox, Rhonda V., and David Lavery, eds. *Fighting the Forces: What's at Stake in* Buffy the Vampire Slayer. Lanham, MD: Rowman & Littlefield, 2002.

8

The Future as Past Perfect
Appropriation of History in the Star Trek *Series*

JUDITH LANCIONI

For a science fiction series set in the future, utilization of the past by the *Star Trek* franchise — *Star Trek* (ST), *Star Trek the Next Generation* (STNG), *Deep Space Nine* (DS9), *Voyager* (VOY) *and Enterprise* (ENT) — has received much scholarly attention. Thomas Richards, for example, argues that the series portrays history as "radically unfinished" and contingent, with each event having many possible outcomes,[1] "for the series recognizes that the past is never past.... History might have been different, and it still might be."[2] According to Lincoln Geraghty, the television series constitutes historical commentary, constructing its own "ideological mediation of future history" that constitutes a "referential, retrospective, socially aware" portrayal of historical events.[3] He argues that the series is "a historical pastiche of the future," with stories located firmly in "contemporary American reality." By presenting the "future as present," its narrative "makes history more identifiable for the people studying it," Geraghty explains. The show "reproduces a historical narrative" through which viewers "can learn about their history and seek to understand their American cultural identity."[4] In fact, the series' use of history legitimates its portrayal of the future. Thus *Star Trek* is "a signifier of the future and a signifier of the past. It acts as a certified history of the real past and a proper history of the soon-to-be real future."[5]

Geraghty further claims that *Star Trek* uses history to create a utopian future by visiting earth-like societies plagued by problems similar to twentieth-century Earth's but no longer present in the Federation universe. For Geraghty, the series constitutes "a moral guide" to the present by dramatizing the mistakes of the past.[6] Katrina Boyd likewise theorizes that the *Star Trek* universe is a utopia, but one that, given the show's firm belief in progress and the continuing perfection of humanity and civilization, is rooted in nineteenth-century ideology.[7]

A close examination of two episodes from *Deep Space 9*, "Far Beyond the Stars" (#137) and "Shadows and Symbols" (#152),[8] explores the viability of these theories about the *Star Trek* franchise's appropriation of history, especially with regard to the implications of human agency. These episodes, in fact, use history in a postmodern manner and are quite different from other history-related episodes. This discussion of the connection between science fiction and history will begin with a survey of various episodes in the *Star Trek* canon that make use of history in a variety of ways and then provide a close reading of the *Deep Space 9* episodes.

Past, Present, and Future

History can be defined as "the continuum of events occurring in succession leading from the past to the present and even into the future,"[9] a definition which is most suitable for science fiction, a genre which consistently links the past, present, and future. Thus, Gary Wolfe uses the term "alternate history" to describe science fiction,[10] a phrase similar to Judith Merril's[11] and Robert A. Heinlein's description of the genre as "speculative fiction."[12] The phrase is especially well suited to those episodes of the *Star Trek* canon that involve history; it corresponds to what Winston Churchill called "the terrible ifs," a phrase he used to describe what might have been if just one element in the historical continuum were altered, leading to a different outcome.[13]

John Sterling suggests that such fictional speculation can "illuminate actual history."[14] One such speculative writer, Gary Wolfe, has explored "what ifs" in science fiction, pointing out that in the genre "time contains infinite branches" in which alternate outcomes are possible. Science fiction frequently employs a "what if" trope, especially in time-travel episodes (though not all time travel has historical import). The trope involves "extrapolation," which Wolfe defines as "the technique of basing imaginary worlds or situations on existing ones...."[15] The "existing" situations explored here are historical, that is, they are rooted in or else allude to specific historical events or eras. Daniel Bernardi points out that some genres excel at incorporating actual history into their narratives and asserts that science fiction is such a genre.[16] He notes that if "*Trek* speaks with one voice, it is the voice of history."[17] Often, says Bernardi, the *Star Trek* universe symbolizes "the future based on the history of the real world. It is our future, and we're constantly cued to understand that fact."[18]

The Canon

Those narrative "cues" encourage viewers to relate to history in a variety of ways. For example, in *Star Trek* canonical history, the diegetic elements from various *Trek* texts combine to create an overall history.[19] As many have observed, tracing a concept through the entire five television series constructs a *Trek* chronicle. The Prime Directive is a perfect example. According to the Prime Directive, Starfleet personnel are forbidden to interfere in the evolution of any planet that has not yet developed to Federation levels. This directive is often cited and sometimes ignored by every captain except Jonathan Archer. In *Enterprise*, the prequel to the other four series, Archer and his crew explore deep space in the 22nd century, over 100 years before the voyages dramatized on the original *Star Trek*. *Enterprise* predates the articulation of the prime directive and so Archer must agonize over whether or not to save a doomed civilization ("Dear Doctor" ENT #12). In another example, the Borg, a collective of other life forms that have been forcefully assimilated and transformed into cybernetically improved drones with a collective consciousness controlled by a queen, play a role in *Star Trek: The Next Generation*, *Deep Space Nine*, and *Voyager*, contributing to faithful viewers' knowledge of Federation history and linking the three series through a sustained story arc. The *Enterprise*, in its various incarnations, contributes as well.

The canonical history might also include the struggle of various crew members to integrate their personal history with their roles in the Federation. These include: Wharf, Klingon security chief and tactical officer on *Star Trek: The Next Generation* and strategic operations officer on *DS9*; B'Ellana Torres, Klingon engineer aboard *Voyager*; Jadzia and Ezri Dax, trills on *Deep Space 9*, who share the consciousness of previous symbiont hosts; Kes, Voyager's Ocampan medical assistant, who has a life span of only nine years; Chakotay, a Native American and first officer aboard *Voyager*; Seven of Five, a human female assimilated by the Borg then dragged back into a human environment by *Voyager*'s Captain Janeway; and Odo, changeling security officer on *Deep Space 9*. They all struggle to achieve both some understanding of the cultures they come from and the Federation's relationships with those cultures, thereby contributing to canonical history.

Many individual episodes contribute to the canonical history as well. For example, "The Cage" (ST #1), provides an account of events that took place thirteen years before James T. Kirk took command of the U.S.S. *Enterprise*. When Spock hijacks the *Enterprise* in order to transport his former captain, Christopher Pike, back to Talos IV, where he had been a captive 13 years earlier, viewers, like the bridge crew of the *Enterprise*, can watch the events of Pike's capture and eventual release, giving them some idea of what the earlier years of space travel were like. Moreover, the mutiny of the usually rational Vulcan Spock invites speculations about the workings of StarFleet and the interpersonal relationships that exist within its bureaucracy.[20] Of course, the best view of the early development of Starfleet is provided by *Enterprise*, which takes place over 100 years before the original *Star Trek*.

Episodes in the *Star Trek* canon also function reflexively to foreground the interconnectedness of the five series. For example, there are episodes in which featured players from one series make an appearance in another, creating a reflexive history. Perhaps the most relevant is "Trials and Tribble-ations" (DS9 #104), which transports the command crew of *Deep Space 9* back in time and onto the *Enterprise* of Captain Kirk. The episode brings together two eras of the *Enterprise*, indicating how members of the Federation honored their own history and traditions. Jadzia Dax, for example, expresses her excitement at being able to interact with the crew of the original *Enterprise* and meet the legendary Captain Kirk.

A more serious example of reflexive history can be found in "Unification I & II" (STNG #207–208), in which Picard and Data must prevent Spock from carrying out his secret mission to establish peace between the Romulans and the Vulcans. In the course of the two-episode story, Spock brings his Vulcan qualities onto the bridge of a new *Enterprise*, creating a diegetic link between the two series. Likewise in "Sarek" (STNG #71), Spock's father engages in emotional behavior which viewers recognize, from what they learned on the original *Star Trek,* to be un-Vulcan-like. Sarek's loss of emotional control is all the more poignant when measured against the lack of emotion exercised by his son in the first series.

The canonical episodes combine to construct a history of the Federation, but earth history plays a role in the *Trek* canon as well. The various functions of history in the *Trek* franchise can be classified into five categories, according to effect: whimsy, allegory, didacticism, illustration, and postmodernism. Numerous instances of such functions can be found for each of these categories.

Approaches to History in Star Trek: Whimsy, Allegory, Didacticism, and Illustration

When Wharf straps on his six-shooter, or Picard dons his trench coat and fedora, or Data assumes his Holmsean haberdashery, humor is afoot; earth history is being used to evoke nostalgia or humor. Whimsy most often comes from immersing the characters in incongruous historical circumstances created on the holodeck, a recreational facility which simulates the times and places of one's choosing and allows crew members to interact within this simulated reality. For example, the Dixon Hill and Sherlock Holmes plot devices in *Star Trek: The Next Generation* utilize historical eras, the twentieth and the nineteenth centuries, respectively, as portrayed in fictional narratives.[21] The props are wonderful and the costumes and characterization enable viewers to see the space travelers in a new light. In another example of holodeck use, "A Fistful of Datas" (STNG #134) presents Wharf as a frustrated father roped in to his son's obsession with the old West. Technology gone berserk meets shoot-out at the O.K. Corral when Data is replicated over and over again. The villains not only look like Data, they have his super-human abilities.

There are also episodes in which a visit to another locale leads to incongruity. For example, in "A Piece of the Action" (ST #46) Kirk and company visit Sigma Iotia II to assess the damage done when, a hundred years earlier, a copy of *Chicago Mobs of the Twenties* was inadvertently left behind. Kirk, McCoy, and Spock find a society fashioned after the early twentieth-century Chicago mob era. The humor comes from the crafty way in which Kirk and company deal with the dozen or more "bosses," each with his own turf.

"Little Green Men" (DS9 #80) also treats the past with whimsical humor. Quark, Rom, and Nog are thrown back in time, ending up in Roswell, New Mexico, in 1947, the place and time when, according to conspiracy theorists, aliens landed and were spirited off by the government. The three Ferengi are identified as aliens and subjected to all sorts of scientific and medical examinations. Their ship is declared a UFO. The absurdity of the situation is heightened by Quark's acquisitive personality and his acerbic comments.

Whimsy is rare in the allegorical episodes — a classification which some have called metaphorical or parabolic. Bernardi uses allegory to designate *Trek* episodes whose diegesis alludes to a particular historical circumstance; that historical circumstance is oblique, operating as metaphor or parable.[22] Many critics have analyzed episodes from the original *Star Trek* as parables about the dangers of the Cold War.[23] Others assert that episodes in the original series reference the 1960s struggle for civil rights, using "its future frontier setting to criticize and theorize about America's social problems...."[24]

In this category, no aspect of the diegesis need involve an actual historical event or era, but plot elements and character development suggest a strong correspondence to historical events occurring around the time the episode was broadcast. For example, in "The Mark of Gideon" (ST #71) Kirk finds himself in a replica of the *Enterprise*, together with a woman named Odona. He learns that germ-free Gideon has become an overpopulated hell. Odona wants to contract Vegan choriomeningitis from Kirk so she can bring natural death to her planet and thus decrease the population. The episode was first broadcast in 1969, in an era when birth control and overpopulation were a matter of concern. In "A Taste of Armageddon" (ST #23), Kirk brings an end to a 500-year-old war fought via computer simulations. Given that the episode was originally broadcast in 1967, it may legitimately be read as an anti-war parable aimed at the superpower involvement in the Vietnam War and stressing its human cost. Similarly, Richard Peltz describes "A Private Little War" (ST #48), in which the Klingons provide advanced weapons to a previously peaceful society, thus altering the balance of power and encouraging war, as a "Vietnam allegory."[25] Broadcast well after the end of the Vietnam War, "The Hunted" (STNG #59), through its portrayal of the violent reactions of soldiers reviled by their society, alludes to the plight of Vietnam veterans whose emotional and psychological needs were ignored. Through the confrontation of two mortal enemies who concentrate on their inconsequential differences rather than their numerous similarities, "Let That Be Your Last Battlefield" (ST #70), first broadcast in 1969, is clearly a parable about racism. Today viewers might also see it as an allegory about ethnic cleansing.

All of these episodes depend on a correspondence between plot and contemporary issues. They make no direct reference to actual historical circumstances but rather function allegorically. Other episodes that do not reference contemporary issues instead allude to earlier history. For example, "Tattoo" (VOY #25) is an allusion to Native American history. Chakotay, the Native American who is first officer in *Voyager*, discovers a cultural symbol that had been used by his ancestors to "heal the land." The planet's inhabitants, the Sky Spirits, who recognize his tattoo and speak his ancestral language, explain that they gave a gift to Chakotay's ancestors to protect and care for the planet but, on a return visit, finding no trace of his ancestors, assume they have been eradicated by other humans. Chakotay convinces them that humans have learned from their mistakes.

Identifying parables can be problematic. For example, Nicholas Sarantakes faults Mark Lagon for reading episodes out of context. Lagon counters that while his interpretation of the episodes may not originally have been relevant, the current context makes them so.[26] This discussion exemplifies a long-standing debate between those who think a text — be it a book, a film, or a television show — has a single meaning and those who think that, within reason, a text can be interpreted according to changing contexts. For instance, "City on the Edge of Forever" (ST #28) can be seen as dramatizing the role of the individual in the making of history. For Sarantakes, however, it is a denunciation of the Vietnam War protesters. Both readings are possible — in different contexts.

Many of these allegorical episodes convey a moral or a political lesson, and in that sense they are allied to didactic history, Bernardi's term for a diegesis that has an instructional or inspirational effect. However, unlike the allegorical episodes, the didactic stories focus on a specific historical event or era, or at least make a recognizable historical allusion. Many of the didactic episodes also involve time-travel, which, as Sean Redmond remarks, provides a vehicle for both cultural and ideological analysis and glorifies the role of the individual, who can achieve "a real and quantifiable difference to the way the world turns out."[27]

One of the earliest didactic episodes is "City on the Edge of Forever" (ST #28). In this episode, a crazed Dr. McCoy tries to escape from Spock and Kirk by jumping through a time portal. In so doing, he alters the timeline, wiping out any traces of the future Federation. Spock and Kirk beam down to twentieth century earth in search of McCoy, materializing in Depression era New York City. Kirk falls in love with Edith Keeler, the social worker who has sheltered them, only to learn that if she is not run over by a speeding car, she will live to become an important pacifist who alters the outcome of World War II. He reluctantly realizes that he must let her die. This plot point illustrates the link the *Treks* frequently make between personal action and historical effect. If Kirk had followed his heart, Hitler would have ruled the world. For some, "City on the Edge of Forever" can also be read allegorically, as oblique political commentary, linking the present to the past: that Keeler's pacifism could change the outcome of World War II sent a covert message to the anti–Vietnam protestors of 1967, when the episode was originally broadcast.

"Past Tense I & II" (DS9 #57–58) also demonstrate a didactic use of history. Due to a transporter malfunction, Sisko, Dax, and Bashir are beamed into the twenty-fourth century, to a San Francisco with a sharp divide between rich and poor. Dax is befriended by a wealthy technocrat who eventually helps her reunite with Sisko and Bashir, who have been arrested and taken to the "Sanctuary District," where the unfortunates of society are confined with little food and no public services. Also, there is little housing available and crime is rampant. These people did not do anything to deserve these conditions, Bashir fumes, beyond just being poor. Sisko realizes that they are in the era when the Sanctuary District erupted with violent riots over intolerable living conditions. "Hundreds of Sanctuary residents will die," he tells Bashir. But it was a "watershed event" in earth's history, thanks largely to the heroism of Gabriel Bell, who saved the lives of hostages seized during the riots. His deeds and his death paved the way for positive change.

When Sisko and Bashir are attacked by thugs, the man who saves them but dies doing so turns out to be Bell. His premature death will alter the timeline. Thus when the riots begin, Sisko feels compelled to impersonate Bell and save the hostages, as history reported, thereby restoring the timeline. As in "City on the Edge of Forever," the episode supports the *Trek* doctrine that one change will alter the timeline and one individual can make things right. Bell's actions were responsible for vast social changes, and Sisko's actions restore those changes. But Sisko and Bell are not the only ones to teach a lesson about individual responsibility.

A female hostage, a clerk at the employment agency where Sisko and Bashir had been processed, confesses that ever since she was reprimanded for breaking the rules to help someone, she has ignored the plight of those whom she processed. Now she regrets that. She represents the role the individual plays in determining the present and ultimately the future. Likewise the belligerent guard who had confronted Bashir later offers to escort Bashir and Sisko through the military cordon and out of the District. The guard says he can not understand how "we" could have let things get so bad. His use of "we" implies both the power and the responsibility of all individuals to promote social justice. The lesson is that individuals must act humanely because institutions will not. His actions contrast with those of the younger guard, who does not want to take responsibility for change, saying, "I just want to get home again."

This insistence on the power of individuals to bring about change contrasts with governmental neglect. When Bashir spots a schizophrenic man sitting on the curb, he fumes at a government that could help but does not care. Later he remarks, "Causing people to suffer because you hate them is terrible ... but causing them to suffer because you've forgotten how to care ... that's even harder to understand." His remarks could be applied to the rich at a cocktail party at the technocrat's office. They have no sympathy for "those people" in the Sanctuary. The elegant dress of the elite and the opulence of the party's setting contrast sharply with the shots of poverty and violence that follow. These people choose not to care and not to interfere, except for the technocrat, who decides to help Dax and enables the rioters to broadcast their message.

The "Sanctuary" District, ironically named, looks like a scene out of the Great Depression (or film portrayals of the era), an allusion to what has been and what could be. Poorly clothed people wander the streets or huddle over open fires to keep warm. And there is hopelessness — no jobs, scarce food, little self-respect. As Bashir and Sisko are processed, the background shots show a number of poor people waiting on benches, a scene which could be found today in the emergency room of many inner-city hospitals or a government employment bureau. In other words, the mise-en-scène suggests ties between today and a possible tomorrow. This social portrait is speculative as well as didactic history — speculating on what earth's future might be given current trends and indicating what individuals must do to take charge of their destiny as a society.

Illustrative episodes reference the role of the individual in society as well. Illustrative history occurs in episodes that foreground the continued relevance of historical issues. The earliest of the illustrative episodes is "Patterns of Force" (ST #50), in which the *Enterprise*, in search of missing Federation historian John Gill, finds itself fired on by Ekos, one of two warring planets (Zeon being the other). Beaming down to the planet, Kirk and Spock discover that Gill, in an attempt to organize Ekosian society, has utilized the model of Nazi Germany and, with himself as Fuhrer, has united the Ekosians in a war against Zeon. In addition to foregrounding the power and responsibility of the individual, the episode illustrates the continued attraction of fascism and enriches the future with the patina of past experience.

The many *Trek* episodes that involve the World War II era can also be read as illustrative. "Storm Front" (ENT #76–77) weaves the war into three story-lines — destroying the Zindi weapon designed to obliterate earth, fighting the temporal Cold War, and thwarting Vosk, a hostile alien who has gone into the past in order to collaborate with the Nazis. After beaming to twentieth-century earth to locate the Zindi super-weapon, the landing party finds itself in an inaccurate version of World War II. The Nazis have taken over the White House and the Eastern seaboard. Resistance fighters help Archer and his crew devise a strategy to prevent Vosk from returning to his own time, armed with knowledge that his return will affect the balance of power in the Temporal Cold War and preserve the false timeline. After several skirmishes with the Nazis and with Vosk, Archer triumphs. The timeline is restored and earth is saved from the Nazis and the Zindi superweapon. In this episode, historical past-time is used to give weight to the present-time of the *Enterprise*— the Temporal Cold War and the threat of the Zindi superweapon. The episode is illustrative because it draws on viewers' knowledge of World War II to give an additional layer of meaning to the future.

World War II is also integrated into the diegesis of "The Killing Game" (VOY #86–87), in which the Voyager crew think they are participating in a holodeck simulation of World War II, only to find they are involved in a real war with the Hirogens. The Hirogens, a war-like race, are fascinated by Nazi culture. Like "Patterns of Force," this episode illustrates the lure of fascism for those who seek power and iron-fisted order.

Theoretical history describes those episodes that use a historical setting to examine the "what ifs" of history and to support the principle of linear history— the principle that if one element is changed, history will be altered. "Future's End" (VOY #50–51) illustrates the complexities of preserving the timeline and introduces the possibility of an alternate history. A twenty-ninth century starship captain named Braxton fires on Voyager, claiming that the starship will be responsible for a temporal explosion that will destroy the entire solar system. Voyager defends itself against his assault, causing a time rift that sends Braxton back to 1967. A man named Henry Starling finds Braxton's ship, the Aeon, and uses its technology to found a company which spearheads the computer revolution of the 1990s. Voyager is catapulted back to 1996, enabling Janeway to execute a plan that restores the time line and returns Voyager and her crew back to the future. In addition to providing a quirky explanation for technological advancement, the episode works very hard to complicate, though not to abandon, the concept of history as linear.

Many theoretical episodes draw from more than one category. For example, "Assignment Earth" (ST #55) employs whimsy and didacticism to dramatize difficulties in determining what constitutes interference in the timeline. When the *Enterprise* travels back to earth to find out what prevented a nuclear cataclysm, it inadvertently beams aboard a man who claims to be a human from a technologically-advanced civilization. He says he is charged with preventing Earth from destroying itself through nuclear proliferation. A skeptical Kirk has the man, Seven, locked up, but Seven escapes and beams down to earth. An orbital bomb is about to be launched by the United States and Seven intends to divert it and make it explode over Asia, thereby convincing the nuclear powers not to launch any more bombs into space. Afraid that Seven will alter history, Kirk and Spock beam down to earth, but they fail to prevent Seven from carrying out his mission. Seven succeeds, however, remarking that his actions have prevented World War III.

The episode is interesting for several reasons. First, it makes clever use of contemporary popular culture through a sly homage to Maxwell Smart, the bumbling secret agent of *Get Smart*. Second, it explores the Federation prohibition against interfering with the timeline, a task which clearly is not as simple as it seems. Third, the episode also raises, albeit humorously, the complicated question of human agency in history—another common *Trek* concern. Do Seven's actions demonstrate the importance of individual initiative in making history? Do Kirk's? Finally, the episode slips in a lesson about the dangers of the arms race.

DS9 and Postmodernism

Jonathan Bignell suggests that science fiction and history are both preoccupied with time, "with representing a future moment, a documented moment in the past, or an arrested time which we can uncover and see."[28] In the original *Star Trek*, the concept of time, and the history it embodies, is linear. In these canonical episodes, past, present, and future are clearly delineated, even if, in an episode like "The Cage," the future precedes the past. Even in the whimsical episodes of the original and much of the other series, the future visits the past, and the distinction between the two is clear. In allegorical episodes, a present narrative overlays a past event, while in the illustrative episodes, the past is used to illuminate the future. For these, sorting out past, present, and future can be complicated. In the allegorical episodes, for example, a narrative that takes place in the future refers to events contemporaneous with the broadcast, but in the past for later audiences. Nevertheless, the concept of a timeline, of history as linear, is straightforward.

Deep Space 9, however, in its sixth and seventh seasons, gradually drew away from linear time to a more postmodern approach to time and history. This shift was accomplished primarily through the character of Captain Benjamin Sisko, Starfleet officer and Emissary to the Bajoran Prophets. Many have analyzed Sisko's conflicted role in what they consider to be a secularized view of religion,[29] but they have not considered the view of time and history instantiated in the Sisko character and his other self, Benny Russell.

"Far Beyond the Stars" (DS9 #137) opens with Captain Sisko dejected over the death of an old friend and fellow officer and thinking about leaving Starfleet. Suddenly he sees a man dressed in a suit and a fedora pass by his window. Later, in a ship's corridor, he sees a baseball player in a New York Giants uniform, who asks him how he liked the game, then opens a door and walks through. Sisko, still in his Starfleet uniform, follows and walks into a busy New York City street in the 1950s. He is promptly hit by a cab and wakes up in sickbay. Dr. Bashir fears that Sisko is experiencing the same synaptic irregularities he had had a year before ("Rapture" DS9 #108). As Sisko peruses the results of his brain scan, they morph into *Galaxy*, a 1950s science fiction pulp magazine. Dressed in a suit and fedora, he is Benny Russell, an African American science fiction writer in New York City during the 1950s. He writes for the science fiction magazine *Incredible Tales*. As Russell, he is inspired to write a story about a space station called "Deep Space Nine," whose commanding officer is Benjamin Sisko. The other writers like the story, but the editor rejects it because its main character is African American: "People won't accept it. It's not believable." A fellow writer suggests Benny frame the story as the dream of a shoe-shine boy or some other disadvantaged Black, a compromise that both Benny and the editor accept. However, the publisher is incensed and has the whole magazine pulped, driving Benny to madness.

In one sense this is an overtly didactic narrative about discrimination in 1950s America. The plot points illustrate prejudicial practices. For example, both Benny and a female writer are excluded from the staff picture because, says the editor, the average American is not ready for a Black or female writer. "It's not personal," the editor explains. "But as far as our readers are concerned, Benny Russell is as white as they are. Let's just leave it that way." When Benny leaves his office with the space-station illustration that had inspired him, he is hassled by two detectives who question his right to be in this neighborhood and his right to wear a nice suit. Later these same two detectives will severely beat Benny, who is distraught over their shooting of his friend. Also, the baseball star explains that he still lived in the old neighborhood because white folks would not want to live next door to him.

In this episode, some Blacks regard discrimination as a fact of life. For example, Benny's friend ridiculed his story because an African American was in charge of the space station. A shoe-shine boy or dishwasher would be more appropriate, his friend notes, laughing, and even then white folks would not be interested.

As it is in other history-based episodes, the issue of human agency is raised. When the other writers chide the editor for rejecting Benny's story, he counters: "I'm a magazine editor — not a crusader. I'm not here to change the world." Benny is, however.

Benny Russell is determined to rewrite the status quo, rejecting his friend's assertion that Blacks will always be dishwashers and shoeshine boys. He ignores his girlfriend's statement that only the present matters, naming Black writers who have made it into the mainstream, as he is determined to do. Telling his girlfriend that he is a writer and determined to remain so, even if he makes no money, he continues to write his Deep Space Nine stories, even after the first one has been rejected.

From the viewers' perspective, however, Benny's mission is to strike a blow against discrimination, as he does literally when his friend is killed by the police and he strikes out at them, only to be badly beaten. That mission is a failure, or so it seems as Benny, strapped to a stretcher, is loaded into an ambulance, presumably to be brought to the asylum in which he appears in "Shadows and Symbols" (DS9 #152). Benny's function, one could argue, is to illustrate the agony of those fighting for civil rights in 1950s America. On the verge of madness, Benny screams: "I'm a human being, dammit!"

Benny's mission is complicated by the Preacher (Sisko's father), who keeps turning up to urge him on to what seems like a different mission. He pleads: "Walk with the Prophets, Brother Benny. Show us the way.... Write the words, Brother Benny." The Preacher ties Benny's mission to the Prophets and to the theme of destiny. "Image in the Sand" (DS9 #151) reinforces the bond between Benny and Sisko and advances this destiny theme. Sisko's struggle to reconcile his role as a Starfleet officer with his designation as the Bejoran Emissary stretches from the first to the last episode of the series and can be viewed as a classic quest narrative. That quest reaches a crisis point in "Image in the Sand," when Sisko learns that his mother was actually his father's first wife, a woman named Sarah. "Maybe learning the truth about my mother is the first step of that journey" toward self-discovery, Sisko tells his father. Later, in "Shadows and Symbols" (DS9 #152), Sisko learns that Sarah's being was usurped by a Prophet, who was actually his mother. He says to her, "What you're telling me isn't easy to accept ... you arranged my birth. I exist because of you." Her reply confirms his dawning sense of destiny: "The Sisko's path is a difficult one." He asks, "But why me? Why did it have to be me?" The prophet answers, "Because it could be no one else."

The destiny theme, and the religious overtones that accompany it here, are certainly not postmodern, but Benny is. As Sisko prepares to travel to the desert of Tyree to look for the Orb of the Emissary, he periodically hears a voice paging Dr. Wykoff (the 1950s version of Cardassian Damar). After a brutal trek through the desert, Sisko locates and unburies the orb. About to open it, he reaches out of frame, pulls his hand back, and finds himself holding a twentieth-century pencil. The next shot shows this same pencil, but this time it is in Benny's hand and writing on a wall. In fact all the walls are covered with closely-spaced script. Benny is dressed in what looks like a hospital gown and is accompanied by Dr. Wykoff, who is beseeching him to stop writing, if he ever wants to escape confinement. The close cuts between Benny and Sisko support the claim, articulated in "Far Beyond the Stars" (DS9 #137), that Benny is part of Sisko's identity as a man and as a prophet, part of his role in history and his destiny. After all, it was Benny whom the Preacher told to "Walk with the Prophets, Brother Benny. Show us the way."

The hospital scene in "Image in the Sand" is not contextualized the way it was in "Far Beyond the Stars." This could be any hospital or asylum anywhere, making Benny a more abstract, symbolic, figure than he was in "Far Beyond the Stars," where only the appearances of the Preacher hinted at Benny's ties to an unimagined future and a supra-personal destiny. Benny is still writing the same story, but it has become even more urgent, more real. In "Far Beyond the Stars," Benny had screamed at his publisher: "You cannot destroy an idea! That future, I created it, and it's real! Don't you understand? It is REAL! I created it and IT'S REAL!" In "Shadows and Symbols, Benny tells Wykoff, "But I haven't finished my story. Captain Sisko has found the Orb of the Emissary.... But he hasn't opened it yet." And indeed he has not. Sisko kneels before the orb, seemingly unable to open it. And as Benny holds a paint roller, urged by Wykoff to paint over his writing, Sisko begins re-burying the orb with sand. Viewers are shown Benny's sentence: "Sisko reaches for the orb box and...." Only when Benny throws down the roller, picks up the pen and finishes the sentence does Sisko open the box. The action recalls Sisko's words at the end of "Far Beyond the Stars": "But I've been wondering ... what if it wasn't a dream? What if this life we're leading... All of this... You and me — everything... What if all this is the illusion?" That question is unburied along with the orb, since it was Benny's writing that made Sisko's action possible. Or rather, as the quick cuts indicate, they are as one — the dreamer and the dream.

In "Shadows and Symbols" Sarah tells Sisko that, as Emissary of the planet Bejor, he has been caught up in the epic battle between Bejor's two spiritual forces — the evil Kosst Amojan and the beneficent Prophets; his vision of Benny in the asylum was false, sent by the Kosst Amojan. But what was false? Benny was real in the first vision, and he wrote stories about Deep Space 9 then. Was it false that his writing could stop Sisko from fulfilling his destiny? But Benny finished the sentence and Sisko opened the Orb, releasing Sarah and freeing the rest of the Prophets. What may be false is that Benny was insane; his obsession with Sisko and with attaining racial equality is not actually insanity. Rather, through a postmodern collapsing of time, space, and consciousness, Benny writes the actions and Sisko performs them.

What function does Benny serve in "Shadows and Symbols"? If indeed he was mad, it might be because of what happened to him in "Far Beyond the Stars," but that does not explain his role in the diegesis. However, Sarah's statement that Benny does not belong in a mental institution, that he is not mad, clarifies his role. If as indicated, Benny is one with Sisko's identity, then Benny's present was Sisko's past and Sisko's present is Benny's future.

There are direct links between past and future. For instance, all the major characters in "Far Beyond the Stars" are played by Deep Space 9 personnel. Willie, the baseball player, appears on the Deep Space 9 deck as the security officer, Worf. At one point, Benny sees Worf in a Klingon uniform instead of in his Willie persona. Also, Dukat and Weyoun are the detectives who almost beat him to death. At another point, Benny briefly finds himself dancing on the deck of the space station with Kassidy, the freighter pilot who is his fiancée, instead of in his New York apartment with his girlfriend, K.C. Hunter, a waitress in a diner. Of course, the fact that both characters are played by the same actress strengthens the link between past and present. When he sits down at his typewriter to begin his story, Benny sees a reflection of Sisko in the window. Finally, in the last scene, when Sisko looks out of his office window, he sees the reflection of Benny looking in at him.

What is the purpose of the complex interweaving of the two stories? Beyond its entertainment value, the casting of space station personnel as earthlings and the periodic appearance of Deep Space 9 crew members in Benny's life tie Sisko and the space station itself to a past injustice that has been rectified through Sisko, the Black hero of Benny's stories. There is no time-travel involved here. Sisko and Benny are linked both spatially and temporally. They exist in each other's time and place. The two are merged. Sisko is Benny. As the Preacher tells him, when Benny questions who he is, "You are the dreamer and the dream." Thus, "Far Beyond the Stars" and "Shadows and Symbols" promote "a mode of awareness, a complex hesitation about the relationship between the imaginary conceptions and historical reality unfolding into the future," as Istvan Csicsery-Ronay has argued for speculative fiction in general.[30]

The character of Benny challenges the linear assumptions of the other history-oriented Star Trek episodes. "The Emissary is corporeal. Linear," Sarah tells Sisko. But Benny/Sisko is not. Time is conflated; the 1950s and the 4600s merge. Benny exists in Sisko's mind, and vice versa. Minutes to others become timeless to Benny/Sisko. Time in "Far Beyond the Stars" and "Shadows and Symbols" exemplifies what Elizabeth Ermath calls rhythmic time, which, instead of linking event to event, is coterminous with an event. This postmodern sense of time transforms the traditional sense of individuality. Individual consciousness "exists only for the same duration and then disappears ... or undergoes transformation into some new state of being."[31] Benny's existence in 1950s America is coterminous with Sisko's on Deep Space Nine in the 4600s. All of the scenes in which the space station and its occupants meld with 1950s New Yorkers support this claim." Far Beyond the Stars" links Sisko and the space station both spatially and temporally to the past — without any space travel. As Jameson observed in "Progress Versus Utopia," science fiction locates our future "in the space on which a sense of the past had once been inscribed."[32]

The Benny persona exhibits another postmodern trait as well. In a discussion of Jameson's adaptation of Lacan's discussion of schizophrenia as "a linguistic disorder," David Harvey explains that the failure to master the linguistic relationship between past, present, and future augurs a similar failure to integrate one's personal history.[33] In the asylum, Benny has no personal history. There is not even one mention of his girlfriend. He is his writing. And he lives in his writing: "the language sequence ... becomes the only site where temporality can be located and where consciousness can be said to exist."[34] The Benny persona lives the postmodern credo that "reality is always shrouded by language."[35] Both his reality and Sisko's exist through language. When Benny stops writing, Sisko stops acting. As Annette Kuhn has observed, science fiction is "a privileged cultural site for the enactment of the postmodern condition."[36]

The postmodern elements in these two episodes go beyond the characterization of Benny to stylistic elements like mise-en-scène and editing. According to Vivian Sobchak, postmodernism can be found in even the most pedestrian science fiction film, when it incorporates a weakened sense of historicity, a *"deflation and inflation of space,"* a *"pervasive conflation of time,"*[37] and a narrative structure that elides past, present, and future.[38] In *Deep Space Nine*, time is conflated through the dual consciousness of Benny and Sisko. Benny's career at *Incredible Tales* and Sisko's confinement in sickbay are coterminous. Sisko's quest for the orb unfolds as Benny writes the story. Space is deflated both literally and figuratively. Viewers see Benny primarily in confined interiors — the office, the diner where his girlfriend works, and one room of his small apartment. He is shown in the street three times, but even then the range of what is shown is limited. The first time, he is being harassed by the police, who question his right to be there; so even this slight expansion of space is figuratively denied him. Another time he is being brutally beaten by the police; again, his right to space is denied. After the beating viewers are shown Benny in a tight two-shot with his girlfriend as she helps him with his hat, glasses, and cane. Figuratively speaking, his personal space has been reduced, since he lacks even the mobility, the access to space, that he had before the beating. When Benny appears again, in "Shadows and Symbols," he is physically confined to his room in the asylum, and then viewers are shown only a small portion of his room. Figuratively speaking, Benny is confined to the story in his head. But the story has space; not limited to 8 × 11 sheets of paper, it covers all the walls of Benny's cell.

Sisko, too, is spatially constricted. Viewers see him first in a dark office with little sense of spaciousness. He is hemmed in by his depression over his friend's death. Then he is increasingly confined to his visions. He is shown in sickbay in a tight body shot, with his hand to his head. And that's where he is — in the vision in his head. Even when he is not trapped within his vision, he is shown in tight spaces — in a dark and narrow corridor with Kassidy, for example. At the beginning of "Shadows and Symbols," Sisko is again constricted — physically, emotionally and psychologically. Most shots are located in a single room of his father's New Orleans restaurant. Sisko is depressed over the closing of the wormhole, with the concurrent loss of access to the Prophets. He is shut inside himself, reluctant to talk to his father or his son. When the action shifts to Tyree, viewers are shown Sisko struggling through an endless expanse of sand, totally oblivious to his father's struggles to keep up. Despite the expanse of the desert, he is shut inside his vision and blind to all else.

In a sense, time and space are compressed when Sarah appears to Sisko. Her image contains the Prophets — non-corporeal entities not bound by space or time but temporarily confined by Sarah's body. Sarah represents both the inflation and the deflation of space and time — she existed in a human body for a time and still borrows that body to communicate with Sisko, but she is out of space and time. Sisko becomes infinite as well. Called to the Fire Caves to defeat the evil Pah-wraiths, enemies of The Prophets, Ben falls into the fire and becomes non-corporeal. When he meets Kassidy for the last time, she asks why he cannot come home. "It's difficult to explain," Ben replies. "It isn't linear... My life ... my destiny." Asked when he will return, Sisko answers, "It's hard to say. Time doesn't exist here. It could be a year. It could be yesterday." So "What You Leave Behind" (DS9 #176), the finale of *Deep Space 9,* ultimately obliterates the concepts of linear space and time, ironic since the many history-oriented *Trek* adventures involved the expanding, but not erasing, viewers' sense of space while maintaining the rigid preservation of the time line that is linear history.

Sobchak observes that science fiction texts are either "conservatively nostalgic about the weakening of historicity — unconsciously revealing that weakness in their very attempts to historicize both the past and future. Or they are primarily celebratory about the conservative value of space...."[39] Ultimately, *Deep Space Nine* leaves Benny and his postmodern potential behind, and by its final episode slips into nostalgia. The Federation finally wins its war with the Dominion, the powerful alliance of The Founders, the Vorta, and the Jem'Hadar bent on destroying the space station as a crucial step in the alliance's expansion. There are sentimental shots of crew members in earlier times and loose ends are tied up. Security Chief Odo returns to his changeling homeland, The Great Link, to cure his fellow ailing changelings. Chief of operations Miles O'Brien and his family go back to earth, where he will teach at the Space Academy. Wharf becomes ambassador to Kronos. Kira Nerys, officer in the Bejoran militia and Bajoran representative to Deep Space 9, who had functioned, informally, as Sisko's first officer, will take charge of the station. The remaining crew members have a black tie farewell party. Last, after Sisko's son Jake has heard the news that his father has died in a fight with Gul Dukat, the former Cardassian officer under the influence of the Pah-Wraiths, he is shown brooding over the model of the house his father was going to build for them.

The show's retreat into sentimentality is also a retreat into religion, with its concept of a confrontation between good and evil being acted out by the battle between Sisko, the servant of the Prophets, and Dukat, the servant of the Pah-Wraiths. By focusing on this epic battle, *Deep Space 9* surrenders any claims to postmodernism in favor of a religious metanarrative: Sisko's struggle with his role as Emissary, his search for his destiny, his trek through the desert for the Orb (his holy grail), his death by fire, and his resurrection as a prophet. At the end of "Far Beyond the Stars," Joseph Sisko quotes from St. Paul: "I have fought the good fight. I have finished the course. I have kept the faith." In "What You Leave Behind," Sarah tells Sisko: "Your time of trial has ended."

This step away from postmodernism was not inevitable. According to the *Deep Space Nine Companion,* Avery Brooks, Ben Sisko on screen, has disclosed that an alternate ending was considered. The last scene would have shown Benny watching the show being filmed as he clutched a script clearly labeled "Deep Space 9," thus transforming the whole series into Benny's "dream."[40] Instead, the ending as written represents a turning away from postmodernism to post-history.

Conclusion

Fredric Jameson has described science fiction as "a way of breaking through to history in a new way, achieving a distinctive historical consciousness by way of the future rather than the past, becoming conscious of our present as the past of some unexpected future rather than as the future of a heroic national past...."[41] The allegorical, the didactic, the illustrative, and the postmodern episodes provide an enriched understanding of the present as well as the past by anticipating a future that alludes to and, directly or indirectly, illuminates past faults and failings. It is not that the future is perfect, but it is the past perfected. In the original *Star Trek* series, the allegorical "Mark of Gideon"(ST #71) created a future world that offered contemporary audiences a fresh understanding of overpopulation and the unforeseen consequences of medical advancement. Today it offers audiences vivid images — bodies crammed against the sides of the replicated Enterprise — that raise difficult questions about the quality of life. Similarly, though set in the future, the virulent racism of "Let This Be Your Last Battlefield" (ST #70) provided a lesson on the ignominy of racism, present in the past, rejected in the future.

Episodes like these support Geraghty's assertion that *Star Trek* constitutes historical commentary and "ideological mediation of future history," that it is "referential, retrospective, socially aware."[42] "Let That Be Your Last Battlefield" (ST #70), for example, provides a better understanding of the immediate present, since it is a powerful metaphor for ethnic cleansing, making viewers "conscious of our present as the past of some unexpected future...."[43] "Patterns of Force" (ST #50) and the two-part "Killing Game" (VOY #86 & #87) dramatize the allure of fascism for future societies, thus illuminating its horrific effectiveness in the past and its potential resurrection in the future — but the future resists the lure. These episodes support Richards's claim that in the *Star Trek* universe, "the past is never past."[44] To find the past (or the present) in the future is certainly unexpected, and it makes viewers conscious that their history is future-oriented. Even the whimsical episodes, by relocating past events into the future, provide viewers with a fresh vision of those events.

"Past Tense I & II" (DS9 #57& #58) and "City on the Edge of Forever" (ST #28), while in different *Star Trek* series, both unfold in a semi-allusionary past rather than in the future. They are located "within a conception of history that holds that science and technology actively participate in the creation of reality...."[45] and criticize a past society that failed to use these tools to produce positive change and achieve social justice. As Dr. Bashir rants in "Past Tense" (DS9 #58), "There were any number of effective treatments for schizophrenia, even in this day and age. They could cure that man now.... Today ... if they gave a damn." Like "Far Beyond the Stars" (DS9 #137), "Past Tense" also stresses the individual's role in creating a just and humane society. When Sisko tries to convince Bashir that "the social problems facing them seem too enormous to deal with," Bashir will have none of it. And indeed, Sisko himself explains that positive social change will be brought about by Gabriel Bell, whose individual actions had tremendous social consequences. Likewise, "City on the Edge of Forever" (ST #28) foregrounds the power of Edith Keeler and Captain Kirk to change history.

"Far Beyond the Stars" (DS9 #137) works somewhat differently in that it presents a moving portrait of the realities of racism located in an actual past. The episode adheres to the *Star Trek* principle that the possibility for change lies in the actions of the individual, but complicates that principle by splitting the individual into two. Benny begins the process of change, but its realization lies in Deep Space 9 and the existence of Sisko. Looking backward into the past viewers see the potential for change; looking forward they are shown its actualization. That Benny and Sisko are merged provides a powerful symbol of the relationship between past and future.

This duality — past wrong and future rectification contained in one person — constitutes a complex approach to the issue of human agency in history. Benny seems to believe firmly in the power of the individual to bring about change. He cites James Baldwin, Richard Wright, Zora Neale Hurston, and Langston Hughes as Black writers who have been or are bringing about change. He believes that his stories can make a difference. Later, that faith becomes an obsession, opening up gaps in the narrative that can be filled in any number of ways — Benny is crazy, Benny has been driven crazy by racism, and Benny represents postmodernity's concern with time, identity, ontology, and epistemology. He is Sisko in the past and Sisko is Benny in the future. As Elizabeth Ermath puts it in her discussion of the conceptualization of time in postmodernism, "What used to be called the individual consciousness has attained a more multivocal and systemic identity."[46] This multivocality is confirmed in "Shadows and Symbols" (DS9 #152), when Sisko's actions are controlled by Bennie's pen. These two episodes — "Far Beyond the Stars" and "Shadows and Symbols" — constitute what Csicsery-Ronay calls "a mode of awareness, a complex hesitation about the relationship between imaginary conceptions and historical reality unfolding into the future."[47] However, "What You Leave Behind" transforms any attempt at exploring historical reality into a religious experience that leaves time, space, and history behind. Thus *Star Trek: Deep Space Nine* is the future perfect because it lies beyond the realm of human experience.

NOTES

1. Thomas Richards, *The Meaning of* Star Trek (New York: Doubleday, 1997), 57.
2. Ibid., 59.
3. Lincoln Geraghty, "Carved from the Rock Experiences of Our Daily Lives: Reality and *Star Trek*'s Multiple Histories," *European Journal of American Culture* 21, no. 3 (2002): 160–76.
4. Ibid., 168.
5. Ibid., 169.
6. Ibid.
7. Katrina G. Boyd, "Cyborgs in Utopia: The Problem of Radical Difference in *Star Trek*," *Enterprise Zones: Critical Positions on* Star Trek, eds. Taylor Harrison et al. (Boulder: Westview Press, 1996).
8. There is variation in the numbering system used to identify specific episodes in the *Star Trek* franchise. This chapter follows the numbering system provided by TV.com.

9. "Definitions of 'History' on the Web," wordnet.princeton.edu/perl/webwn.
10. Gary Wolfe, "Coming to Terms," *Speculations on Speculation: Theories of Science Fiction*, eds. James Gunn and Matthew Candelaria (Lanham, MD: The Scarecrow Press, 2005), 14.
11. Merrill discussed in Vivian Sobchack, *Screening Space: The American Science Fiction Film*, 2d ed. (New Brunswick, NJ: Rutgers University Press, 2001), 18.
12. Heinlein quoted in James Gunn, "Introduction," *Speculations on Speculation: Theories of Science Fiction*, eds. James Gunn and Matthew Candelaria (Lanham, MD: The Scarecrow Press, 2005), ix.
13. Martin Arnold, "Making Books: The 'What Ifs' That Fascinate," *New York Times*, December 21, 2000, late ed., E3.
14. Sterling quoted in Arnold, E3.
15. Wolfe, 16.
16. Daniel Leonard Bernardi, Star Trek *and History Race-ing: Toward a White Future* (New Brunswick, NJ: Rutgers University Press, 1998), 81.
17. Ibid., 117.
18. Ibid., 97.
19. Ibid., 97–102.
20. Memory Alpha points out that in this unused pilot episode, Spock exhibits a wide range of "human" characteristics that would later be eliminated from his character. For additional information, see <http://www.memory-alpha.org/en/wiki/The_Cage_%28episode%29#Story_and_production>.
21. For examples, see "Elementary Dear Data" (#29) and "The Big Goodbye" (#113).
22. Bernardi, 97–102.
23. For example, see Allan W. Austin's detailed analysis of "The Omega Glory" (ST #52) in this volume.
24. Geraghty, 164.
25. Richard J. Peltz, "On a Wagon Train to Afghanistan: Limitations on *Star Trek*'s Prime Directive," *University of Arkansas at Little Rock Law Review* 25.3 (2003): 634–679.
26. Nicholas Evan Sarantakes, "Cold War Pop Culture and the Image of U.S. Foreign Policy: The Perspective of the Original *Star Trek* Series," *Journal of Cold War Studies* 7, no. 4 (Fall 2005): 76; Mark P. Lagon, "'We Owe It to Them to Interfere': *Star Trek* and U.S. Statecraft in the 1960s and the 1990s," *Extrapolation* 34 (Fall 1993): 251–264.
27. Sean Redmond, "The Origin of the Species: Time Travel and the Primal Scene," *Liquid Metal: The Science Fiction Film Reader*, ed. Sean Redmond (London: Wallflower Press, 2004), 114.
28. Jonathan Bignell, "With Eyes Uplifted: Space Aliens as Sky Gods," *Liquid Metal: The Science Fiction Film Reader*, ed. Sean Redmond (London: Wallflower Press, 2004), 138.
29. See, for example, Star Trek *and Sacred Ground: Explorations of* Star Trek, *Religion, and American Culture*, eds. Jennifer E. Porter and Darcie L. McLaren (Albany: State University of New York Press, 2000). Of special interest in this volume is Peter Linford's essay, "Deeds of Power: Respect for Religion in *Deep Space Nine*," 77–100.
30. Istvan Csicsery-Ronay, Jr., "The SF of Theory: Baudrillard and Haraway," *Science Fiction Studies* 18, no. 3 (Nov. 1991). DePauw Archives <http://www.depauw.edu/sfs/back issues/55/icr55art.htm>.
31. Elizabeth Ermarth, *Sequel to History: Postmodernism and the Crisis of Representational Time* (Princeton: Princeton University Press, 1992), 53.
32. Fredric Jameson, "Progress Versus Utopia; or, Can We Imagine the Future?" *Science-Fiction Studies* 9, 2, 150.
33. David Harvey, *The Condition of Postmodernity* (Oxford: Basil Blackwell, 1989), 53.
34. Ermath, 181.

35. Joyce Oldham Appleby, Lynn Hunt, and Margaret Jacob, *Telling the Truth About History* (New York: W.W. Norton, 1995), 214.
36. Annette Kuhn, "Intertexts Introduction," *Alien Zone: Cultural Theory and Contemporary Science Fiction Culture,* ed. Annette Kuhn (London: Verso, 1990), 178.
37. Vivian Sobchack, *Screening Space: The American Science Fiction Film*, 2d ed. (New Brunswick, NJ: Rutgers University Press, 2001), 254.
38. Ibid., 273.
39. Ibid.
40. "What You Leave Behind." Memory Alpha <http://www.memory-alpha.org/en/wiki/What_You_Leave_Behind_%28episode%29>. See also "Ben Sisko," Wikipedia <http://en.wikipedia.org>.
41. Jameson quoted in Anders Stephanson, "Regarding Postmodernism — A Conversation with Frederic Jameson, Interview 4 July 1986," *Social Text* #17 (Autumn 1987), 43.
42. Geraghty, 160.
43. Stephanson, 60.
44. Richards, 59.
45. Csicsery-Ronay, <http:www/depauw.edu/sfs/backissues/55/icr55art.htm>.
46. Ermath, 53.
47. Csicsery-Ronay, <http:www/depauw.edu/sfs/backissues/55/icr55art.htm>.

BIBLIOGRAPHY

Appleby, Joyce Oldham, Lynn Hunt, and Margaret Jacob. *Telling the Truth About History*. New York: W. W. Norton, 1995.
Arnold, Martin. "Making Books: The 'What Ifs' That Fascinate." *New York Times*. December 21, 2000, late ed., E3.
"Ben Sisko." Wikipedia. <http://en.wikipedia.org/wiki/Benjamin_Sisko>.
Berman, Judith. "Science Fiction without the Future." *Speculations on Speculation*, eds. James Gunn and Matthew Candelaria, 331–42. Lanham, MD: The Scarecrow Press, 2005.
Bernardi, Daniel Leonard. *Star Trek and History: Race-ing Toward a White Future*. New Brunswick, NJ: Rutgers University Press, 1998.
Bignell, Jonathan. "With Eyes Uplifted: Space Aliens as Sky Gods." *Liquid Metal: The Science Fiction Film Reader*, ed. Sean Redmond, 136–144. New York: Wallflower Press, 2004.
Boyd, Katrina G. "Cyborgs in Utopia. The Problem of Radical Difference in *Star Trek*." *Enterprise Zones: Critical Positions on Star Trek*, ed. Taylor Harrison, et al., 95–114. Boulder: Westview Press 1996.
"The Cage." Memory Alpha. <http://www.memory-alpha.org/en/wiki/The_Cage_%28episode%29>.
Csicsery-Ronay. "The SF of Theory: Baudrillard and Haraway." *Science Fiction Studies* 18 (November 1991). DePauw archives. <http://www.depauw.edu/sfs/backissues/55/icr55art.htm>.
"Definitions of History on the Web." wordnet.princeton.edu/perl/webwn.
Ermarth, Elizabeth. *Sequel to History: Postmodernism and the Crisis of Representational Time*. Princeton: Princeton University Press, 1992.
"Far Beyond the Stars." Wikipedia. <http://en.wikipedia.org/wiki/Far_Beyond_the_Stars>.
Franklin, H. Bruce. "*Star Trek* in the Vietnam Era." *Science Fiction Studies* 21 (March 1994): 24–34.
Fredericks, Casey. *The Future of Eternity*. Bloomington: Indiana University Press, 1982.

Geraghty, Lincoln. "'Carved from the Rock Experiences of Our Daily Lives': Reality and *Star Trek*'s Multiple Histories." *European Journal of American Culture* 21, no. 3 (2002): 160–76.
Gunn, James. "Introduction." *Speculations on Speculation: Theories of Science Fiction*, eds. James Gunn and Matthew Candelaria, ix–xi. Lanham, MD: The Scarecrow Press, 2005.
Harvey, David. *The Condition of Postmodernity*. Oxford: Basil Blackwell, 1989.
Jameson, Fredric. "Progress Versus Utopia; or, Can We Imagine the Future?" *Science-Fiction Studies* 9.2 (1982): 147–158.
Kuhn, Annette, ed. *Alien Zone: Cultural Theory and Contemporary Science Fiction Culture*. London: Verso, 1990.
Lagon, Mark P. "'We Owe It to Them to Interfere': *Star Trek* and U.S. Statecraft in the 1960s and the 1990s." *Extrapolation* 34 (Fall 1993): 251–264.
Linford, Peter. "Deeds of Power: Respect for Religion in *Deep Space Nine*." Star Trek *and Sacred Ground: Explorations of* Star Trek, *Religion, and American Culture*, edited by Jennifer E. Porter and Darcie L. McLaren, 77–100. New York: State University of New York Press, 2000.
Peltz, Richard J. "On a Wagon Train to Afghanistan: Limitations on *Star Trek*'s Prime Directive." *University of Arkansas at Little Rock Law Review* 25, no. 3 (2003): 634–679.
Porter, Jennifer E., and Darcie L. McLaren, eds. Star Trek *and Sacred Ground: Explorations of* Star Trek, *Religion, and American Culture*. Albany: State University of New York Press, 2000.
Redmond, Sean. "The Origin of the Species: Time Travel and the Primal Scene." *Liquid Metal: The Science Fiction Film Reader*, ed. Sean Redmond, 114–115. London: Wallflower Press, 2004.
Richards, Thomas. *The Meaning of* Star Trek. New York: Doubleday, 1997.
Sarantakes, Nicholas Evan. "Cold War Pop Culture and the Image of U.S. Foreign Policy. The Perspective of the Original *Star Trek* Series." *Journal of Cold War Studies* 7, no. 4 (Fall 2005): 74–103.
Sobchack, Vivian. *Screening Space. The American Science Fiction Film*, 2d ed. New Brunswick, NJ: Rutgers University Press, 2001.
Stephanson, Anders. "Regarding Postmodernism — A Conversation with Frederic Jameson." *Social Text* 17 (Autumn 1987): 29–54.
"What You Leave Behind." Memory Alpha <http://www.memory-alpha.org/en/wiki/What_You_Leave_Behind_%28episode%29>.
Wolfe, Gary. "Coming to Terms." *Speculations on Speculation*, eds. James Gunn and Matthew Candelaria, 13–22. Lanham MD: The Scarecrow Press, 2005.

Star Trek Series Cited and Episodes Discussed

Star Trek (ST). Executive Producer Gene Roddenberry. Network: NBC. Studio: Desilu. Aired September 8, 1966–June 3, 1969.
  "Assignment Earth." #55. Aired March 29, 1968.
  "The Cage." #1. Made as the pilot episode but not released until 1986, to celebrate *Star Trek*'s 20th anniversary. See Memory Alpha <http://alpha.org> for more information.
  "City on the Edge of Forever." #28. Aired April 6, 1967.
  "Let That Be Your Last Battlefield." #70. Aired January 10, 1969.
  "Mark of Gideon." #71. Aired January 17, 1969.
  "Patterns of Force." #50. Aired February 16, 1968.
  "A Piece of the Action." #46. Aired January 12, 1968.
  "A Private Little War." #48. Aired February 2, 1968.
  "A Taste of Armageddon." #23. Aired February 23, 1967.

Star Trek Next Generation (STNG). Executive Producers Gene Roddenberry, Rick Berman, Ira Steven Behr, Brannon Braga, Michael Piller, and Jeri Taylor. Network: syndicated. Studio: Paramount. Aired September 28, 1987–May 23, 1994.
    "The Big Goodbye." #113. Aired January 11, 1988.
    "Elementary Dear Data." #29, Aired December 5, 1988.
    "A Fistful of Datas." #134. Aired November 9, 1992.
    "The Hunted." #59. Aired January 8, 1990.
    "Sarek." #71. Aired May 14, 1990.
    "Unification I." #207. Aired November 4, 1991.
    "Unification II." #208. Aired November 11, 1991.

Deep Space Nine (DS9). Executive Producers Ira Steven Behr, Rick Berman, Michael Piller, and Jerri Taylor. Network: syndicated. Studio: Paramount. Aired January 3, 1993–June 2, 1999.
    "Far Beyond the Stars." #137. Aired January 11, 1998.
    "Image in the Sand." #151. Aired September 30, 1998.
    "Little Green Men." #80. Aired November 13, 1995.
    "Past Tense I." #57. Aired January 2, 1995.
    "Past Tense II." #58. Aired January 9, 1995.
    "Rapture." #108. Aired December 30, 1996.
    "Shadows and Symbols." #152. Aired October 7, 1998.
    "Trials and Tribble-ations." #104. Aired November 4, 1996.
    "What You Leave Behind." #176. Aired June 2, 1999.

Voyager. Executive producers Rick Berman, Kenneth Biller, Brannon Braga, Michael Piller and Jeri Taylor. Network: UPN. Studio: Paramount. Aired January 16, 1995 — May 23, 2001.
    "Future's End I. #50. Aired November 6, 1996.
    "Future's End II. #51. Aired November 13, 1996.
    "Killing Game." #86. Aired March 4, 1998.
    "Killing Game." #87. Aired March 4, 1998.
    "Tattoo." #25. Aired December 6, 1995.

Enterprise (ENT). Executive Producers Rick Berman and Brannon Braga. Network: UPN. Studio: Paramount. Aired September 26, 2001–May 13, 2005.
    "Dear Doctor." #12. Aired January 23, 2002.
    "Storm Front I." #76. Aired October 8, 2004.
    "Storm Front II." #77. Aired October 15, 2004.

9

Too Close for Comfort?
Exploring the Construction of Near Future Historical Narratives in Science Fiction Television

KORCAIGHE P. HALE

I read a book once. It said that it was the end of history—everything important had already happened. Maybe the Big Death reset history and it's starting up again....
　　　　　　　　　　　　　　　—Jeremiah, "The State of the Union"

If this chest is what we think it is, it's going to force us to revise most of our current thinking about ancient history.
　　　　　　　　　　　　　　　—seaQuest, "Something in the Air"

If someone had gotten to Hitler, or Stalin, or the guy who reprogrammed the AI, how many more would be alive?
　　　　　　　　　　　　　　　—Space: Above and Beyond, "Eyes"

You always hear people yapping about how it was all different before the Pulse. Land of milk and honey, blah, blah, blah, blah. With plenty of food and jobs, and things actually worked. I was too young to remember, so, whatever.
　　　　　　　　　　　　　　　—Dark Angel, "Pilot"

In 1932, historian Carl Becker proposed that all people, regardless of their background or training, employ the tools of the historical trade to keep track of their lives and, in so doing, construct their own narratives of the past.[1] He argued for a simplification of history that would "reduce it to its lowest terms."[2] History, he observed, was simply "the memory of things said and done."[3] This definition stripped away the idea that careful research could produce an objective historical record, or history "as it really happened."[4] Becker also suggested that, in fact, there were two kinds of history: "the actual series of events that once occurred; and the ideal series that we affirm and hold in memory."[5] All historians need to consider the effect of memory, but the practitioners of contemporary history are especially affected by this phenomenon. Memories interfere with the reconstruction of a single or dispassionate historical record of recent events because too many people remember events "as they happened" from their own perspective, and that makes careful historical analysis difficult.[6] Eventually, cultural memories of the past fade into that which Becker termed "a once valid but now discarded version of the human story, as our now valid versions will in due course be relegated to the category of discarded myths."[7] Any construction of the present is also fragile; time continues inexorably, so technically the "present" can never exist. Instead, we situate ourselves within an historical milieu, using the past to frame and illustrate the present. Becker used the philosophical term the "specious present" to describe this phenomenon.[8] The "specious present" also extends into the future: not only is the present situated by what *has been* done, Becker suggests, but also by expectations of what *will be* done.[9]

How does the construction of history apply to science fiction television? In some ways, science fiction is history inverted. Inasmuch as we all situate ourselves within an historical milieu, science fiction shows set in the future have to situate themselves historically in relation to the present. Some science fiction which is set in the far future has the same freedom of extrapolation and documentation that historians of ancient civilizations, who create histories out of scattered artifacts, do. Perhaps the best example of this is in the final episode of the fourth season of *Babylon 5*, which imagines society a millennia into the future.[10] The "near future" science fiction program, however, attempts to take the present and extrapolate into the future just a little, retaining a recognizable social environment. Its "history" needs to be clearly defined, explaining how the future developed within a few decades. These programs face obstacles similar to those of contemporary history. Too many viewers potentially have a "memory" of that future's past, which in turn could act as a critical filter to their acceptance of the posited near future.

Four television shows broadcast in the last two decades have been set in early or mid-twenty-first century Earth: *Space: Above and Beyond, seaQuest DSV/2032* (hereafter *seaQuest*),[11] *Dark Angel,* and *Jeremiah*. Each of these shows engages history in a different manner. Both *Space* and *seaQuest* assume a linear path of history; the programs establish a general historical narrative extrapolated from the time the shows were broadcast. *Space* has more leeway in this respect, and several more decades of history to "fill." Given the greater amount of historical distance involved, it is probably not surprising that the program uses more overt historical parallels to emphasize its ties to the past and to the present. In contrast, *seaQuest* approaches its future history from a relatively narrow examination of the early 1990s. The storylines of *seaQuest* are visible mirrors of the issues prevalent in the news and in the minds of its writers — what they saw in the early 1990s as potential future problems. After all, writers of the history of the future have the same dilemmas of selection and perspective as do writers of the history of the past. Yet, by extrapolating roughly twenty years from its broadcast date, the show's writers imagined a future that is quickly becoming the present. Thus, many of what its creators assumed would become major world issues and events in the intervening years have not come to pass. History itself has outpaced *seaQuest*'s future past.

The other two shows examined, *Jeremiah* and *Dark Angel*, treat history as a cyclical phenomenon, and each posits a future "break" in their history. They both assume a post-apocalyptic future that returns humanity to a similarly situated moment in the past, rather than extrapolating a linear future from the time the shows were broadcast. *Dark Angel* contains both overt and subtle references to the Great Depression, and its creators have suggested that the show was a deliberate attempt to re-imagine that period.[12] *Jeremiah*'s historical parallel stretches even further, nicknaming the future apocalyptic plague the "Big Death" (mirroring the "Black Death" outbreak of the fourteenth century) and having characters reference it as well.

Space: Above and Beyond: *War Springs Eternal*

The larger sense of history in *Space* is situated in the idea of repetition: wars of the future are very much like wars of the past.[13] Although an assumed and inherent history is embedded within the premise, there is little sense of progress or historical movement. *Space* follows a squadron of Marine recruits fighting an interstellar war against bug-like aliens in the future "Chig War." Despite being set several decades into the future, the program seems to suggest a certain technological stagnation, one without flying cars and high-tech environments. Thus, the Marine recruits go to basic training on an ordinary (albeit armored) school bus. The decades of intervening history are suggested quickly by means of flashbacks and vignettes showing the development of artificial intelligence and its attempted destruction of humanity (recounted as the A-I wars) as well as advances in genetic engineering that allowed for the creation of "in vitro" soldiers (who are grown in tanks). But in many ways the issues these events introduce are simply repeats of twentieth century woes, including a debate about "in vitro rights," for example, that deliberately recalls the battle over civil rights in the United States in the late 1950s and the 1960s.

Space borrows liberally from more than one moment in history, but most of the deliberate historical references stem from World War II. Throughout the season, the squadron finds itself in situations reminiscent of iconic World War II moments, and in most of the episodes the show both overtly refers to the historical event and subtly mirrors it as well. The series is bookended, for example, by famous wartime speeches. In the pilot episode, the UN Secretary General invokes Winston Churchill's "never was so much owed by so many to so few" speech in recognizing the achievements of the squadron,[14] and at the end, in "Tell Our Moms We Done Our Best," a commander repeats President Roosevelt's 1941 remark about days that will live in infamy.[15] The war in the Pacific, and the bloody experience of the U.S. Marine Corps in particular, provides the focal point for many of the historical antecedents.[16] References to the Doolittle Raid on Tokyo,[17] the Marine assaults on Iwo Jima and Guadalcanal,[18] and a discussion of the overall strategy of "planet-hopping maneuvers," recasting the Pacific War's island-hopping strategy, continually look back to World War II.[19] The episode "Star Dust" replays the World War II secret mission "Operation Mincemeat," undertaken to provide disinformation to the Germans before the assault on Sicily.[20]

A sense of timelessness and eternity exists in *Space*'s use of military memories, especially when the references stray beyond World War II. In "The River of Stars," characters specifically recollect the World War I Christmas truce of 1914 and then, in effect, recreate it when the squadron is lost behind enemy lines at Christmas and only make it back to Earth territory with the help of anonymous enemy forces.[21] "Never No More" re-stages the dogfights of World War I and refers to the Red Baron, featuring an enemy fighter nicknamed "Chiggie von Richthofen" that attacks with impunity. "Toy Soldiers" references both the fictional heroism of John Wayne and the real-life World War I Marine hero Dan Daly.[22] Throughout the show, characters also quote war literature from the ages: memoirs from soldiers fighting the American Civil War and Vietnam, letters from the kamikaze pilots of World War II,[23] and literary classics from Shakespeare's *Henry V* to Homer's *Iliad*.[24] In other episodes, on-screen quotes are shown from people as varied as Stephen Crane, Robert Louis Stevenson, and John Wilkes

Booth.²⁵ All of these various references allow the creators to reinforce the idea that war, whenever it is fought, is timeless and eternal. As a result, a sense of continuity and, really, historical inevitability reinforces *Space*'s perceived past.

Space uses casual cultural references to historical artifacts to illustrate that it really is the future. These are primarily centered on pop culture. In the pilot, for example, a character mentions a "twentieth-century history class" where he learned about "The Pink Floyd." Compact discs have become obsolete; one of the Marines gets a shipment from an "antiques" shop containing a boom box and the CD "Under the Big Black Sun" by the band X. And the references stretch further back into the twentieth century: in one episode a character plays Johnny Cash's "Folsom Prison Blues" and in another, the squadron commander watches W.C. Fields films.²⁶

The historical cultural artifacts are scattered, nearly randomly through the series, and as documents of the past they impose far less upon the viewer than the overt military parallels. The randomness of the historical moments highlighted in the program extends *Space*'s specious present almost limitlessly—it fuses the past, present, and future into an amalgamation of the eternal history of war.

seaQuest: *An Idealized Past in a Hopeful Future*

If *Space*'s future history suggests the unchanging nature of war and the repetition of historical parallels, loosely compiled in a nominally future environment, *seaQuest* instead imagines a specific short-term future, its specious present limited to the moment of the early 1990s. Broadcast from 1993 to 1996, *seaQuest* is steeped in the issues of that decade. The premise of the show is that the technology of the future has advanced to the point where undersea colonization and exploration is possible, land-based environmental problems have made it necessary, and increasingly intransigent politics over the use of undersea resources has forced the creation of a future UN-inspired collective security group called the "United Earth Oceans Organization" (UEO). The massive submarine *Seaquest* has been assigned to protect the undersea territory of the UEO and to undertake scientific research. The UEO spends significant time mediating between political extremes, represented by preservationists and capitalists. As such, it is targeted both by those who want to strip the oceans of their resources and by those who argue that its efforts are simply inadequate. In the world of *seaQuest*, terrorism is the weapon of choice for renegade environmentalists and predatory undersea entrepreneurs alike.

seaQuest strikingly expresses the New World Order idealism of the early 1990s even as it uses "stock villains" from that period. The most visible idealist iconography, explored through the prism of the early 1960s, references John F. Kennedy's short presidency. The pilot episode, "To Be or Not to Be," opens with a vast establishing shot that scans from the galaxy, to an external view of the earth, to a bird's eye view, and finally, to the oceans, during which an unnamed voice proclaims:

> It's because we all came from the sea, and it is an interesting biological fact that all of us here have in our veins the exact same percentage of salt in our blood that exists in the ocean, and therefore we have salt in our blood, in our sweat, in our tears, we are tied to the ocean. And when we go back to the sea, whether it is to sail or to watch it we are going back from whence we came.

In the context of the show, the unidentified speaker is calling for undersea exploration on a scale similar to that of space. But the voice is easily identified as that of President Kennedy. The speech is taken out of context from remarks Kennedy made at the 1962 America's Cup Dinner given by the Australian ambassador to the United States.[27] He was talking about a sailing contest, but the use of his speech in the opening episode of *seaQuest* imbues the show with a sense of history.[28] In the third season the allusion to Kennedy's presidency becomes far more overt. In the episode "Second Chance" the submarine is transported through a "space-time sphere" back to October 1962 in the midst of the Cuban Missile Crisis and must ensure a peaceful resolution for history to remain untainted.

For all of its pretensions to the future, *seaQuest*'s history remains mired in the problems of the early 1990s, and all too often its cast of bad guys closely mirrors those real-life "villains" who occupied the media spotlight at the time *seaQuest* was broadcast. For example, in the episode "Treasures of the Mind" the boat's crew discovers the lost library at Alexandria and hosts a conference of nations, all of which demand access to or control of the artifacts. The Libyan representative is intransigent and argumentative, at one point even threatening to attack the UEO submarine instead of negotiating. The other representatives, from Italy, Greece, Egypt, and so forth, appear far more reasonable. When the program was broadcast in 1993, Libya was widely identified as a rogue nation and a state sponsor of terrorism. Infamously, it was alleged to have colluded in the bombing of PAN AM flight 103 in 1988, which crashed in Lockerbie, Scotland, killing all aboard. In 1991 several Libyans were charged in the bombing, and throughout the rest of the decade Libya refused to allow their extradition. The issue was not resolved until 1999 when Colonel Qaddafi began to take a more accommodating line to the West.[29] Showing the Libyans as less enlightened than the rest of the region hearkens perhaps more obviously to the early 1990s than the 2020s.

In "Hide and Seek," *seaQuest* shows another stock villain of the early 1990s. The episode features William Shatner as exiled dictator Milos Tezlof, a war criminal from southeastern Europe charged with the crime of ethnic cleansing (mirroring the problems of the former Yugoslavia). Having escaped from prison, he was being hunted by the "Serbo-Croatian alliance" to be put on trial for his crimes. In 1993, as Yugoslavia was imploding into a civil war, widespread reports surfaced of regional leaders — Milos Tezlof's predecessors, perhaps — engaging in ethnic cleansing. Likely the assumption of a similar future history centering on this area seemed plausible at the time.[30] In the same way, "The Good Death" assumes the continued presence of death squads in the "Amazonian confederation," and at one point *Seaquest*'s captain, Nathan Bridger, mentions that the region had been "killing kids for decades." In 1993 stories about children in the *favelas* being murdered by death squads appeared regularly.[31]

As in *Space*, *seaQuest* uses historical artifacts to illustrate its distance from the past. In this perceived future companies had "stopped making CDs,"[32] which in the early 1990s might have seemed a vast advance in recording technology. In "Whale Song," a character decides to make a cheeseburger, a difficult prospect in part because cattle farming had been outlawed (too much methane production) and he had to use long-frozen ground beef. He uses a commemorative "Nolan Ryan III" bat to fuel the grill and sings Jimmy Buffett's "Cheeseburger in Paradise," as he cooks, all of which is played as farce. In "The Last Lap of Luxury," Bridger and his boss discuss their taste in music:

> BRIDGER: I've heard this story a hundred times. The day you skipped summer school and went to Woodstock. Dre picked you up while you were hitchhiking and you went to the concert together.
> ADM. NOYCE: Yeah ... the last great rock concert.
> Bridger: I don't know. I was only eight. When it came to rock and roll, I was a U2 man anyway.
> NOYCE: A derivative rock band at best. They couldn't pack The Who's lunch.

Woodstock is, of course, iconic; the show's writers could easily assume their viewers could identify the reference, not least because the commemorative concert Woodstock II was held in August 1994.[33] While the larger sense of history in *Space* is that of the eternal nature of war, *seaQuest*'s history in turn is limited to a particular contemporaneous bubble. The show's imagined future's "specious present" extends not very far from the time of its creation, and centers more upon the short-term specific memory of its age than the imagination of a general linear narrative.

Dark Angel: *Apocalypse Light*

Dark Angel shares with *seaQuest* a tendency to reflect its broadcast age in its portrayal of future history, although in its case that reflection is blurred by its post-apocalyptic premise. *Dark Angel* is set ten years after an electromagnetic pulse ("the Pulse") has destroyed the computers of the United States and rendered it a "third world country." It is also ten years after a daring escape by genetically altered "super-soldier" children from a secret military base. The show follows one of them, Max Guevara, who works as a bike messenger and sometime thief in Seattle. She is searching for her "siblings," her fellow escapees, helped by a local "cyber journalist," Logan Cale, who broadcasts illegally under the *nom de guerre* "Eyes Only." His goal is to fight the rampant corruption and the excesses of the police state created in the wake of the Pulse. Creators James Cameron and Charles Egbee have said that the rush of late-1990s "Y2K" hysteria inspired the show.[34] They present a re-imagined Depression,[35] albeit one with few direct evocations of the United States in the 1930s. The society is polarized, and for the average citizen, basic necessities as well as luxuries are difficult to obtain. Max's roommate accepts "real coffee" in barter for language lessons, lamenting that it has been a long time since she had seen quantities of the stuff; when Max gives Logan a grapefruit as a gift, he remarks, "We must be in a recovery." A suitor of Max's gives her a quart of motor oil, to the envy of her fellow bike messengers, and everywhere cars have extra gas tanks welded onto their roofs, perhaps indicating that gasoline is scarce and therefore hoarded.[36]

Although it nominally refers to the historical moment of the Great Depression, the imagery is more reminiscent of stereotypes of late twentieth century "third world" dystopias. In the pilot episode, Max lives as a squatter in an abandoned building. The city is visibly under martial law and divided into easily controllable "sectors," and Max and her roommate are regularly shaken down by corrupt cops in order to keep their apartment. Later, Max and Logan investigate a local operation that smuggles emigrants *out* of the United States to Canada and try to find a missing journalist long assumed to have been "disappeared" by the government.[37] If the oblique references to classic "third world" scenes were not enough, at various times the characters remind themselves of their plight, remembering the United States before it became "just another broke superpower," discussing the "huddled masses yearning to get by," and, at one point, commenting that "I'm just a young capitalist in a failing economy."[38]

Overall, *Dark Angel* contains far less of a clear historical narrative than either *seaQuest* or *Space*. Most of the show's historical clues to a perceived past occur in off-hand references, some of which are never fully explained. For example, early in the series one of Max's neighbors is dying of "Balkan War Syndrome." Later in the series, riots, such as the Tallahassee food riots, are common and an influenza epidemic apparently occurred in 2011.[39] Perhaps the most developed future history concerns the "May 22 Movement," a future terrorist organization that adopted the ideals of Ted Kaczynski (the Unabomber) and named the movement after his birth date.[40] In "Prodigy," the May 22 Movement takes hostages at a scientific conference in order to protest genetic engineering, which allows the television news to fill in the history. These future terrorists apparently saw the Pulse as the fulfillment of the Unabomber's desired destruction of the "morally bankrupt technocratic state;" their announced goal is to continue his work.

Dark Angel makes some historical references to the late 1990s, similar in form to *seaQuest*'s references to the earlier years of that decade. The frequent mention of the Unabomber in particular reflects the issues of its broadcast age, as does casual references to wars in the Balkans. In "Meow," a character notes that a satellite-based defense system nicknamed "Star Wars" had been launched in 2005; in "Cold Comfort," reference is made to the prevalence of villages in Africa still fighting Ebola.[41] More generally, the placement of the show in Seattle, the incarnation of the 1990s high-tech boom, provides a vivid contrast by showing the city as a broken-down police state, complete with rundown buildings, homeless people on every corner, and the iconic Space Needle dark and covered in graffiti. Culturally, *Dark Angel* engenders a few ties to the decade in which it was broadcast. In "Shortie's in Love," for example, one of the bike messengers suggests that as "it's been thirty years ... grunge is due for a revival" and in several episodes characters are competing, watching, or betting on "extreme sports" such as bike jumping, skateboarding, and so forth.[42]

Rather than constructing a deliberate and overarching historical narrative, *Dark Angel* concentrates on developing the history of an individual — reducing a society's history to its component parts. In that respect *Dark Angel* exemplifies Becker's imagining of an everyman historian: Max has no larger sense of history than herself, and few historical documents other than her memory with which to sort out her past. For Max, at least, history is in part the shared past of family. But for her, history is also a place: she has filled in her past and established a historical narrative for herself simply by remaining in a single location, Seattle. In more than one episode, she argues that the city is her home — a place where she has developed a history — and refuses to leave, even when it seems to be essential for her survival.[43]

Jeremiah: *Apocalypse Past*

Like *Dark Angel*, *Jeremiah* is set in a post-apocalyptic future. In *Jeremiah*, however, the apocalypse is nearly total: a bio-weapon virus has killed almost "everyone over the age of innocence." The sudden break from linear history allowed the show to speculate more deeply on the possibilities of a post-apocalyptic future and to imagine a world further removed from the present than that of *seaQuest* and *Dark Angel*. The show is set fifteen years after the apocalyptic event, known as the "Big Death." The main character, Jeremiah, is searching for his father (who may have survived the Big Death). Jeremiah and his partner, Kurdy, work for a group based out of NORAD's headquarters at Cheyenne Mountain that wants to reconstitute the nation. The first season examines their attempts to reconstruct the history of the plague and to determine whether it would return, as well as Jeremiah's own quest to understand his personal history. By the second season he has untangled his history, and now the main characters are making history by creating a new government "out of the ashes of the old."

Jeremiah's construction of a historical future is very nearly self-contained. After an apocalypse that brought "six billion dead in six months," the survivors became scavengers and, in many cases, nomads. Any post–Big Death recorded history remained largely fragmented, and news stories were spread by hearsay or emerged as myth. In one episode, characters discuss several rumors circulating that a new religion had appeared among children born after the Big Death. It is only when communities begin to try to coalesce into a single organized entity that there is a concerted effort to record history. One of the characters uses a pinhole camera to document the meetings of the new "founding fathers, " and chroniclers are shown traveling the country, spreading tales of the world for later generations to remember.[44]

Although the show evokes a new "Middle Ages," only a few direct references to the Black Death plague of the fourteenth century and the resulting history emerge from it. In one example, the leader of Cheyenne Mountain, Marcus Alexander, notes the role of churches in preserving knowledge after the Black Death:

> Some historians say that the Renaissance would never have happened if the Black Death hadn't happened first. They never considered the possibility that the Renaissance also wouldn't have happened if the churches had just sat on all of those books, waiting for the right day.... If we wait, we lose. The Renaissance never comes.[45]

Oblique references to the Middle Ages in *Jeremiah* are far more common. The first season is a quest saga, in itself emblematic of medieval chronicles. Also, in more than one episode, like in the Middle Ages, books are revealed as treasured and rare things. In one episode a community brags that it has "eighty books," and in another, a self-appointed librarian defends his collection of books with his life.[46] In a similar fashion, some survivors revere and remember art. In the episode "Mother of Invention" one community leader is discovered to be storing art objects on the sly (when other groups are seeking tools and practical information). The woman defends her choice to preserve the art, explaining: "It's our history in inks and oils and stone."[47]

Jeremiah avoids presentism by leaving out obvious anachronisms. Its future history explores the destruction of the framework of the past, something that the other shows do not attempt. The national government does not survive the Big Death, and in its place small communities, of various stripes, emerge. While some of the towns the characters encounter are relatively intact, with working small town governments, others are police states or oligarchic tyrannies. In the second season, several groups establish a nominal alliance, in part to defend against the rise of a Hitlerian messianic figure expanding from his base of operations on the East Coast. The deliberate use of propaganda posters and Potemkin villages by the demagogue "Daniel" offers one of the more overt historical parallels, as is the heroes' response: before the armed showdown between the nascent alliance and the attacking forces of Daniel, Kurdy raises the symbolic, if defunct, U.S. flag above alliance headquarters.[48]

Specific artifacts appear only as memories or recovered treasures. In chance moments, characters remind themselves of the products and cultural artifacts of their past including movies like *Jaws*, *Alien*, *Mad Max*, and *Star Wars*, as well as food like Necco wafers, rock candy, pizza, and babyback ribs. The lack of regular references to late twentieth century and early twenty-first century artifacts helps maintain the conceit that the Big Death had created a new world. In *Jeremiah* the imagined future past is fragmented; after the Big Death historical narratives are passed along as rumor and hearsay. *Jeremiah* has little or no specious present, as Kurdy notes:

> There wasn't no other time. Not for me. And not for most everybody else. I don't remember what went on before, and I don't give a shit. As far as I'm concerned, the only world that matters is this one. This is the one I've got to live in. Now, what came before and what came after, other people's shit, that's not my problem.[49]

The End of the Future

None of the shows surveyed survived more than three seasons. High costs and poor ratings were at least in part reasons for their failure. Although respected by critics, *Space* never gained a strong viewership and was not renewed after just one season.[50] Episodes of *seaQuest*, like *Space* and *Dark Angel*, were expensive to produce, which meant that lower ratings made cancellation more likely.[51] *Dark Angel* was canceled amid falling ratings in its second season, in part to make room in the Fox schedule for Joss Whedon's *Firefly*.[52] Of the four, *Jeremiah* alone might have beaten the odds; its ratings were climbing in its second season, but J. Michael Straczynski, its creator, probably doomed the show when he announced that he would not be staying with the program for a third year.[53]

But in their quest for success at a commercial level, each of these shows also seemed to develop potentially fatal alterations of their premise. Likely *seaQuest*'s creators contributed to the series' demise by constantly tweaking the show, first concentrating on future "science fact," before moving on to examine the paranormal and aliens and then, finally, in the truncated third season, shifting the time frame ahead a further decade.[54] The turn to the supernatural in the second season put off some viewers,[55] especially since in more than one instance *seaQuest* encountered mythical creatures.[56] *Dark Angel*, too, shifted to a more supernatural story line in its second season, including genetic mutants of all stripes, in addition to the attractive super-soldiers introduced in the first season. Although *Space* in general maintained a cohesive military-oriented premise, it addressed the paranormal in its later episodes, when one of the characters discovers that she has "psi" powers.[57] *Jeremiah* also flirted with unexplainable phenomena in its second season, in particular with the addition of a character that seemed to have both foreknowledge and a higher agenda.[58] It is possible that in all cases "upping the sci-fi quotient" or adding a fantasy dimension narrowed their potential audiences.

The shelf-life of any show trying to gain popularity is potentially short, and even more so for those trying to tackle the near-future. For those viewers who were not so bothered by the supernatural elements which all of these shows introduced, it is possible that the nearness of the future might have been jarring. There might be *too much* that is familiar, and that familiarity, coupled with the enhanced "sci-fi" quotient, as it were, potentially weakens the suspension of disbelief all science fiction shows require. And this is a problem that does not go away after the show has been canceled: the historical presentism of *seaQuest* is more visible (and potentially cringe-inducing) now than it was while the show was on the air, and *Dark Angel*'s references to grunge and street sports link it more closely to the decade in which it was broadcast than might have been imagined at the time.

A larger problem here is the question of plausibility: how likely and believable are the future histories that near future shows conceive? The narrow vision of shows such as *seaQuest* and, to a point, *Dark Angel* potentially limits the imagination of the viewer — by extrapolating not very far into the future, and by attempting to create a fully realized future, in effect the shows themselves weaken their ability to weave a believable narrative. By removing the premise from the recognizable extension of the immediate specious present, however, both *Space* and *Jeremiah* overcame that particular limitation of time.

As the "what-if" scenarios of history buffs intent upon imagining a different historical narrative, counterfactuals are the bane of historians. Yet, all of science fiction exists within this same milieu: hovering at the edge of "what may be." The counterfactuals in history are innumerable, and like a theoretical multiverse, every historical moment is possible. Perhaps that is where near future shows fall short: by limiting the possibilities of the future they reduce the attraction of their vision. And, if earlier versions of the past eventually become historical myths, perhaps the future, too, has a certain mythology that simply has not happened yet. Like obscenity: we'll know it when we see it. The specious present, after all, incorporates the cultural memory of the past. Why should it not envelop a cultural memory of the future?

Notes

1. For the full text of his speech, see Carl Becker, "Everyman His Own Historian," *The American Historical Review* 37.2 (1932): 221–236.
2. Ibid., 221.

3. Ibid., 223.

4. Early twentieth-century historians followed Leopold von Ranke's dictum that narrative should show history as it really happened; i.e., that there is an objective history to be discovered, and competing narratives perhaps only illustrate that a true narrative has not been discovered yet. For a discussion of how different approaches to history developed over the century, see George G. Iggers, *Historiography in the Twentieth Century: From Scientific Objectivity to the Postmodern Challenge* (Hanover, NH: Wesleyan University Press, 1997).

5. Becker, 222.

6. On the study of history and memory, see for example Jacques LeGoff, *History and Memory* (New York: Columbia University Press, 1992); and Pierre Nora, ed., *Realms of Memory: The Construction of the French Past. I. Conflicts and Divisions* (New York: Columbia University Press, 1996).

7. Becker, 231. For example, consider Great Britain during the London Blitz, preserved in the general cultural memory as the people standing together against the bombs, united in their defense of the city. This perceived solidarity stems from early accounts of the war, most especially Winston S. Churchill's memoirs, published shortly after the war. Recently, Clive Ponting re-examined what he termed the "myth of 1940" and determined that it was not evident that Londoners indeed stood together during the Blitz. Crime rates rose sharply during the war, and factory workers, even those in armament industries, regularly went on strike. His efforts complicate the history of wartime Britain but have yet to make a dent in the historical and cultural memory of the British home front. For the complete study, see Clive Ponting, *1940: Myth and Reality* (Chicago: Ivan R. Dee, 1991).

8. Becker, 226.

9. Ibid., 227.

10. "The Deconstruction of Falling Stars," *Babylon5*.

11. The official logo and name of the show is written as "seaQuest," although many critics and commentators changed it to the more-grammatical rendering "Seaquest," which is also how the name of the boat itself is spelled. Therefore references to the show will be "seaQuest" and of the boat, "Seaquest."

12. See the documentary *Dark Angel: Genesis* from *Dark Angel—The Complete First Season*.

13. The executive producers of the show, Glen Morgan and James Wong, attributed the inspiration of the show and its recurring military themes to taking a 'Fiction of War' class at Loyola Marymount University. "'Space' series mixes love and war," *The Boston Herald*, November 12, 1995, 7.

14. The original quote from Churchill is from his tribute to the Royal Air Force, House of Commons, August 20, 1940, during the Battle of Britain at http://www.winstonchurchill.org/i4a/pages/index.cfm?pageid= 388#so_much_owed.

15. The phrase "A date which will live in infamy" was uttered by Franklin D. Roosevelt when he requested a declaration of war against Japan, December 8, 1941, before a joint session of Congress. A facsimile of the original document and an audio clip is at http://www.fdrlibrary.marist.edu/tmirhdee.html

16. For specific details on the assault on Guadalcanal, see John Whiteclay Chambers, ed., *The Oxford Companion to American Military History* (New York: Oxford University Press, 1999), 304. For more on this battle and American strategy in the Pacific War, see for example David Kennedy, *Freedom from Fear: The American People in Depression and War, 1929–1945* (New York: Oxford University Press, 1999): 543–564.

17. "Hostile Visit."

18. "Star Dust" and "Sugar Dirt," respectively.

19. "Sugar Dirt."

20. The original World War II mission, "Operation Mincemeat," is outlined in Peter

Kross, *The Encyclopedia of World War II Spies* (Fort Lee, NJ: Barricade Books, 2001), 176–78. The mission concerned planting false details on a dead soldier, suggesting that the main Allied strike in the Mediterranean would not come at Sicily as it eventually did with Operation Husky.

21. The Christmas truce episode occurred on the Western Front in December 1914, when the troops on either side of the trenches put down their weapons and mingled for the holiday. See for example Martin Gilbert, *The First World War: A Complete History* (New York: Henry Holt, 1994): 117–119.

22. Sgt. Major Daniel Joseph Daly was twice awarded the Medal of Honor. For more information, the U.S. Marine Corps Historical Division maintains a biography at http://www.tecom.usmc.mil/HD/Whos_Who/ Daly_DJ.htm.

23. All from "Hostile Visit."

24. "Toy Soldiers" and "The Angriest Angel," respectively.

25. "Toy Soldiers" and "Eyes," respectively. The Booth quotation is particularly effective because at first the screen shows the words: "Tell my mother I died for my country. I did what I thought was best." Only after the line has been displayed for a moment does the attribution appear at the bottom of the screen.

26. "Pilot," "The Dark Side of the Sun," "Ray Butts," and "R&R," respectively.

27. "Remarks at the America Cup Dinner Given by the Australian Ambassador," Newport, Rhode Island, September 14, 1962 (John F. Kennedy Presidential Library and Museum website).

28. *seaQuest* is not the only program that makes a point of mentioning Kennedy. In the *Space* episode "The Farthest Man from Home," the Marines are watching a documentary on the History Network, entitled "A Century Beyond Dallas"; as the show is set in 2063, it is referencing Kennedy's assassination.

29. In many film and television shows, Libyans were "bad guys" throughout the 1980s and 1990s. News of the indictment of the Libyans came in late 1991. See for example Eloise Salholz, et al., "Who Paid for the Bullet," *Newsweek*, November 25, 1991, 26. For the eventual extradition of two Libyan agents for trial, see articles from *USA Today* and the *New York Daily News*, April 6, 1999.

30. The Yugoslavian Civil War only "ended" with the Dayton Accords in 1995; in 1993–94 fighting was still raging throughout the area. For general information on the conflict and the creation of the Dayton agreement, see for example Peter Huchthausen, *America's Splendid Little Wars: A Short History of U.S. Engagements from the Fall of Saigon to Baghdad* (London: Penguin, 2004), 185–211.

31. The routine slaughter of children in poor areas of South America, in particular Brazil, filled the news pages of the early 1990s. See for example "When Death Squads Meet Street Children," *The Economist*, July 31, 1993, 39.

32. "The Devil's Window."

33. There were two commemorative (and competing) concerts planned, and therefore a good deal of press on the rivalry. In the end, the less commercially-viable concert was cancelled. For details, see the *New York Times* articles of February 27, April 2, and June 6 (all 1994). A general piece about the event can be found in *Newsweek*, August 22, 1994, 64.

34. Bernard Weinraub, "Bio-Tweaked and On the Run, but Her Heart Will Go On," *New York Times*, Nov. 19, 2000, 13.4.

35. See the documentary *Dark Angel: Genesis* from *Dark Angel—The Complete First Season*.

36. "Prodigy," "C.R.E.A.M.," and "Heat," respectively.

37. "Heat" and "C.R.E.A.M.," respectively.

38. "Pilot," "Flushed," and "C.R.E.A.M.," respectively.

39. "Pilot," "C.R.E.A.M.," "Haven," and "Shortie's in Love," respectively.

40. For an overview of the Unabomber, see CNN's special report at http://www.cnn.com/SPECIALS/1997/unabom. Ted Kaczynski was arrested in April 1996 and his trial lasted from November 1997 to May 1998.

41. In 2000–01, a massive (425 cases) and well-publicized outbreak of Ebola occurred in Uganda—the largest at that moment in history. For the coverage in major magazines, see for example Stefan Lovgren, "A Killer Virus Pays a Visit," *U.S. News and World Report*, October 20, 2000, 39, and Simon Robinson, "A Trip Inside an African Hot Zone," *Time*, October 30, 2000, 8.

42. The X-Games, which transformed sidewalk culture into a serious industry, began in 1995, and expanded rapidly. A cover story in *U.S. News and World Report*'s June 30, 1997, issue considered the cultural significance of the phenomenon, and for a backlash defense of "traditional sports" see Richard Hoffer, et al., "Xtremely Xasperating," *Sports Illustrated*, November 16, 1998, 29.

43. In "Cold Comfort," in particular, she faces the prospect of capture if she stays in the city, rather than escaping to Canada.

44. "The Red Kiss," "Deux Ex Machina," and "The Mysterious Mister Smith," respectively.

45. "Firewall."

46. "The Red Kiss" and "Out of the Ashes," respectively.

47. "Mother of Invention."

48. "Voices in the Dark" and "The State of the Union," respectively.

49. "The Long Road."

50. Tom Bierbaum, "Review: Space: Above and Beyond," *Variety*, September 25, 1995, 42; Brian Lowry, "New Fox time slots set to take up 'Space,'" *Daily Variety*, March 28, 1996, 29.

51. *seaQuest* averaged $1.5 million per episode; *Space* averaged more than $2 million per episode; and the *Dark Angel*'s series pilot alone cost $10 million. Andy Meisler, "'seaQuest': Time to Sink or Swim," *New York Times*, October 10, 1993, 2.1; Tom Bierbaum, "Review: Space: Above and Beyond," *Variety*, September 25, 1995, 42; Bernard Weinraub, "Bio-Tweaked and on the Run, but Her Heart Will Go On," *New York Times*, November 19, 2000, 13.4.

52. Just before the second season finale, *Dark Angel* ranked 123rd among all primetime programs. See Eric Deggans, "Finale may be all that can save 'Dark Angel,'" *St. Petersburg Times*, May 2, 2002, 1D.

53. KJB, "Jeremiah's Future in Doubt?" *IGN FilmForce* (November 7, 2003). <http://movies.ign.com/articles/458/458473p1.html>; "JMS to Quit *Jeremiah*?" *Sci-Fi Wire* (July 28, 2003). <http://www.scifi.com/scifiwire/2003-07/28/10.30.tv>

54. Jefferson Graham, "Changes as 'seaQuest' fishes for more viewers," *USA Today*, April 29, 1994, 3D; Bob Sokolsky, "'seaQuest DSV' changes days, direction and captain in fall," *The Press-Enterprise*, August 13, 1995, TV03; Todd Everett, "Review: seaQuest 2032," *Daily Variety*, October 16, 1995, 2.

55. Alan Bash, "Support for 'seaQuest' sinking fast," *USA Today*, March 9, 1995, 3D; Susan Karlin, "On-Line 'seaQuest' viewers push for changes," *Electronic Media*, March 13, 1995, 10.

56. In "Treasures of the Mind" the crew discovers the library at Alexandria, in "Meltdown" the warming oceans thaw out a prehistoric reptile, in "Lostland" they discover the lost city of Atlantis, in "Watergate" they uncover 'Minerva's' tomb, and in "Something in the Air" they find (and open) Pandora's box.

57. "Level of Necessity."

58. "The Mysterious Mister Smith."

Bibliography

Books

Becker, Carl. "Everyman His Own Historian." *The American Historical Review* 37, no. 2 (Jan. 1932): 221–236.
Chambers, John Whiteclay, ed. *The Oxford Companion to American Military History.* New York: Oxford University Press, 1999.
Churchill, Winston S. *The Second World War.* New York: Houghton Mifflin, 1947–53.
Gilbert, Martin. *The First World War: A Complete History.* New York: Henry Holt, 1994.
Huchthausen, Peter. *America's Splendid Little Wars: A Short History of U.S. Engagements from the Fall of Saigon to Baghdad.* London: Penguin, 2004.
Iggers, George G. *Historiography in the Twentieth Century: From Scientific Objectivity to the Postmodern Challenge.* Hanover and London: Wesleyan University Press, 1997.
Kennedy, David. *Freedom from Fear: The American People in Depression and War, 1929–1945.* New York: Oxford University Press, 1999.
Kross, Peter. *The Encyclopedia of World War II Spies.* Fort Lee, NJ: Barricade Books, 2001.
LeGoff, Jacques. *History and Memory.* New York: Columbia University Press, 1992.
Nora, Pierre, ed. *Realms of Memory: The Construction of the French Past. I. Conflicts and Divisions.* New York: Columbia University Press, 1996.
Ponting, Clive. *1940: Myth and Reality.* Chicago: Ivan R. Dee, 1991.
Reynolds, David. *In Command of History: Churchill Fighting and Writing the Second World War.* New York: Random House, 2005.

Magazine and Newspaper Articles

Bash, Alan. "Support for '*seaQuest*' Sinking Fast." *USA Today*, March 9, 1995, sec. 3D.
Bierbaum, Tom. "Review: *Space: Above and Beyond.*" *Variety*, September 25, 1995, 42.
"By the Time They Got to..." *Newsweek*, August 22, 1994, 64.
Deggans, Eric. "Finale may be all that can save '*Dark Angel.*'" *St. Petersburg Times*, May 2, 2002, 1D.
Everett, Todd. "Review: *seaQuest 2032.*" *Daily Variety*, October 16, 1995, 2.
Graham, Jefferson. "Changes as '*seaQuest*' Fishes for More Viewers." *USA Today*, April 29, 1994, sec. 3D.
Hoffer, Richard, et al. "Xtremely Xasperating." *Sports Illustrated*, November 16, 1998, 29.
Karlin, Susan. "On-Line '*seaQuest*' Viewers Push for Changes." *Electronic Media*, March 13, 1995, 10.
K.J.B., "*Jeremiah*'s Future in Doubt?" *IGN FilmForce*, November 16, 2003. http://movies.ign.com/articles/458/458473p1.html.
Lovgren, Stefan. "A Killer Virus Pays a Visit." *U.S. News and World Report*, October 30, 2000, 39.
Lowry, Brian. "New Fox Time Slots Set to Take up '*Space.*'" *Daily Variety*, March 28, 1996, 29.
Meisler, Andy. "'*SeaQuest*': Time to Sink or Swim." *New York Times*, October 10, 1993, 2.1.
Robinson, Simon. "A Trip Inside an African Hot Zone." *Time*, October 30, 2000, 8.
Salholz, Eloise. "Who Paid for the Bullet." *Newsweek*, November 25, 1991, 26.
Sci-Fi Wire "JMS to Quit *Jeremiah*?" *Sci-Fi Wire*, July 28, 2003.http://www.scifi.com/scifiwire/2003-07/28/10.30.tv
Sokolsky, Bob. "'*seaQuest DSV*' Changes Days, Direction and Captain in Fall." *The Press-Enterprise*, August 13, 1995, TV03.

"'Space' Series Mixes Love and War." *The Boston Herald,* November 12, 1995, 7.
Weinraub, Bernard. "Bio-Tweaked and on the Run, but Her Heart Will Go On." *New York Times,* November 19, 2000, 13.4.
"When Death Squads Meet Street Children." *The Economist,* July 31, 1993, 39.

VIDEOGRAPHY

2003 Babylon5: *the Complete Fourth Season.* DVD. U.S.: Warner Home Video.
2004 Jeremiah: *The Complete First Season.* DVD. U.S.: MGM Entertainment.
2005 seaQuest DSV: *Season One.* DVD. U.S.: Universal Studios.
2005 Space: Above and Beyond: *The Complete Series.* DVD. U.S.: 20th Century–Fox.
2007 Dark Angel—*The Complete First Season.* DVD. U.S.: 20th Century–Fox.
2007 Dark Angel: *The Complete Second Season.* DVD. U.S.: 20th Century–Fox.
2007 Jeremiah: *The Complete Second Season.* iTunes. U.S.: MGM Entertainment.
2007 *seaQuest DSV: Season Two.* DVD. U.S.: Universal Studios.

10

"The Future Is the Past"
Music and History in Firefly

Kendra Preston Leonard

In the television series *Firefly*, set in 2517, music of the American West is used to establish a rough-and-ready frontier feeling. The show's music is neither composed in a new sound, representing music of the future, nor derived from today's more common genres. Rather, *Firefly*'s music is based on that of New World colonists and Westward expansionists. This chapter examines the uses of eighteenth- and nineteenth-century North American musical genres in *Firefly* in developing the show's "space western" feel and discusses how these genres interact with non–Western musical forms used in the show, creating a perhaps unintended atmosphere of American colonialism that both evokes a nostalgia for the past and maintains its societal boundaries and hierarchies.

Created by Joss Whedon, best known for *Buffy the Vampire Slayer*, *Firefly* aired in 2002 on the Fox Network. Fox executives, uncomfortable with the show's space-western premise, ran episodes out of order, frequently changed the show's air time, and finally cancelled the show after eleven episodes. Fans rallied around the show, resulting in the 2005 production of a motion picture (*Serenity*) based on the series.

Firefly chronicles the lives of the nine crew members and passengers of *Serenity*, a "Firefly-class" spaceship. Their world is one in which Earth is a long-abandoned homeland; people of all ethnicities now live in a large system of planets that have been engineered ("terraformed") for human habitation. The system is ruled by the Alliance, a merger of American and Chinese superpowers. This amalgamation of cultures has resulted in the use of both English and Chinese in everyday language and the fusion of Western and Eastern influences in visual art, medicinal practices, and behavioral codes.

Whedon credits reading Michael Shaara's Civil War book *The Killer Angels* with the inspiration for the show, saying,

> It's a very detailed account of the Battle of Gettysburg that I read in London when I was on one of my vacations where I didn't write anything, but I did come up with *Firefly* and a couple other shows.... The minutia of the Battle of Gettysburg and the lives of the people in it really made Firefly just pop out of my head. I want to get into people's lives this intimately. I want to do it in the future and show that the future is the past. So I built the structure of the world and the look of the show on the Reconstruction Era.[1]

Whedon's vision of a post–civil war universe extended beyond the logistics of a single time period and grew into a more complete construct with the addition of carefully chosen locations and visuals. By shooting scenes in the California desert among scrub brush, old mining towns, and ranches, many locations are signifiers of the untamed lands common to television and film Westerns. Weapons, clothing, and occupations are also indicative of a nineteenth century frontier life: revolvers rest in leather holsters; missionaries in white collars carry worn Bibles.

At the same time, the Eastern and futuristic influences on the show's look and feel are never far from view. Chinese is spoken frequently. Clothes are often in Asian styles or with Asian elements, including tunics with Mandarin collars and tee-shirts with Chinese text on them. Costume designer Shawna Trpcic writes that she borrowed heavily from "World War Two and the Old West, 1876 and the American Civil War, 1861, mixed in with 1861 samurai Japan."[2] Advertisements, too, are given a hybridized treatment, featuring English and Chinese while incorporating design elements from early twenty-first century Japanese and Japanese-influenced materials. Saucer-eyed animated animals, anime-style drawings of women and weapons, and strange translations are all present in ads and other text-bearing products in the *Firefly* universe. While the futuristic elements are kept to a minimum, they are necessarily present. Though the spaceships are often rusty, they are nonetheless capable of travel between worlds. Medical tools are shown to be evolved versions of present-day scalpels, syringes, and scanners.

The integration of East and West is not unusual for film and television Westerns. Film aficionados know that the origins of many Westerns are Japanese. In discussing the music of spaghetti Westerns, a major influence on *Firefly*'s scores, Royal S. Brown writes that "the mythology that dominates these westerns is neither the 'bourgeois myth' of earlier westerns nor purely the antimyth of the revisionist westerns, but rather a broader mythology that has multicultural origins (such as Japanese) in general and such filmic origins as Kurosawa's *The Seven Samurai* (1954), which inspired John

Sturges's 1960 *The Magnificent Seven* (with its famous score by Elmer Bernstein), which in turn led to Leone's first western, *Per un pugno di dollari* (*A Fistful of Dollars*), 1964, described by David Cook as 'a direct, almost shot-for-shot copy of Kurosawa's *Yojimbo* (1961).'[3] As is the case in these iconic film Westerns, *Firefly*'s music incorporates numerous multicultural elements, creating a rich aural tapestry that nevertheless remains recognizable as having been influenced by the genre's earliest scores.

Despite the integration of cultures presented in *Firefly*, its music is firmly situated in the Western genre. Much of the music in the series relates directly to the Western landscape depicted in the show. Like producers of television westerns in the past, the producers of *Firefly* rely on collective audience understanding and memory to assist them in creating a frontier in space.

Music has long been associated with geography. For instance, the sound and lyrics of Delta Blues and Southern Rock provide instant identification of location and even history. As John Connell and Chris Gibson write, "Artists or even whole communities can represent themselves and their experiences of place through music, in much the same way as literature or art."[4] Just as nationalistic composers promoted specific genres and harmonic language to construct musical identities, such as Bartok's use of Hungarian folk elements, musicians for synthesized states also create music that could come to stand for an entire geographical region and even a particular period of time. This use of music is exactly what composers did in writing for early television and movie Westerns.

Will Wright notes that almost all Americans are familiar with "gunfights, saloon brawls, schoolmarms, dance-hall girls, [...]; horses, cattle railroads; white hats and black hats."[5] Audiences who know these constructs also recognize the sounds of the Western as created by Ennio Morricone and Nino Rota. The coding of Western sounds can be traced to scores for theatre organs in the silent film era, but truly came into its own in the 1930s and 40s with the advent of the synchronized film score.[6] Westerns typically included the sound of a pan flute or pipe — or, in the case of Morricone, a person whistling — echoing the loneliness of a barren Western landscape; a motif played on a harmonica; or a ballad accompanied by a guitar and fiddle. *Firefly*'s primary composer, Greg Edmonson, obviously had these iconic elements in mind when he wrote for the show.

Non-diegetic Music

American colonial-era and Western musical styles and forms occur in both diegetic and non-diegetic ways in *Firefly*. While there is a considerable amount of diegetic music, the show's non-diegetic theme song, written by Whedon, firmly establishes its musical atmosphere. The show's theme song reflects Whedon's post–Civil War vision, seeking an artistic and historical context in which to place the show's characters Mal and Zoe (the ship's captain and first mate), who were on the losing side of an interstellar war for independence:

> It's a song of life in defeat, and that's kind of what the show is about. It's about people who have been either economically or politically or emotionally beaten down in one way or another and how they cling to each other and how they fail each other and how they rebuild themselves. I wrote it so it could be sung as a Civil War lament....[7]

Indeed, the song could be from the American Civil War. Edmonson, who composed the majority of the music for *Firefly*, has said of the theme, "I think Joss always saw this as a lone black man sitting on a front porch, kind of like Leadbelly, singing this post-apocalyptic song."[8] The recording used for the show features blues singer Sonny Rhodes and an accompaniment that — while over-orchestrated for the tastes of Whedon and Edmonston — still retains the flavor of one man and a guitar.[9] The song is in the 12-bar blues form common to most popular American music, providing a familiar touch for audiences. The language too gives listeners a hint of the world they will soon experience: dropped g's at the ends of words and "ain't" make clear that these space dwellers will not speak with the carefully enunciated Shakespearean delivery of Patrick Stewart's Jean-Luc Picard.

The repeated use of elements from the main theme in the show's incidental music is a continual aural reminder of the show's dusty, hardscrabble setting. Quotes and timbral references from the main theme are often heard in background music, especially when the crew is preparing to leave a planet for space or making an escape from a sticky situation. In other cases, the music is direct accompaniment to actions that would not be out of place on any frontier.

In the first episode, "Serenity," the extended opening scene, or teaser, shows the defeat of Mal's regiment in the war for independence.[10] Music is first heard as Alliance ships drop bombs and tracer rockets — shown in slow motion against the disbelief in Mal's eyes — down into the arena of battle: a slow lament on a solo violin. The music has an Appalachian folk quality to it; the tune sounds like it could be from an Irish or Scottish dirge brought to the Americas by settlers. The atmosphere is one of a losing battle in those mountains, rather than on an unfamiliar planet, and the use of a solo instrument emphasizes the isolation of the independent fighters. Whedon has said of the music, "The idea of the instrumentation was to highlight the sparseness of their environment and the teeniness of them," and this initial musical elegy does exactly that.[11]

The violin returns, this time accompanied by a guitar, in the second segment of the teaser. The crew is illegally salvaging materials from a wrecked spaceship; all goes well until the appearance of an Alliance cruiser. Music is used to illustrate the crew's apprehension of being sighted and the speed at which they need to complete the job. This time the music is quicker, featuring the violin as the solo instrument while the guitar provides rhythm and adds harmonic depth to the violin's tune. The music is distinctly American in flavor and based on the melodies and harmonic language associated with the Appalachians and the American West. Diatonic in nature, the music occasionally sidesteps to modal melodic forms as it recalls folk music of the British Isles. As the crew boards the Firefly and the ship makes its escape, strummed guitars bring the sequence to a bluesy end, cadencing along with the violin's melody line, a variation on the lost battle music of the teaser's first half. The music heard here exemplifies Whedon's view of a life in defeat; the audience is reminded that the loss of independence is never far from Mal and Zoe's minds, not by visual flashback, but by the repeated musical theme from the battle sequence.

Nondiegetic scene-setting music is also a key element in the teaser to the episode "The Train Job."[12] The scene opens in a bar, where a belly dancer in the traditional bedlah costume of skirt, beaded hip scarf, and bra works the room to the strains of a repeating pentatonic melody played on a bamboo flute accompanied by a drum and plucked string instrument, possibly an oud. This diegesis firmly places the dancer in an Eastern social setting, although the tavern's visual treatment — and that of its patrons — is a hybrid of East and West. For instance, Asian paper lanterns hang over a bar, patrons wear denim and other sturdy work clothes reminiscent of the American gold rush, servers appear in cartoonishly applied geisha-like make-up and kimonos, Westernized into a style drawn from Japanese manga and anime, and men share a hookah at a table in the center of the room. There is obvious use of Chinese in the scene, both in polite conversation, as Mal orders a drink from the bar, and sarcastically, later in the scene. The music of the belly dancer ends when a patron in Western garb orders the musicians to "shut up" so that he can make a toast. An altercation between Mal, Zoe, and Jayne, *Serenity*'s mercenary crew member, and the patrons erupts, along with music Edmonson later labeled "Big Bar Fight."

The bar fight could, visually speaking, be anywhere and any time, with the exception of the holographic window through which Mal is thrown. There are no futuristic laser guns: fists and the occasional barstool are the weapons of choice. The music of the fight, though, places the brawl firmly into a nineteenth-century border setting, particularly the Kentucky border, due to the bluegrass sound used. The timbre of a bluegrass-derived resonator guitar and a wailing violin using slow slides establishes the tension before the fight erupts. Then, a heavy drumbeat, and a quickly picked guitar and banjo, accompany a bluegrass fiddle, whose line mirrors the action as the punches fly. The harmonic progressions of the accompaniment are simple, and the fiddle's seemingly improvised solo echoes the melody line from the *Firefly* theme.

The guitar motifs repeat as the fight intensifies, and the rolling, unpredictable line of the fiddle emphasizes that the outcome of the fight is in no way guaranteed for the show's heroes. As the patrons push Mal, Zoe, and Jayne towards a cliff edge, the pacing of the fiddle's tune slows, mimicking the uncertainty of the situation. The music stops as the three look over the cliff edge and wait for their rescue by the ship. As the trio boards the ship, the music returns to offer harmonic and scenic resolution, the fiddle playing a standard harmonic cadence.

Two other brief instances of nondiegetic music used to continue the tone of Western settlement life occur in the episode "Shindig," when the crew docks on one of the major Alliance city-planets, Persephone, to restock and look for work.[13] As they depart the ship and stroll through the city streets, the visual juxtaposition of East and West is again present, but mitigated by the cowboy-style Western music underneath. Persephone appears to be a late twentieth-century city, with brick buildings, concrete skyscrapers, and advertising that would be familiar to any city-dweller, with the exception of live models in storefronts and the occasional spaceship passing overhead. As in the bar fight sequence of "The Train Job," both Chinese and English are used in signs and conversation, and the clothes of the city crowds speak to a number of ethnicities.

Underlying the relative exoticism of the city, however, is the familiar sound of guitar and fiddle. The music is lively but not rushed, and its major-key tonality reflects the happiness of the crew to be out of the confines of the small ship and exploring a new place. At the end of the same episode, the ship's hold is filled with cattle, and again, the fiddle and guitar are heard in a ballad-like melody similar to "Red River Valley" and other songs of the American West. The lowing of the cattle — heard clearly amid the instruments — reminds viewers that while the ostensible location may be space, the true place of the story is the frontier.

Close listening reveals that the non-diegetic music of *Firefly* provides a soundscape that remains close to the show's Western roots. It underlies both action scenes and dialogue to make the show's premise of life in a rough and unpredictable age entirely familiar to audiences; just as they recognize the scrub brush and horses as motifs of the hardship of expansion, so do they recognize the music as a shared indicator of the life led by *Serenity* and her crew.

Diegetic Music

In addition to creating an aural backdrop reinforcing the show's concept, music plays a significant part in the storylines of several episodes. Like the non-diegetic music of the show, this music also evokes the atmosphere of the American west. Two examples of communities celebrating with music and dance occur in the episodes "Safe" and "Our Mrs. Reynolds."[14] Both episodes deal with the cultures created by colonists on terraformed planets; in both cases, the communities are isolated and devoutly religious.

In "Safe," *Serenity* lands on Jiangyin, a planet where the audience's first glimpse of life is three men skinning a rabbit. Dressed in homespun clothes, they carry knives and have obviously been hunting for most of the day. The ship's medic, Simon, steps into cow dung as the crew disembarks and shoos off their cargo of cattle. The planet is obviously a rural one, with no cities to speak of, just a dusty main street visually reminiscent of a spaghetti Western. Although there is a blend of East and West in the town's dry goods — branding irons, post-hole diggers and other supplies for farming and ranching sit alongside Asian-inspired carvings and painted plates — and citizenry, the culture is one of the American frontier: the men hunt, women tend to shops and children, and the living is plain, if not a little brutal.

Simon and his troubled sister River wander the town, and when she suddenly disappears, Simon follows the sound of music to find her dancing with the colonists. Musicians and dancers are gathered under a tent in the middle of a lush green field — a direct contrast with the dusty streets shown moments earlier. Women in long skirts and heavy boots dance with men in work clothes; a variety of ethnicities are represented in the faces shown circling about in the dance. The music is a traditional Scottish jig called "The Sailor's Wife," arranged by Edmonson. Those not dancing clap and whoop to the tune as musicians, who are shown with a violin, wood flute, and a pipa, or Asian lute, perform at the side of the dance platform. River joins in the dance and whirls about with the men and women of the settlement. The music is quick and sprightly; these colonists are enjoying themselves despite the harsh realities of their lives.

Because of the instantly recognizable sound of the jig, the scene places this small planet within the cultural sphere of some of America's earliest settlements, those of the Scots and Irish in Virginia and North Carolina. The mostly-traditional instruments used—a woodwind, violin, and plucked strings—add to the verisimilitude, as does the costuming of the dancers in habitual eighteenth-century garb, especially for the women. While multiethnic visuals are present, such as the decorations on the tree that serves as the tent's main post, some of the men's clothing, and the brief appearance of the Asian lute, the music still clearly delineates a setting from the frontier of the American colonies. This aural setting is a bit earlier than the Western soundscapes previously discussed, and there is a reason for the older music's use: part of the plot depends upon the archaic beliefs of a group of the colonists who, in their religion, are highly superstitious and believe in the supernatural. They live a much plainer life than even those in the struggling town and have been known to kidnap individuals with skills they need—in this case, Simon's medical expertise. Drew Z. Greenberg, who wrote the episode, describes the settlers' community as

> a small community. Falling down gray wood shacks. A frontier town that lost the battle with the forest and was overrun. The general look is Appalachian village. A few beaten-looking people sit in front of the shacks: thin men cooking on crude clay ovens, grim-faced tattered women tending to dirty children in sack-dresses.[15]

The desired primitive "Appalachian" feel of the scene is accomplished by using music associated with that region, and the idea of a more primitive colonial setting is likewise fulfilled by the older form of folk music used here.

In the episode "Our Mrs. Reynolds," the initial opening teaser music is non-diegetic and has a more distinctly hybrid sound to it.[16] Edmonson said of the music that Fox executives were trying to "get rid of all the Western elements.... So as it fades from black, I had a sitar playing and then I had Chinese vocals, just purely to say, 'This is not a Western Western. It's a different Western, it's a different planet, it's a different universe.'"[17]

However, the musical diegesis during the first scenes of the episode does not remain true to Edmonson's original intention here. At a celebration that follows the first scene of the teaser, members of this community — also religious and somewhat primitive — dance to music played in a true Western style. Neither Scottish jig nor bluegrass, this soundscape is that of a Wild West barn dance, and the dancers follow patterns that mimic Western square dance forms. The instrumentation is familiar: fiddle, plucked strings, and a bass are clearly heard. The atmosphere of the dance, which takes place in a dusty clearing lit by torches, draws heavily from the collective television audience imagination of the Old West. Without an obvious clue as to the actual place and time, an inexperienced viewer would situate the scene firmly in Oklahoma or Texas circa 1880. Later in the scene a woodwind, likely a wood flute, is added to the instruments, and the music becomes more ballad-like, while still retaining the harmonic and rhythmic flavor of the American West. The dance becomes a circle dance, also appropriate to the time period evoked. This community is slightly more modern than the one depicted in "Safe," and the more recent music helps indicate this to the audience.

Newly-created music is also present in the *Firefly* universe, but it too draws on American musical traditions for form, harmonic language, and even text. In "Jaynestown," the crew visits Higgins' Moon, where the primary industry is making mud bricks.[18] In Canton, the main settlement, they discover that Jayne, the ship's hired mercenary, is celebrated as a Robin Hood–like folk hero, complete with a mud statue and a folk ballad. While it turns out that Jayne's charitable act of throwing gold down to the workers — or "mudders" — was inspired by the need to relieve his escape ship of weight rather than out of the goodness of his heart, the folk legend remains intact. When Mal, Zoe, Jayne, and Wash, the ship's pilot, stop for a drink in a muddy, subterranean bar, they hear about Jayne's so-called good deeds from a mudder with a guitar.

Written by scriptwriter Ben Edlund, "The Hero of Canton" is what is known as a "border ballad." Border ballads are the musical stories of border raiders, livestock rustlers, and outlaws, chronicling their exploits and daring escapes. Although traditional Scottish and English border ballads lack the chorus — an element present in "The Hero of Canton" — they do include most of the other elements of Edlund's song, including half-spoken, half-sung narrative text, which clearly describes the "common folk," the oppressive authority, and the hero of the song. Despite the fact that Higgins' Moon is far from the borders of England and Scotland, the music indicates that all of the small worlds in the *Firefly* universe are border lands, just as lawless and unstable as they were on Earth-that-was.

Non-Western Music

There are two recurring entities in *Firefly* for which non–Western music (in both the sense of non–American West and non-global West) is always used: the elegant Companion (courtesan) Inara; and the Reavers, bands of men who terrorize remote areas of space, raping, killing, and mutilating anyone they can catch. These two extremes — the exotic, erotic, and feminine and the barbaric, aggressive, and insane — are represented by musical forms and timbres with long traditions of depicting the Other.

Inara is based on a traditional figure of the Middle East: the dusky-skinned, bejeweled woman clothed in veils and flowing caftans, highly trained in dance, music, swordplay, conversation, and love-making. This exotic construct has been popular among Western audiences since the first reports of Turkish harems and Japanese geisha and oiran were received in Europe. Nineteenth-century poetry, paintings, and music depicting non–Western women ranged from idealized portraits to eroticized odalisques. Music composed to suggest women of these worlds was hugely popular in the mid-nineteenth century, when both instrumental music and opera looked to the Orient for inspiration. Ralph P. Locke writes that such music "vividly evokes images of curvaceous women dancing with supple arm and torso movements; the beckoning quality is intensified by the curling melody's being given to a solo oboe, perhaps understood as the equivalent of the Arab *mujwiz*."[19] Such musical evocations became common fare for depicting women outside of the Western sphere; Franz Waxman's scores for *Sayonara* and *My Geisha* are replete with examples of Westernized imitations of Asian music. Even today musical depictions of Asian women in film often rely on stereotypical musical elements including the pentatonic scale, gong-like percussion, and sinuous, winding melodies. As Ellie M. Hisama notes in one study of Orientalism in recent popular music, "Asian female identity has long been linked with prostitution and naughty sex."[20]

As Christina Rowley has written, despite the futuristic time frame, some gender roles in *Firefly*, Inara's among them, are based on "conventional ('here-and-now') notions of gender" or even earlier interpretations.[21] Indeed, Inara's position is similar to that of a nineteenth-century Japanese oiran, a woman with training similar to that of a geisha in calligraphy, conversation, dance, music, and poetry but who, unlike a geisha, does engage in sex with her clients. She is from the planet Sihnon, a name redolent of Asian culture, and is shown to be a practicing Buddhist. Her costumes are rich and varied, but always suggest traditional Asian designs, albeit from a variety of ethnicities. Her shuttle — which she rents from Mal — is a smaller spacecraft that docks onto the larger ship and is capable of short-range travel; it too serves as her living quarters. Her shuttle's interior also is bedecked in fabrics and styles borrowed from nineteenth-century Asia. A pipa rests near a Buddha; draperies and candles suggest intimacy and the exotic. Dee Amy-Chinn has suggested that while other female characters, such as Zoe and Kaylee, benefit in both characterization and camera gaze from second wave feminism, Inara is excluded by virtue of her appearance:

> Her appearance is always womanly and over the course of the series she appears dressed in a range of beautiful costumes all of which have an Oriental feel to them and which are designed to showcase (and thus fetishise) parts of her body.... Within the text, her grooming rituals facilitate her location as the object of the male gaze.... But this is the classic, rather than the heterosexpositive postfeminist, male gaze proposed by Projansky as the text offers no evidence that Inara is aware of the camera's gaze or is deliberately playing to it....[22]

Appearance alone does not isolate Inara. Inara's music almost always features the pipa (or a guitar substituting for one), along with violin and a wood flute. Her music is pentatonic and deftly mimics Chinese melodic forms. Slow in tempo and quiet, it is the most complete aural acknowledgement of the East in the *Firefly* universe's mixed culture of East and West. However, the music itself is not as fully integrated as is the Western music used elsewhere. Where Western music might be played on Eastern instruments, or with an interpolation of Eastern melody or modality, Inara's music lacks reciprocal hybridity: with the exception of replacing a pipa with a guitar (which happens only rarely), her music never includes aspects of the American genres used by Edmonson. The overall culture may include elements of both East and West, but for the Eastern feminine, these remain unblended. Inara's music sets her aside; as Hisama relates, in an analysis of Asian musical characteristics in popular song, "a pentatonic scale associated with traditional music of east Asia ... is meant to evoke the 'sound of the Orient' and reinforces the narrator's dominant position."[23] In this case, the pentatonicism also promotes the audience's Western gaze, or, as Derek Scott writes, "When Orientalism appropriates music from another culture, it is not simply used to represent the Other; it is used to represent our own thoughts *about* the Other," a view already sustained by the strong presence of the Western/American elements the series.[24] Although her character is integral to the series, Inara's separateness is marked by her unique and isolating living quarters, dress, profession, and music, ultimately signifying her as both apart from the rest of the crew and apart from the audience, the classic feminine Other.

Inara is not the only Other in *Firefly*. Flying in ships gruesomely ornamented with the skeletons of their victims, Reavers are a subculture of violent, aggressive, and irrational former colonists who have left civilization to terrorize settlements and ships alike. Reavers and their behavior are described by Zoe in the show's first episode: "If they take the ship, they'll rape us to death, eat our flesh and sew our skins into their clothing and if we're very very lucky, they'll do it in that order."[25]

Edmonson says that the music he composed for the Reavers "was just meant to be disturbing."[26] Their theme is a persistent, rhythmic percussion over a low drone accompanied by a static, high-pitched line; it is meant to sound both mechanical and barbaric — music without melody or harmony. The percussion used is a variety of instruments, some manufactured for the purpose and others found. Edmonson described some of the percussion used in the show's music as "a guy beating on found percussion — a hubcap, a can,"[27] and "pieces of metal, wood boxes, and ethnic instruments, all played with brushes and sticks."[28] The image of the violent Eastern Other, from its origins in the *style turc* and *style hongrois* to present-day lyrics about Middle Eastern "barbarism," is no less pervasive in popular culture than that of the erotic Eastern Other. Like Inara, the Reavers are exoticized through their appearance, societal isolation, and music.

Both Others in *Firefly* are represented by unique musical approaches that helps audiences recognize the distinctions between the Others' different living and behavioral patterns and those of the rest of the show's characters To emphasize this difference, Inara's and the Reavers' music is always framed by the show's established Western soundtrack. There is little interaction between these spheres of musical representation; while Inara is occasionally present when Western music signifying the rest of the crew is heard, she is usually on the margins of the scene. For the Reavers, there is no overlap; within the series, there is little recognition that they are even human.

Conclusion

Firefly offers audiences a future drawn from a contemporary youth culture of Japanese manga and American action movies; a setting in which the elements of life are a little distant but not unfamiliar; a political world that is bleak but plausible; and a soundscape that, for the most part, provides audiences with forms, harmonic languages, and timbres easily identified as "native" to North American culture. The majority of the well-designed music of the show unequivocally sets it in a time of human expansion and frontier challenges. Furthermore, even the sounds of the Other are not unfamiliar to audiences, but refer to widely accepted late twentieth/early twenty-first century signifiers for such. Yet, the completely integrated culture Whedon and the show's other creative consultants envisioned fails to materialize in part because of the show's musical dichotomies. While the rigid enforcement of the show's musical boundaries may be a boon to audiences, who rely, even subconsciously, on aural cues for greater understanding of events and dynamics in the show, close analysis shows the music ultimately portrays American colonialism through a nostalgic and thus uncritical soundscape that emphatically preserves the divisions between cultures.

NOTES

1. SciFi.com, interview with Joss Whedon, August 2002. Accessed at http://www.scifi.com/scifimag/october2002/transcripts.
2. Shawna Trpcic, "Costume Design," in Joss Whedon, Firefly: *The Official Companion, Volume One* (London: Titan Books, 2006), 150.
3. Royal S. Brown, *Overtones and Undertones: Reading Film Music* (Berkeley: University of California Press, 1995), 227.
4. John Connell, *Sound Tracks: Popular Music, Identity, and Place* (New York: Routledge, 2003), 117.
5. Will Wright, *Sixguns and Society: A Structural Study of the Western* (Berkeley: University of California Press, 1977), 2.
6. David Bordwell, *The Classical Hollywood Cinema: Film Style & Mode of Production to 1960* (New York: Routledge, 1988), 34.
7. Joss Whedon, "The Ballad of Serenity," in Firefly, 33.
8. Greg Edmonson, quoted in Joss Whedon, "The Ballad of Serenity," in Firefly, 33.
9. Helen San, interview with Greg Edmonson for Tracksounds.com, 2002. Accessed at http://www.tracksounds.com/specialfeatures/Interviews/interview_greg_edmonson.htm.
10. "Serenity," *Firefly*, Joss Whedon, Twentieth Century–Fox Television, 2002.
11. Joss Whedon, "Into the Black," in Firefly, 13.
12. "The Train Job," *Firefly*, Joss Whedon, Twentieth Century–Fox Television, 2002.
13. "Shindig," *Firefly*, Joss Whedon, Twentieth Century–Fox Television, 2002.
14. "Safe" and "Our Mrs. Reynolds," *Firefly*, Joss Whedon, Twentieth Century–Fox Television, 2002.
15. "Safe," *Firefly*, 138.
16. "Our Mrs. Reynolds," *Firefly*, Joss Whedon, Twentieth Century–Fox Television, 2002.
17. "Our Mrs. Reynolds," *Firefly*, 156.

18. "Jaynestown," *Firefly*, Joss Whedon, Twentieth Century–Fox Television, 2002.
19. Ralph P. Locke, "Cutthroats and Casbah Dancers, Muezzins and Timeless Sands: Musical Images of the Middle East," *The Exotic in Western Music*, ed. Jonathan Bellman (Boston: Northeastern University Press, 1998), 115.
20. Ellie M. Hisama, "Postcolonialism on the Make: The Music of John Mellencamp, David Bowie, and John Zorn," *Popular Music*, 12.2 (May 1993): 99.
21. Christina Rowley, "Firefly/Serenity: Gendered Space and Gendered Bodies," *British Journal of Politics and International Relations* 9 (2007): 318.
22. Dee Amy-Chinn, "'Tis Pity She's a Whore: Postfeminist Prostitution in Joss Whedon's *Firefly*," *Feminist Media Studies*, 6.2, 178.
23. Hisama, 92.
24. Derek Scott, "Orientalism and Musical Style," *The Musical Quarterly*, 82.2 (Summer 1998): 314.
25. "Serenity," *Firefly*, Joss Whedon, Twentieth Century–Fox Television, 2002.
26. Helen San, interview with Greg Edmonson for Tracksounds.com, 2002. Accessed at http://www.tracksounds.com/specialfeatures/Interviews/interview_greg_edmonson.htm.
27. Ibid.
28. Greg Edmonson, quoted in Joss Whedon, "The Ballad of Serenity," Firefly*: The Official Companion, Volume Two* (London: Titan Books, 2007), 33.

BIBLIOGRAPHY

Amy-Chinn, Dee. "'Tis Pity She's a Whore: Postfeminist Prostitution in Joss Whedon's *Firefly*." *Feminist Media Studies* 6, no. 2 (2006): 178.
Bordwell, David. *The Classical Hollywood Cinema: Film Style & Mode of Production to 1960*. New York: Routledge, 1988.
Brown, Royal S. *Overtones and Undertones: Reading Film Music*. Berkeley: University of California Press, 1995.
Connell, John. *Sound Tracks: Popular Music, Identity, and Place*. New York: Routledge, 2003.
Edmonson, Greg. Interviewed by Helen San. Tracksounds.com, 2002. Accessed at http://www.tracksounds.com/specialfeatures/Interviews/interview_greg_edmonson.htm.
_____. "The Ballad of Serenity." Firefly*: The Official Companion*, Volume Two. London: Titan Books, 2007.
Hisama, Ellie M. "Postcolonialism on the Make: The Music of John Mellencamp, David Bowie, and John Zorn." *Popular Music* 12, no. 2 (1993): 99.
"Jaynestown," *Firefly*. DVD. Directed by Marita Grabiak. 2002, Los Angeles: Twentieth Century–Fox Television, 2002.
Locke, Ralph P. "Cutthroats and Casbah Dancers, Muezzins and Timeless Sands: Musical Images of the Middle East." *The Exotic in Western Music*, ed. Jonathan Bellman. Boston: Northeastern University Press, 1998, 115.
"Our Mrs. Reynolds," *Firefly*. DVD. Directed by Vondie Curtis-Hall. 2002, Los Angeles: Twentieth Century–Fox Television, 2002.
Rowley, Christina. "Firefly/Serenity: Gendered Space and Gendered Bodies." *British Journal of Politics and International Relations* 9 (2007): 318.
"Safe," *Firefly*. DVD. Directed by Michael Grossman. 2002, Los Angeles: Twentieth Century–Fox Television, 2002.
Scott, Derek. "Orientalism and Musical Style." *The Musical Quarterly* 82, no. 2 (1998): 314.

"Serenity," *Firefly*. DVD. Directed by Joss Whedon. 2002, Los Angeles: Twentieth Century–Fox Television, 2002.
"Shindig," *Firefly*. DVD. Directed by Vern Gillum. 2002, Los Angeles: Twentieth Century–Fox Television, 2002.
"The Train Job," *Firefly*. DVD. Directed by Joss Whedon. 2002, Los Angeles: Twentieth Century–Fox Television, 2002.
Trpcic, Shawna. "Costume Design." In Firefly*: The Official Companion*. Vol. 1. London: Titan Books, 2006.
Whedon, Joss. "The Ballad of Serenity." *Firefly*. Los Angeles: Twentieth Century–Fox, 2002.
_____. Firefly*: The Official Companion, Volume One*. London: Titan Books, 2006.
_____. Firefly*: The Official Companion, Volume Two*. London: Titan Books, 2006.
_____. Interviewed by SciFi.com. August 2002. Accessed at http://www.scifi.com/scifimag/october2002/transcripts.
Wright, Will. *Sixguns and Society: A Structural Study of the Western*. Berkeley: University of California Press, 1977.

11

The Battle for History in *Battlestar Galactica*

JANICE LIEDL

From its first incarnation as a 1970s space opera to its re-imagining as a twenty-first century sci-fi drama, *Battlestar Galactica* carries with it a weighty sense of the past. The original series evoked ancient Earth cultures from Greeks and Egyptians to the Toltecs and Mayans, arguing that all of these had their origins in a common, extra-terrestrial source: a thirteenth tribe of interstellar humanity. With its protagonists' stated goal being "a shining planet known as Earth," the original *Battlestar Galactica* dizzyingly posited a universe filled with futuristic technology and alien threats.

Relaunched in a 2003 mini-series by Ronald D. Moore and David Eick, the new *Battlestar* takes a very different tack towards the characters and universe while retaining a few essential elements from the original show. Both versions focus on "rag-tag fleets" fleeing the destruction of their home worlds. Characters are no longer saddled with mythological names such as "Apollo" and "Athena," but those symbolically-charged names are recycled as pilot call-signs in the military system. The futuristic universe teeming with alien encounters in the original series gives way to an unpopulated emptiness offering little shelter or hope for the fugitive remains of humanity.

The greatest transformations from old series to new are in the origins and aims of the Cylon antagonists. Originally, the Cylons were the relentless mechanical creations of an alien race that had long been at war with the Colonial humans, fighting their war from beyond the grave through their robots. In the new series, the Cylons began as the war machines of the Colonies, the twelve human settlements. These war machines had rebelled against their creators, sparking a devastating war that faded into distant memory among the Colonies after an armistice of more than forty years. While colonial humanity grew complacent, the Cylons evolved a new aspect: twelve humaniform models indistinguishable from the people that had created them. These new forms allow the Cylons to infiltrate and overtake their opponents but not simply to effect their destruction. The reality of their aims, unfolding over the show, is more complex.

Post-colonial analysis helps to untangle the complicated relationship between the antagonistic groups of Colonial humans and mechanical Cylons in *Battlestar Galactica*, the new series. Indistinguishable from Colonial humanity, the Cylons are both other and self, destroyers and preservers. They consider themselves to have evolved beyond humanity but face a limited future, replicating only in exact duplicates of their few existing models. Thus, when the Cylons destroy billions of Colonials in a coordinated nuclear attack on the Colonies, they preserve a number of survivors in hopes of achieving sexual reproduction by interbreeding with their foes. The Cylons appropriate humanity's worlds, forms, and even their history.

The Cylons consider themselves the rightful heirs and interpreters of the Colonial's prophetic texts that speak of cycles of destruction, rebirth, and renewal. "Humanity's children are returning home today," coldly noted the Cylon known as Number Six, while she approvingly witnessed the destruction of most of Colonial humanity.[1] This statement establishes the tone for the new *Battlestar Galactica* as well as the series' dynamic. The Cylon rebellion may have brought them liberty, but, as with many other colonized peoples, that freedom has brought them no peace with their past. They are like Edward Said's "colonized people who had freed themselves on one level but remained victims of their past on another."[2] The Cylons are obsessed with their creators, whom they see as a source of evil and corruption they must counter but cannot eradicate because they remain dependent upon the humans in surprising ways. Both groups stake their futures on claims to a common history derived from the Colonials' mythical forebears, which the Cylons reinterpret as more properly applying to them.

Hegel suggested that the first battles in history were battles sparked by the desire to be recognized as a human being, to challenge the master/slave dialectic; post-colonial theory would make this battle a battle *for* history, particularly in the colonized people's struggles to regain and rearticulate a subsumed or dismissed history.[3] In *Battlestar Galactica* this fight manifests as the desires of both Cylons and Colonials to be recognized as the more authentic people, worthy as heirs to the legacy of prophetic and newly-contested history.

A Common History

> *All this has happened before. All this will happen again.*
> — Book of Pythia, Colonial sacred scripture

Both humans and Cylons lay a claim to a common past: the Colonials because it is their history; the Cylons because they were created by man and thus claim humanity's history as their own precursor. Little by little, the viewers become privy to a past which resonates with motifs from their own history. And, as the show develops, it becomes more and more difficult to see the story as a simple struggle between good (humans) and bad (Cylons) because the very complex historical background revealed in the show leaves neither untainted.

Two significant events mark the recent history of the human Colonials, both relating to the Cylons. The first is the Cylon War of two generations past that began when the complex, networked war machines of the feuding colonies turned on their masters and launched a war that lasted over twelve years, forcing the colonies to abandon more advanced computer systems because those were the Cylons' tools. The second major event was, ironically, sparked by the Cylon War: the unification of the fractious, warring twelve colonies of humanity under the Articles of Colonization, commemorated on the holiday of "Colonial Day." On the surface, both events ended with the triumph of humanity: the Cylons signed an Armistice and the Colonies became united.

However, the subsequent years were not without event. The Colonies were plagued with racism, violent political protest, terrorism, and the holding of political prisoners. The Twelve Colonies had not found true peace, but only a ceasefire with their enemy and a superficial integration at home. The failure of humans to build a society that lived up to their ideals and expectations would be one of the greatest charges laid against the Colonials by the Cylons. During this time, the Colonials lost their fear of the Cylons. Nevertheless, the Cylons, although uncommunicative, were not quiescent. Their time was spent building up their military power as well as perfecting the "evolved" humaniform they would use to infiltrate and defeat their former masters.

The Cylons seemingly disappeared at the end of the war, inspiring complacency among the Colonials. On the eve of renewed conflict, the Twelve Colonies were superficially united in peace and prosperity but divided and vulnerable to an enemy they did not expect. About to be decommissioned and repurposed as an educational vessel, complete with a souvenir shop, the battlestar *Galactica* in the series' outset embodied Colonial humanity's stasis and self-satisfaction. Wars and war-machines were being relegated to the dustbin of history. The cautious actions and carefully limited technology of the past, as showcased on this aged vessel, were swept away to make room for modern networks of convenience and centralizing control.

At the outset of the new series, celebrity scientist Dr. Gaius Baltar and Education Secretary Laura Roslin advocate for these modern conveniences. Only the old ship's commander, Bill Adama, sees value in preserving more than the appearance of the past, and it is only that anti-modernist bent that saved *Galactica* and her crew when Cylon technology infiltrated all of the newly-networked systems of the Colonies' defenses. By the end of the miniseries, the Colonials are homeless and hopeless except for Adama's chimerical promise of a refuge out of their own quasi-mythological history: Earth, the home of a long-lost thirteenth colony.

But the road to that refuge is neither clear nor undisputed. The Cylons continue to harry the survivors of the colonies desperately seeking the way to Earth. Particularly as described by the Cylons, humanity is deeply flawed, unworthy of a privileged position in the universe. And, to some extent, the history revealed in the series does condemn Colonial humanity. Hidden behind the façade of unity and peace at the series' outset, a history of imprisoned dissidents and endemic racism alludes to American actions past and present. The Cylons' return is only the first challenge the Colonials face. Their past has rendered the Colonials, in Cylon eyes, unworthy to live or, at least, to remain the heirs to prophecy and history as promised in their heritage. The Cylons toy with strategies of annihilation, interpolation, and domination, all in the name of assuming the prophesized position of "chosen people" in the traditions shared by themselves and the Colonials.

Although the series regularly asserts that the Cylons have a plan, three seasons have failed to articulate this with any clarity. What is evident, however, is that the Cylons are engaged in a complex redefinition of their own status in the universe, particularly in regards to the culture that gave birth to them. That redefinition might easily result in the annihilation of humanity. Given the near total depopulation of the Colonies and the small number of survivors making up the fleet, humans are against the ropes. Even worse, their Cylon offspring stand in utter opposition to their self-proclaimed parents on many issues, including religious beliefs. Humans evoke significant contradictions for the Cylons who struggle with opposing impulses towards destruction and assimilation throughout the series. Number Six, the first humanoid Cylon introduced in the show and one of the main characters throughout, ambiguously confronted a Colonial functionary at the series' outset with the question "Are you alive?"[4] But overall, the Cylons seem less to doubt humanity's life force than humanity's right to existence based upon their dubious record.

This dialectic between Colonial creators and their antagonistic Cylon progeny represents an extreme manifestation of the resentment conjured in the relationship between colonizers and the colonized, but an extremity that is relatively common in science fiction and fantasy. As Greg Grewell suggests, a fear of colonization underlies much of science fiction television's representation of humanity's relationship with the Other:

> The literature of earthly colonization, produced largely by colonizing Europeans and Americans, and those early colonists' constructions of an "other" have informed ways the science fiction industry has understood its relationship to more recently constructed Others.[5]

Created by humans and adopting a human form, at first glance the Cylons do not appear to fit Grewell's category of Science Fiction Others. Their very assertion of distinctiveness, of other-ness, coupled with their adoption of human form places them in a new and intriguing place: they are both self and other, human and alien. Yet, they are all the more terrifying than conventional science fiction opponents; Cylons are identical to Colonial humans except at the microscopic level. Couple this perfect and disquieting replication with their implacable desire to destroy that which made them, and the Cylons have become the colonizer's worst nightmare: an Other that can no longer be easily distinguished from the self.

What makes a human a human? How is a Cylon, virtually indistinguishable from a Colonial in form, not a human? These are questions that the series invites viewers to consider but for which it offers, as yet, no clear answer. Every Cylon is first presented to the viewer as a presumptive human, from the mysterious blonde at Armistice Station in the mini-series (an incarnation of Number Six) to four of the final five who discover their own Cylon identity through the siren call of a musical motif, drawing them simultaneously to the same place and the same realization in "Crossroads, Part II." One lesson for the viewer is the same as it is for the Colonials: trust no one. This lesson is hammered home early on in the show when scientist Baltar develops a blood test to distinguish humans from Cylons and is immediately tasked by President Roslin to test Commander Bill Adama and vice versa.[6]

The Colonials can never assuage their fear of finding more Cylons among them as well as other copies of those already known and ranged against them. They know there are only twelve humaniform Cylon models (but potentially an infinite number of each). Seven of those (the Significant Seven) are known to the humans by the start of the third season and four more (of the Final Five) were revealed in the season finale, but only to themselves, leaving the potential for (and anxiety about) undiscovered Cylons to remain high among the general Colonial population.[7] Through the technology of a resurrection ship, Cylons have a practical kind of immortality: as long as they die within range of one of these facilities, their consciousness can be "downloaded" into a new body.

The reason for Adama's early acceptance of the existence of humaniform Cylons becomes evident when his personal history is explored in "Razor." During the Cylon War, a young Bill Adama stumbled upon a secret Cylon facility where humans were imprisoned and literally dissected by their mechanical foes.[8] His memory of that discovery remains vivid, decades later, and provides a compelling explanation for his refusal to accept modern technologies vulnerable to Cylon takeover as well as his ready suspicion of trader Leoben and publicist Doral. The sterile statements of the show's introduction describing the Cylons as beings who rebelled and evolved takes on a darker tone when the show reveals that the means of that evolution lay in tearing apart already existing individual humans and building a first humaniform prototype, the Hybrid, from their experiments on captives.

Adama's past is not without missteps of his own: he is revealed to have possibly triggered the Cylon's latest wave of aggression when he sent a patrol over the armistice line into Cylon territory (and then, under orders, abandoned that pilot). More than once, his closest relationships are shown to be, knowingly or unknowingly, with Cylons, in particular an individual Number Eight, Sharon Agathon, and, later, his second-in-command, Saul Tigh. Adama sees all of Colonial humanity as deeply flawed, a position he articulates before the Cylon attacks:

> Why are we as a people worth saving? We still commit murder because of greed, spite, jealousy. And we still visit all of our sins upon our children. We refuse to accept the responsibility for anything that we've done. Like we did with the Cylons. We decided to play God, create life. When that life turned against us, we comforted ourselves in the knowledge that it really wasn't our fault, not really. You cannot play God then wash your hands of the things that you've created. Sooner or later, the day comes when you can't hide from the things that you've done anymore.[9]

The Cylons demonstrate a comparably ambivalent attitude towards their Colonial enemies. The very existence of humaniform Cylons embodies the mechanical race's desire to become that which they are working to destroy. This mimesis of the humans by the Cylons reveals a contradiction at the heart of their existence. Cylons revel in their perfect mimicry of the human form while proclaiming the inferiority of the originators of the form they adopt. Their assumption of the outward form of humanity threatens their own cultural surety as much as their former masters' complacency. Homi Bhabi identified the challenge of the colonized mimic:

> ... the repetition of *partial presence*, which is the basis of mimicry, articulates those disturbances of cultural, racial, and historical differences that menaces the narcissistic demands of colonial authority. It is a desire that reverses in part the colonial appropriation by now producing a partial vision of the colonizer's presence.[10]

Bhabi's description of a partial presence helps explain Cylon representation of humanity. They adopt the form, literally the outward seeming of their enemy, but as camouflage, not as conversion. On the contrary, the Cylons revealed as such early in the series repeatedly avow disdain for or seek to differentiate themselves from the Colonials. They adopt their human form to move among the Colonials, unseen and unsuspected as an enemy within.

The Cylon adoption of human form is not without consequences for humans as well as for themselves. Graham Huggan contends "[m]imicry (disruptive imitation) and mimesis (symbolic representation) clearly play a variety of overlapping roles within a colonial context."[11] For the humans, the greatest challenge is countering the disruptive effects of Cylon mimicry which weakens the bonds of trust among themselves. This fear results in further demonization of suspected Cylons. The Colonials casually revile Cylons as "toasters" or "skin jobs," subject them to torture, and even attempt to annihilate them entirely through a viral infection. For the Cylons, the consequences of mimicry and mimesis include becoming entangled with humans on a personal level such as Leoben Conoy's mystical obsession with Colonial pilot Kara Thrace or Caprica Six's desperate devotion to Baltar both in life and in her imaginings. The taking of human form also leaves the Cylons open to the very flaws and missteps they so bitterly reject in their makers as they find emotions and individual opinions challenging the unified consensus they expected to maintain. What begins in mimesis and mimicry ends with Cylons trapped in the structures of human-like emotions, conflicts, and disappointments. By assuming human form and appropriating human history, the Cylons have become essentially human themselves.

Annihilation

> "But parents have to die. It's the only way children come into their own."
> — Doral (Number Five) after the colonies' destruction ("Bastille Day")

If the Cylons are humanity's children, this is a very dysfunctional family. The rebellion that sparked the Cylon war can be seen as the ultimate act of teenage rebellion and the renewal of that conflict some forty years later as a renewed manifestation of the family crisis. From the perspective of the shocked remnants of Colonial humanity, however, the Cylons are not angry children, seeking redress for their parents' wrongs, but the merciless enemies of humanity bent on their annihilation. After destroying most of the population of the Colonies — literally billions of people — the Cylons continue to hunt down the surviving humans. Usually less than 50,000 by a running count maintained throughout the series, the survivors banded together in the rag-tag fleet under the protection of *Galactica*. Later, they were joined by a second battlestar, *Pegasus*, and a handful of resistance fighters retrieved from the ruins of the old Colonies.

Not content with the havoc they have wreaked, the Cylons infiltrate and terrorize the Colonial refugees in their panicky flight from their home worlds. "Litmus" featured a Cylon suicide bomber (a copy of Number Five) operating in the fleet who narrowly missed assassinating Bill Adama while bombs planted by the sleeper agent Boomer sabotaged the fleet's water supply in "Water." The most devastating attack on the fleet is carried out by Gina, a version of Number Six who had been brutalized by the *Pegasus* crew. At the end of the second season, she commits suicide by detonating a nuclear device that kills thousands of civilians on several ships.[12] All the while, Cylon ships shadow and pick away at the fleet. Thus, it appears the Cylons will destroy the last remnants of Colonial humanity, given their great advantages in terms of technology, numbers, and preparation. The Cylons seem to be engaged in a total war to bring about the end of Colonial humanity.

After the devastation of the Colonies and the many subsequent attacks upon the fleet, the Colonials have good cause to believe they are targeted for extermination. Therefore the Colonials view the Cylons' return and the devastating success of their surprise attack as a justification for total war on their part, putting aside their own civilized traditions. In the mini-series, Adama attacks a mysterious arms trader, Leobon Conoy, when the fleet stops at Ragnar Anchorage to rearm the helpless, decommissioned battlestar. Adama manages to kill Conoy, whom he denounces as a Cylon, and later abandons another suspected Cylon in the weapons depot, publicist Aaron

Doral. Doral was identified as a Cylon on a whim by Gaius Baltar, frantic to turn suspicion from his own complicity in the initial attacks. Only in the final moments of the mini-series are their Cylon identities confirmed for the viewers when copies of Leobon and Doral, along with other Cylons, rescue their fellow. It takes even longer before the Colonials themselves are certain these first suspects are, indeed, Cylons.

When Colonials are certain of Cylon identity, most are quick to act against their enemies. After Cylons prove vulnerable to an ancient virus discovered on yet another "signpost" to Earth, even one of the more conscientious and principled individuals, Lee Adama, Bill's son and the fleet's chief pilot, finds it within himself to propose a Cylon genocide. His plan to wipe out the Cylons with a deliberate infection is only stymied through the intervention of a fellow pilot, Karl Agathon, who is married to a Cylon and, thus, unwilling to accede to this desperate tactic.[13] Lee Adama takes up the role of Colonial conscience when he resigns from the military and acts as Gaius Baltar's advocate in a treason trial. Addressing the judges, Lee blames himself and, by extension, all of the Colonials, for the infiltration of the colonies' defense system that led to humanity's annihilation and the ongoing problems of fugitive humanity.[14]

Civilians also advocate extreme measures against the Cylons and those who side with them. President Roslin personally urges the pre-emptive destruction of a civilian ship suspected of carrying a Cylon bomb, the *Olympic Carrier*.[15] She also orders Cylon captive Leoben to be dumped out of an airlock in "Flesh and Bone." The President is far from the only Colonial to embrace ruthless measures, whether under the protection of law or not. Most notably, after the evacuation of New Caprica, an unofficial tribunal secretly seeks out and "tries" those who aided the Cylons in power, a rough justice that only ends when they realize they nearly executed their chief informant inside the Cylon-directed government, Felix Gaeta.[16]

Repeatedly, both Cylons and Colonials attempt the complete annihilation of their enemy. Each justifies this on the basis of history. Colonial humans, as creators of the Cylons, see themselves justified in destroying a flawed, mechanical creation. Cylons, who see human history as a record of failure, consider that justification for obliteration. Yet neither side seems completely comfortable with that analysis, holding back, time and again, from utterly annihilating the other. Thus, the Cylons have perhaps concluded that the Cylon agenda can be better served by assuming the place of humanity, rather than seeking to destroy it.

Interpolation

> *"It's real. The scriptures, the myths, the prophecies, they're all real."*
> — Laura Roslin on the discovery of Kobol ("Kobol's Last Gleaming I")

Spiritual history is the tie that binds Colonials and Cylons as old traditions are reinterpreted and appropriated by the Cylons. According to Michael Taussig, mimesis can function as an avenue to access sacred realities otherwise beyond reach.[17] Number Six, in particular, repeatedly refers to the need to adopt human form and master sexual reproduction as part of the commandments of the Cylon God. Their mimesis appropriates parts of the Colonial heritage for their own, from the human form to the human elements of prophetic history, as reinterpreted from their own, privileged position of monotheistic certainty. At the same time that the Cylons disdain human weaknesses, both physical and moral, they seek to appropriate and redefine the spiritual traditions of their enemy. The struggle between the two groups becomes a battle for legitimacy as much as supremacy and spills over into a metaphysical contest for who is the "chosen people" of prophecy. The Cylons see themselves as the logical and superior inheritors of a grand tradition and the apparatus that goes with this. Thus, the old Colonies are being resettled — literally replanted — by the new Cylon masters, in "Downloaded."

That the battle might not only be fought with weapons of war but also with a struggle to control history and the mechanisms of society resonates with Western cultures' complicated histories. The question of what modes and forms these challenges take is significant. As Linda Hutcheon has shown in her critique of the national model in literature, authors in formerly colonized non-western cultures are "bound to replicate the mechanisms responsible for rendering [them] marginal in the first place," although this internalization of the narratives of progress and national destiny were some of the very forces that led to their oppression at the outset.[18] When the Cylons seek to engage humans on and in their own terms of reference, they replicate these dualities of marginalization: master/slave, ruler/ruled, and chosen people/outcasts.

This battle for control of history between Colonials and Cylons is beautifully engaged in the first season episode "The Hand of God." Both Colonial and Cylon actions are based on and justified by an ancient book of prophecies, *The Scrolls of Pythia*. Due to the secular turn of the dominant Caprican Colonial culture, Pythia's writings are more known of than studied, but they still are widely recognized as a key element in the sacred scrolls underlying the religious traditions of all the Twelve Colonies. Composed some 3600 years before the events of the show, these scrolls tell of a cycle of exile and discovery that is elementary knowledge for any citizen. The current series of events are considered to be the third in a sequence which form the bedrock of the polytheistic faith's belief in the cyclical nature of history: "All this has happened before, and all this will happen again."

Among many other events, Pythia prophesized: "And the Lords anointed a leader to guide the caravan of the heavens to their new homeland. And unto the leader, they gave a vision of serpents, numbering two and ten, as a sign of things to come."[19] This seemingly straightforward description should make it easy to determine if one filled the role of Pythia's prophesized leader. However, two candidates emerge with equally viable claims to be the leader predicted in the Sacred Scrolls: Laura Roslin and Gaius Baltar.

Both Roslin and Baltar are considered the fulfillment of prophetic interpretation from a Colonial and Cylon viewpoint, respectively. When President Roslin confesses to having seen twelve snakes writhing on the podium during a press conference, her spiritual advisor, Priestess Elosha, interprets this in the light of the scriptures that spoke of a prophesized leader's vision of twelve serpents. Further verification that the scriptures refer to Roslin comes from another passage in the texts that describes the leader as having a wasting illness. As Roslin's character is well-established at this point to be suffering from cancer (in fact, taking a hallucinogenic drug to treat her illness, which leaves open the possibility that her vision is merely the product of her medication), she reluctantly accepts the possibility that she is the dying leader of prophecy.

Dr. Gaius Baltar also found a prophetic interpretation for his role in a grand scheme of destiny beginning with the destruction of the Twelve Colonies. On the eve of the attack, Baltar discovered that his lover was a Cylon who had used his connections to compromise the entire Colonial defense system. Wracked with fear that his treachery would be discovered, Baltar escaped the ruins of Caprica but could not elude his link to the Cylons, manifesting itself as a vision of his former lover only he can see and hear. The virtual Number Six in his head, who has been driving him towards an acceptance of the Cylon God, offers an interpretation of Baltar as the prophesized leader of the sacred texts for a Cylon destiny. Thus, with her encouragement, Baltar directs twelve Colonial Vipers to destroy a Cylon base, proving his vital expertise regarding the Cylon enemies to the Colonials among whom he must live.[20] Baltar embraces this vision of himself as a savior with a secret twist: the salvation he brings is reserved for worshippers of the one, true God of the Cylons.

The first season's climax revolves around the discovery of Kobol, a presumed mythical planet from which the twelve colonies had been exiled after an earlier catastrophe.[21] This discovery further cements the historicity of the Sacred Scrolls and the fabled Earth mentioned therein for both the Cylon and Colonial causes. Among the members of the fleet, President Roslin's role as prophet is reinforced by her momentary double-vision of the intact ancient City of the Gods instead of the scans of ruins those around her see. Baltar's mystical position also strengthens when he crash-lands on the planet with other Colonials after a Cylon ambush and is led by his virtual Number Six into a seemingly intact building in the ancient city in which he gazes upon a mystical vision of a child his companion tells him is "the first of a new generation of God's children," whom Baltar is to protect. Baltar increasingly ties himself to the Cylons' monotheistic faith and the assumption of the Scrolls' prophesized destiny, even taking refuge with them after the fall of New Caprica.[22] Again, the rival camps and leaders demonstrate how Colonials and Cylons can equally claim the heritage of history as justifying their actions and aims.

Kobol is significant not just because it confirms the existence of the historical world of the Sacred Scrolls and the position of the prophets thereof, but also because it holds the first in a series of keys to finding Earth. Laura Roslin's determination to fulfill the prophecy drives her to suborn the fleet's best pilot, Starbuck, to go back to Caprica to retrieve the Arrow of Apollo, a prized relic that scripture promises will reveal the way to Earth if properly employed at a site on Kobol. This action creates a catastrophic split amongst the Colonials: Commander Adama orders the arrest of the president which leaves the fleet leaderless when he, himself, is shot twice by the sleeper Cylon, a trusted pilot known as Boomer.

While that incarnation of Number Eight almost eliminates Adama as leader of the rag-tag fleet when her Cylon programming is activated, another turns her back on the Cylons and becomes integral to the Colonial discoveries on Kobol and humanity's future. She is the one who enables Starbuck's retrieval of the Arrow of Apollo from Caprica, abandons the other Cylons on the homeworlds, and escapes to the fleet with her human romantic partner and Starbuck. This Cylon attempts to demonstrate her loyalty to the Colonials by helping them find the way to Athena's tomb, disabling a Cylon attack on the group, and thwarting another, internal assassination attempt against Adama. Pregnant with a human–Cylon child and married to a human pilot, Karl "Helo" Agathon, Sharon Agathon represents a new hope for the Cylons (who are incapable of sexual reproduction) and a perilous future for the Colonials who consider forcible abortion of the anticipated child.[23] Thus, despite her supportive actions, some Colonials remain firmly convinced that her work with the fleet is only to further the Cylon cause of replacing the Colonials as the agents of prophecy.

The events of "The Hand of God" and the discovery of Kobol confirm for both Cylons and Colonials the reality of the mythic past. The Colonials assume they are the ones of whom the Sacred Scrolls speak: their leader the one prophesized, their people the ones destined to reach Earth. Cylons see themselves as the equal, if not more valid, fulfillment of that past and work to interpolate themselves into the domain of prophecy, once thought the private preserve of Colonial humankind.

Domination

> "We're here to find a new way to live in peace, as God wants us to live!"
> — Boomer (Number Eight) on seizing New Caprica ("Occupation")

Just when the Colonials think they have found safe haven from the Cylons, on a marginally habitable planet they dub "New Caprica," the Cylons reappear. Humanity is utterly vulnerable but not destroyed. Instead, convinced by the evangelical arguments of human sympathizers within their midst, Caprica Six and Boomer, the Cylons begin an occupation. This new situation creates a fascinating dynamic wherein the previously colonized Cylons become the occupying power. In "Counter-Terror Culture: Ambiguity, Subversion, or Legitimization," Christian Erickson argues that this sequence becomes critical "for examining occupation and resistance" under occupation; the humans have founded a resistance network that uses suicide bombings, sabotage, and assassination to disrupt the occupation forces of human collaborators and their Cylon overlords.[24] With the military vessels in the fleet outnumbered, some humans on New Caprica adopt terror tactics as their only hope against what they see as a tyrannical Cylon rule. Others choose to collaborate with the Cylon leaders, most significantly the recently-elected President Baltar. In response, the Resistance network metes out harsh justice to collaborators, even long after the occupation has ended.

The Cylon rule does not provide the peace they originally promised. Although the Cylons present their occupation as benevolent oversight, they imprison many of the humans, including prominent dissident and current

Vice President, Tom Zarek, along with former pilot Kara Thrace, aka Starbuck, who was identified by Leoben as having a "destiny." Another prisoner, Colonel Tigh, Adama's second-in-command, loses an eye during his time in the Cylon prison. As the Resistance progresses, the Cylon suppression becomes more violent and oppressive, with a round-up of suspected dissidents who are driven off to an isolated site where they are to be executed.[25] Although the Cylons had decried humanity's past actions, once the Cylons are established in power over the Colonials they, too, resort to deplorable methods to maintain their rule.

The failure of Cylon rule is a significant development in the show, revealing the first discernable weakness in Cylon surety. By the end of their tenure on New Caprica, the Cylons have lost their certainty that they do not have the failings of humans before them. The experience of occupation further polarizes the Cylon community as some are hardened against the Colonials they had previously hoped to live with in peace while others begin to identify with the downtrodden captives. Boomer becomes disaffected with humanity as a result of Resistance attacks. Along with other Cylons, she turns on Caprica Six, once celebrated for bringing the destruction of the Colonies through her influence with Gaius Baltar but now an outcast for promoting Colonial/Cylon cooperation. For the first time, the Cylons appear bitterly divided on matters ranging from the policies and even the advisability of occupation to whether there is a God. In the aftermath of New Caprica, one Cylon model, Number Three, is "boxed" or permanently discontinued as a response to her relentless search for God and other secrets of the Cylon faith. The occupation shook the Cylon's faith in themselves, if not in their mission.

Both Cylons and Colonials have been shamed by the depths they plumbed seeking to dominate their opponents, which sometimes causes reevaluation of what actions to take. "It's not enough to survive. One has to be worthy of surviving," Adama concludes after discussions with the Cylon captive Sharon Agathon, who questions whether humanity deserves to live. He then calls off a practical but unethical assassination plot against Admiral Cain, ruthless leader of the second battlestar, *Pegasus*. This insight further drives Adama to make more thoughtful choices in the show, aware both of the weight of history and the potential for historical judgment in the future.[26]

Accommodation

> *"Then history will have to make its judgments. And since history's first draft will be written in our logs...."*
> *"I guess I've got some writing to do."*
> — Bill and Lee Adama, commanders of *Galactica* and *Pegasus* ("Razor")

As the series progresses, the line between Colonial and Cylon blurs. There are commonalities and crossovers. The human traitor Baltar defects to the Cylons and then back again; the Cylon Caprica Six turns to the Colonials for refuge. Among the Colonials, Bill Adama, in particular, stands out as one who sees value in understanding and even coming to terms with the Cylons.

Sharon Agathon is a significant incarnation of Number Eight among the Cylon humanoid models. Her character repeatedly challenges the presumptions of what it means to be human in this world, often very directly in her confrontations or conversations with Bill Adama. Although another copy of Number Eight, Boomer, attempted to assassinate Adama at the end of season one, this version, who bonded with her co-pilot, Karl Agathon, while on the run on Caprica, becomes pregnant and throws her lot in with Colonial humanity. This version of Number Eight bears the first known human/Cylon child and also becomes a close confidante of Bill Adama over the course of seasons two and three. Although ostensibly a prisoner of the Colonials, once she engineers an escape from the ruins of Caprica for herself, her lover, and Thrace, Sharon Agathon repeatedly demonstrates her trustworthiness so that she is eventually made an officer by Adama and given the call-sign Athena.

Adama's protectiveness towards this copy of Number Eight that he has come to know further blurs the barriers between Colonial and Cylon. For the first time, we see the suggestion of a concept of reciprocal accommodation between Colonials and Cylons on more than a personal level. However, this accommodation is based upon mutual respect emerging between two individuals, and it is on the individual level that the greatest changes occur for both sides.

Athena builds the most significant bridge between the Colonials and Cylons not only with her close integration with the fugitive Colonial fleet but as the mother of the human–Cylon hybrid, Hera. This child has been invested with great significance by both Cylons and Colonials. Hera is the only known offspring of a humaniform Cylon and a Colonial human. (Although the last episode of season three reveals Chief Tyrol as a Cylon, making his young son, Nicholas, another possible human/Cylon hybrid.)[27] The birth of Hera and the prospect of other such children literally unites the two groups, making some sort of accommodation between the Cylons and the Colonials possible, if not inevitable.

Kara Thrace also bridge gaps between the two groups, although less willingly. Already noteworthy as an ace pilot, Starbuck, and insubordinate officer, her character became entangled with the Cylons when Leoben spoke of her special destiny in their first encounter, binding them together and linking Kara to higher powers, whether the gods of the Colonials or his one God.[28] Both Cylons and Colonials seem to have accepted this special distinction for Kara and sometimes vie in attempting to bring her under their control. Leoben, in his many incarnations, fixates on Kara, seeking not only her love but her acceptance of this destiny. Leoben is not the only Cylon focused on Starbuck. Sam Anders, a resistance fighter she married after rescuing him from the ruins of Cylon-occupied Caprica, discovers he is a Cylon at the end of the third season.[29]

After seeming to die when after her ship explodes, Kara later reappears in the final moments of the season three finale. Asserting that she's found Earth, it seems as if her special destiny is clear. Yet, cautionary foretelling that spills from the lips of the original humaniform Cylon, the Hybrid, suggests that Kara's destiny is less propitious. He warns one of the Colonials that she will lead the human race to its end: "She is the herald of the apocalypse. The harbinger of death. They must not follow her."[30] That warning goes unheeded until much later when another Hybrid elaborates on that prophecy to Kara's horror.[31] Starbuck's return might help bring Cylons and humans closer together, but it could very well divide the two groups with concerns over her loyalty and her potential.

Ultimately, it is the search for Earth that might force the greatest accommodation between the two groups. From the start, the Colonials considered the Sacred Scrolls as their preserve, viewing the further guidance derived from visits to sites mentioned in the texts, Kobol and The Temple of Five, as directed solely to the survivors of the Twelve Colonies. The Cylons challenged this presumption, finding equally valid contexts for themselves in the Sacred Scrolls. When Cylons and humans contest the meaning of the Temple of Five in "The Eye of Jupiter" and "Rapture," each side believes they have the right, as the chosen people of prophecy and history, to follow the guideposts to Earth, but it appears that they each have only part of the puzzle. Colonials and Cylons seem to need each other to proceed in their search. This feeling leads eventually to a joint voyage by the

Colonial fleet and a Cylon faction to a desolated planet they believe is Earth.[32] It appears inevitable that the two groups will come to terms on that common, contested ground or in their journeys beyond.

Having taken on the form of humans, Cylons originally believed that they needed only to master the very human art of reproduction to have an uncontestable claim as humanity's heirs. It appears the Cylons can only achieve that goal and perhaps their ultimate destiny by working with their once-despised creators. At the same time, it seems that Colonial humanity, decimated by the Cylon attacks, might only have a viable future through intermarriage and cooperation with their destroyers. Perhaps the oppositional positions of the combatants have become impossible: each side has to embrace the other in order to achieve the ends promised in prophecy, let alone to survive. The race for Earth is not just one for survival, but an evolving dialectic between rival groups for control of contested destinies arising out of their claims on history. Only when they cooperate, accepting the other's rights to the past and present, will Cylons and Colonials be able to achieve their promised future.

Notes

1. *Battlestar Galactica: The Miniseries*, DVD, executive prods. Ronald D. Moore and David Eick (2003; Universal Studios, 2004).

2. Edward Said, "Representing the Colonized: Anthropology's Interlocutors," *Critical Inquiry* 15, no. 2 (1989): 207.

3. For one articulation of the problems of colonized people's history, see Anne Norton, "Ruling Memory," *Political Theory* 21, no. 3 (1993): 457.

4. *Battlestar Galactica: The Miniseries*.

5. Greg Grewell, "Colonizing the Universe: Science Fictions Then, Now, and in the (Imagined) Future," *Rocky Mountain Review of Language and Literature* 55, no. 2 (2001): 26.

6. "Tigh Me Up, Tigh Me Down," Battlestar Galactica: *Season One*, DVD, executive prods. Ronald D. Moore and David Eick (2004; Universal Studios, 2005).

7. For a discussion of how the Cylons are seen and understood by the show's creators, listen to Ronald D. Moore and Terry Dresbach, "Frak Party Q&A Podcast" April 4, 2007. http://media.scifi.com/battlestar/downloads/podcast/mp3/frak_party/frak_party_podcast.mp3 (accessed November 28, 2007).

8. Battlestar Galactica: *Razor*, DVD, executive prods. Ronald D. Moore and David Eick (2007; Universal Studios, 2007).

9. *Battlestar Galactica: The Miniseries*.

10. Homi Bhabi, "Of Mimicry and Man: The Ambivalence of Colonial Discourse," *October, Discipleship: A Special Issue on Psychoanalysis* 28 (1984): 129.

11. Graham Huggan, "(Post)Colonialism, Anthropology, and the Magic of Mimesis," *Cultural Critique* 38 (1997–1998): 95.

12. "Lay Down Your Burdens, II," Battlestar Galactica: *Season 2.5*, DVD, executive prods. Ronald D. Moore and David Eick (2005; Universal Studios, 2006).

13. "A Measure of Salvation," Battlestar Galactica: Season Three, DVD, executive prods. Ronald D. Moore and David Eick (2007; Universal Studios, 2008).
14. "Crossroads I and II," Battlestar Galactica: Season Three, DVD, executive prods. Ronald D. Moore and David Eick (2007; Universal Studios, 2008).
15. "33," Battlestar Galactica: Season One, DVD, executive prods. Ronald D. Moore and David Eick (2004; Universal Studios, 2005.)
16. "Collaborators," Battlestar Galactica: Season Three. executive prods. Ronald D. Moore and David Eick (2007; Universal Studios, 2008).
17. Michael Taussig, *Mimesis and Alterity: A Particular History of the Senses* (London: Routledge), 1993, 84–85.
18. Linda Hutcheon, "Rethinking the National Model," *Rethinking Literary History: A Dialogue on Theory*, eds. Linda Hutcheon and Mario J. Valdes (New York: Oxford University Press, 2002) 10–11.
19. "The Hand of God," Battlestar Galactica: Season One, DVD, executive prods. Ronald D. Moore and David Eick (2004; Universal Studios, 2005.)
20. Ibid.
21. "Kobol's Last Gleaming, I and II," Battlestar Galactica: Season One, DVD, executive prods. Ronald D. Moore and David Eick (2004; Universal Studios, 2005).
22. "Exodus, II," Battlestar Galactica: Season Three, DVD, executive prods. Ronald D. Moore and David Eick (2007; Universal Studios, 2008).
23. "Epiphanies," Battlestar Galactica: Season 2.5, DVD, executive prods. Ronald D. Moore and David Eick (2005; Universal Studios, 2006).
24. Christian Erickson, "Counter-Terror Culture: Ambiguity, Subversion, or Legitimization?" *Security Dialogue* 38, no. 2 (2007): 207.
25. "Precipice," Battlestar Galactica: Season Three, DVD, executive prods. Ronald D. Moore and David Eick (2007; Universal Studios, 2008).
26. "Resurrection Ship, II," Battlestar Galactica: Season 2.5, DVD, executive prods. Ronald D. Moore and David Eick (2005; Universal Studios, 2006).
27. "Lay Down Your Burdens, II."
28. "Flesh and Bone," Battlestar Galactica: Season One, DVD, executive prods. Ronald D. Moore and David Eick (2004; Universal Studios, 2005).
29. "Crossroads II," Battlestar Galactica: Season Three, DVD, executive prods. Ronald D. Moore and David Eick (2007; Universal Studios, 2008).
30. Battlestar Galactica: *Razor*, DVD, executive prods. Ronald D. Moore and David Eick (2007; Universal Studios, 2007.)
31. "Faith," Battlestar Galactica: Season 4.0, DVD, executive prods. Ronald D. Moore and David Eick (2008; The SciFi Channel, 2008)
32. "Revelations," Battlestar Galactica: Season 4.0, DVD, executive prods. Ronald D. Moore and David Eick (2008; The SciFi Channel, 2008)

Bibliography

Battlestar Galactica: The Miniseries. DVD. Executive prods. Ronald D. Moore and David Eick. 2003; Universal Studios, 2004.
Battlestar Galactica: Season One. DVD. Executive prods. Ronald D. Moore and David Eick. 2004; Universal Studios, 2005.
Battlestar Galactica: Season 2.5. DVD. Executive prods. Ronald D. Moore and David Eick. 2005; Universal Studios, 2006.
Battlestar Galactica: Season Three. DVD. Executive prods. Ronald D. Moore and David Eick. 2007; Universal Studios, 2008.

Battlestar Galactica: Razor. DVD. Executive prods. Ronald D. Moore and David Eick. 2007; Universal Studios, 2007.
Battlestar Galactica: Season 4.0. DVD. Executive prods. Ronald D. Moore and David Eick. 2008; The SciFi Channel, 2008.
Bhabha, Homi. "Of Mimicry and Man: The Ambivalence of Colonial Discourse." *October, Discipleship: A Special Issue on Psychoanalysis* 28 (Spring 1984): 125–133.
Erickson, Christian. "Counter-Terror Culture: Ambiguity, Subversion, or Legitimization?" *Security Dialogue* 38.2 (2007): 197–214.
Grewell, Greg. "Colonizing the Universe: Science Fictions Then, Now, and in the (Imagined) Future." *Rocky Mountain Review of Language and Literature* 55.2 (2001): 25–47.
Huggan, Graham. "(Post)Colonialism, Anthropology, and the Magic of Mimesis." *Cultural Critique* 38 (Winter 1997-1998): 91–106.
Hutcheon, Linda. "Rethinking the National Model." *Rethinking Literary History: A Dialogue on Theory*, eds. Linda Hutcheon and Mario J. Valdes, 3–49. New York: Oxford University Press, 2002.
Norton, Anne. "Ruling Memory." *Political Theory* 21.3 (Aug. 1993), 453–463.
Moore, Ronald D., and Terry Dresbach. "Frak Party Q&A." April 4, 2007. http://media.scifi.com/battlestar/downloads/podcast/mp3/frak_party/frak_party_podcast.mp3.
Said, Edward. "Representing the Colonized: Anthropology's Interlocutors." *Critical Inquiry* 15.2 (Winter 1989): 205–225.
Taussig, Michael. *Mimesis and Alterity: A Particular History of the Sense.* New York: Routledge, 1993.

Suggested Readings in Science Fiction and Fantasy Television

DAVID C. WRIGHT, JR.

This select bibliography includes some of the works cited in the book's chapters and well as other writings on science fiction and fantasy television. While wide-ranging, the list is by no means comprehensive. The list's bias is toward more scholarly works; articles in magazines and fanzines, as well as on web sites, are not included. Also, studies of animated and children's series (not necessarily the same), as well as research on horror shows, are generally not incorporated.

Abbott, Stacey, ed. *Reading* Angel: *The TV Spin-off with a Soul.* London and New York: I.B. Tauris, 2005.
Adare, Sierra, ed. *Indian Stereotypes in TV Science Fiction: First Nations Voices Speak Out.* Austin: University of Texas Press, 2005.
Anderson, Steve. "Loafing in the Garden of Knowledge: History TV and Popular Memory." *Film & History* 30, no. 1 (2000): 14–23.
Bacon-Smith, Camille, ed. *Enterprising Women: Television Fandom and the Creation of Popular Myth.* Philadelphia: University of Pennsylvania Press, 1992.
_____. *Science Fiction Culture.* "The Rebirth of the Clinic: The Body as Alien in *The X-Files.*" Philadelphia: University of Pennsylvania Press, 1999.
Badley, Linda. "The Rebirth of the Clinic: The Body as Alien in *The X-Files.*" In *Deny All Knowledge: Reading* The X-Files, edited by David Lavery, Angela Hague, and Marla Cartwright, 148–167. Syracuse: Syracuse University Press, 1996.
Baker, Neal. "Creole Identity Politics, Race, and *Star Trek: Voyager.*" In *Into Darkness Peering: Race and Color in the Fantastic*, edited by E.A. Leonard, 119–129. Westport, CT: Greenwood Press.
Barron, Neil, ed. *Anatomy of Wonder: A Critical Guide to Science Fiction.* New York and London: R.R. Bowker, 1987.
_____, ed. *Fantasy and Horror: A Critical and Historical Guide to Literature, Illustration, Film, TV, Radio, and the Internet.* Lanham, MD: Scarecrow Press, 1990.
_____, ed. *Fantasy Literature.* New York: Garland, 1990.

Battis, Jes, ed. *Investigating* Farscape: *Uncharted Territories of Sex and Science Fiction.* London and New York: I.B. Tauris, 2007.
Beeler, Stan, and Lisa Dickson. *Reading* Stargate SG-1. New York and London: I.B. Tauris, 2006.
Bernardi, Daniel, ed. Star Trek *and History: Race-ing Toward a White Future.* New Brunswick, NJ: Rutgers University Press, 1998.
Bignell, Jonathan. "Space for 'quality': negotiating with the Daleks." In *Popular Television Drama,* edited by Jonathan Bignell and Stephen Lacey, 76–92. Manchester: Manchester University Press, 2005.
_____, and Andrew O'Day, *Terry Nation.* Manchester: Manchester University Press, 2005.
Booker, M. Keith, ed. *Science Fiction Television.* Westport, CT: Greenwood Press, 2004.
Bould, Mark. "Film and Television." In *The Cambridge Companion to Science Fiction,* edited by Edward James and Farah Mendlesohn, 79–95. Cambridge and New York: Cambridge University Press, 2003.
_____. "This Is the Modern World: *The Prisoner,* Authorship, and Allegory." In *Popular Television Drama,* edited by Jonathan Bignell and Stephen Lacey, 93–109. Manchester: Manchester University Press, 2005.
Boyd, Katrina G. *Imagined Spaces: Entertainment and Utopia in Science Fiction Films and Television Series of the 1980s and 1990s.* PhD diss., Indiana University, 2001.
Brynen, Rex. "Mirror, Mirror? The Politics of Television Science Fiction." In *It's Showtime! Media, Politics and Popular Culture,* edited by David Shultz, 73–100. Baltimore: Peter Lang, 2000.
Butler, David, ed. *Time and Relative Dissertations in Space: Critical Perspectives on* Doctor Who. Manchester and New York: Manchester University Press, 2007.
Buxton, David, ed. *From* The Avengers *to* Miami Vice: *Form and Ideology in Television Series.* Manchester and New York: Manchester University Press, 1990.
Cartmel, Andrew. *Through Time: An Unauthorized and Unofficial History of* Doctor Who. New York: Continuum, 2005.
Chaires, Robert H., and Bradley Chilton, eds. Star Trek *Visions of Law and Justice.* Dallas: Adios Press, 2003.
Cook, John R., and Peter Wright, eds. *British Science Fiction Television: A Hitchhiker's Guide.* London and New York: I.B. Tauris, 2006.
Cornell, Paul, Martin Day, and Keith Topping, eds. *X-Treme Possibilities: A Comprehensively Expanded Rummage through Five Years of* The X-Files. London: Virgin, 1998.
Cumberland, Sharon, ed. *"*Private Uses of Cyberspace: Women, Desire and Fan Culture.*" MIT Communications Forum.* July 28, 2005. http://www.web.mit.edu/comm-forum/paper/cumberland.html.
Cussutt, Michael. "The Feedback Loop: Science Fiction and Television." In *Reading Science Fiction,* edited by James Gunn, Marleen S. Barr, and Matthew Candelaria, 72–84. New York: Palgrave Macmillan, 2008.
Delasara, Jan, ed. *PopLit, PopCult, and* The X-Files: *A Critical Exploration.* Jefferson, NC: McFarland, 2000.
Edgerton, Gary R., and Peter C. Rollins, eds. *Television Histories: Shaping Collective Memory in the Media Age.* Lexington: The University Press of Kentucky, 2001.
Espenson, Jane, and Glenn Yeffeth, eds. *Finding* Serenity: *Anti-Heroes, Lost Shepherd and Space Hookers in Joss Whedon's* Firefly. Dallas: BenBella Books, 2005.
Ferguson, Kathy E., Gilad Ashkenazi, and Wendy Shultz. "Gender Identity in *Star Trek.*" In *Political Science Fiction,* edited by Donald M. Hassler and Clyde Wilcox, 214–233. Columbia: University of South Carolina Press, 1997.
Franklin, H. Bruce, ed. "*Star Trek* in the Vietnam Era." *Science-Fiction Studies* 21 (1994): 24–34.

Fulton, Roger, ed. *The Encyclopedia of TV Science Fiction*, 2d. ed. London: Boxtree, 2000.
Gentejohann, Volker, ed. *Narratives from the Final Frontier: A Postcolonial Reading of the Original* Star Trek *Series*. New York: Peter Lang, 2000.
Geraghty, Lincoln. *Channeling the Future: Essays on Science Fiction and Fantasy Television*. Lanham, MD: Scarecrow Press, 2009.
_____. *The Influence of* Star Trek *on Television, Film, and Culture*. Jefferson, NC: McFarland, 2008.
_____. "A Truly American Enterprise: Star Trek's Post-9/11 Politics." In *New Boundaries in Political Science Fiction*, edited by Donald M. Hassler and Clyde Wilcox, 145–156. Columbia: University of South Carolina Press, 2008.
_____, ed. *Living with* Star Trek: *American Culture and the* Star Trek *Universe*. New York and London: I.B. Tauris, 2007.
Ginn, Sherry, ed. *Our Space, Our Place: Women in the Worlds of Science Fiction Television*. Lanham, MD: University Press of America, 2005.
Gottlieb, Anthony, ed. "A Love That Dare Not Compute Its Name." *The New York Times*, June 8, 2008.
Greenberg, Harvey Roy, ed. "Introduction: Fantastic Voyages." *Journal of Popular Film and Television* 30, no. 3 (Fall 2002): 122–124.
Gregory, Chris, ed. Star Trek: *Parallel Narratives*. London: Macmillan, 2000.
Gunn, James, Marleen S. Barr, and Matthew Candelaria. *The Feedback Loop: Science Fiction and Television*. New York: Palgrave Macmillan.
Gwenllian-Jones, Sara, and Roberta E. Pearson, eds. *Cult Television*. Minneapolis: University of Minnesota Press, 2004.
Harrison, Taylor, Elyce Rae Helford, Kent A. Ono, and Sarah Projansky, eds. *Enterprise Zone: Critical Positions on* Star Trek. Boulder: Westview Press, 1996.
Hassler, Donald M., and Clyde Wilcox, eds. *New Boundaries in Political Science Fiction*. Columbia: University of South Carolina Press, 2008.
Helford, Elyce Rae, ed. *Fantasy Girls: Gender in the New Universe of Science Fiction and Fantasy Television*. Lanham, MD: Rowman & Littlefield, 2000.
Heller, Lee. "The Persistence of Difference: Postfeminism, Popular Discourse, and Heterosexuality in *Star Trek: The Next Generation*." *Science-Fiction Studies* 24 (1997): 226–244.
Henderson, Mary. "Professional Women in *Star Trek*, 1964–1969." *Film & History* 24, nos. 1–2 (February–May 1994): 48–59.
Hersey, Eleanor, ed. "Word-Healers and Code Talkers: Native Americans." *Journal of Popular Film and Television* 26, no.3 (Fall 1998).
Hockley, Luke. "Science Fiction." In *The Television Genre Book*, edited Glen Creeber, 26–31. London: British Film Institute, 2001.
Hodges, F. M, ed. "The Promised Planet: Alliances and Struggles of the Gerontocracy in American Television Science Fiction of the 1960s." *The Aging Male* 6, no. 3 (September 2003): 175–182.
Howe, David J., and Stephen James Walker, eds. Doctor Who: *The Television Companion*. London: BBC, 1998.
_____, and _____. *The Television Companion: The Unofficial and Unauthorized Guide to* Doctor Who. London: Telos, 2003 (revised edition of Howe and Walker 1998).
Iaccino, James F., ed. "*Babylon 5*'s Blueprint for the Archetypal Heroes of Commander Jeffery Sinclair and Captain John Sheridan with Ambassador Delenn." *Journal of Popular Culture* 34, no. 4 (Spring 2001): 109–120.
Inness, Sherrie A., ed. *Action Chicks: New Images of Tough Women in Popular Culture*. New York: Palgrave Macmillan, 2004.
James, Edward, and Farah Mendlesohn, eds. *The Parliament of Dreams: Conferring on Babylon 5*. Reading: Science Fiction Foundation, 1998.

Jancovich, Mark, and James Lyons, eds. *Quality Popular Television: Cult TV, the Industry and Fan.* London: British Film Institute, 2003.

Jenkins, Henry. "*Star Trek* Rerun, Reread, and Rewritten: Fan Writing as Textual Poaching." In *Close Encounters: Film, Feminism, and Science Fiction,* edited by C. Penley, E. Lyon, L. Spigel, and J. Bergstrom. Minneapolis: University of Minnesota Press, 1991.

_____, and John Tulloch, eds. *Science Fiction Audiences: Watching* Doctor Who *and* Star Trek. London: Routledge, 1995.

Johnson, Catherina. *Telefantasy.* London: British Film Institute, 2008.

Johnson-Smith, Jan, ed. *American Science Fiction TV:* Star Trek, Stargate, *and Beyond.* Middletown, CT: Wesleyan University Press, 2005.

Kulman, Martha, ed. "The Uncanny Clone: *The X-Files*, Popular Culture, and Cloning." *Studies in Popular Culture,* 26, no. 3 (2004): 75–88.

Lagon, Mark P. "'We Owe It to Them to Interfere': *Star Trek* and U.S. Statecraft in the 1960s and the 1990s." In *Political Science Fiction,* edited by Donald M. Hassler and Clyde Wilcox, 234–250. Columbia: University of South Carolina Press, 1997.

Lancaster, Kurt, ed. *Interacting with* Babylon 5: *Fan Performance in Media Universe.* Austin: University of Texas Press, 2001.

Lavery, David, Angela Hague, and Marla Cartwright, eds. *Deny All Knowledge: Reading* The X-Files. Syracuse: Syracuse University Press, 1996.

Lewis, Lisa A., ed. *The Adoring Audience: Fan Culture and Popular Media.* London: Routledge, 1992

Mason, Francis, ed. "Nostalgia for the Future: The End of History and Postmodern 'Pop' T.V." *Journal of Popular Culture* 29, no. 4 (Spring 1996): 27–40.

Milner, Andrew, ed. "Postmodern Gothic: *Buffy,* the *X-Files* and the Clinton Presidency." *Continuum: Journal of Media & Cultural Studies* 19, no.1 (March 2005): 103–116.

Muir, John Kenneth. *An Analytical Guide to Television's* Battlestar Galactica. Jefferson, NC: McFarland, 1998.

_____. *An Analytical Guide to Television's* One Step Beyond, *1959–1961.* Jefferson, NC: McFarland, 2006.

_____. *A Critical History of* Doctor Who *on Television.* Jefferson, NC: McFarland, 1999.

_____. *Exploring* Space: 1999: *An Episode Guide and Complete History of the Mid–1970s Science Fiction Television Series.* Jefferson, NC: McFarland, 2001.

_____. *A History and Critical Analysis of* Blake's 7, *the 1978–1981 British Television Space Adventure.* Jefferson, NC: McFarland, 1999.

Pearson, Roberta E. ed. "Kings of Infinite Space: Cult Television Characters and Narrative Possibilities." *Scope: An Online Journal of Film Studies* (August 2003). http://nottingham.ac.uk/film/journal/articles/kings-of-infinate-space.htm.

Peltz, Richard J., ed. "On a Wagon Train to Afghanistan: Limitations on *Star Trek's* Prime Directive." *University of Arkansas at Little Rock Law Review* 25, no.3 (2003): 634–679.

Penley, Constance, ed. *Close Encounters: Film, Feminism and Science Fiction.* Minneapolis: University of Minnesota Press, 1991.

Porter, Jennifer E., and Darcee L. McLaren, eds. Star Trek *and Sacred Ground: Explorations of* Star Trek, *Religion, and American Culture.* Albany: State University of New York Press, 1999.

Potter, Tiffany, and C.W. Marshall, eds. *Cylons in America: Critical Studies in* Battlestar Galactica. London: Continuum, 2008.

Pounds, Michael C., ed. *Race in Space: The Representation of Ethnicity in* Star Trek *and* Star Trek, the Next Generation. Lanham, MD: Rowman & Littlefield, 1999.

Presnell, Don, and Marty McGee, eds. *A Critical History of Television's* The Twilight Zone, *1959–1964.* Jefferson, NC: McFarland, 1998.

Relke, Diana M.A. *Drones, Clones, and Alpha Babes: Retrofitting* Star Trek's *Humanism, Post 9/11.* Alberta: University of Calgary Press, 2006.

Richards, Thomas, ed. *The Meaning of* Star Trek. New York: Doubleday, 1997.
Roberts, Graham, and Phillip M. Taylor, eds. *The Historian, Television and Television History.* Luton: University of Luton Press, 2001.
Roberts, Robin. *Sexual Generations:* Star Trek: The Next Generation *and Gender.* Urbana: University of Illinois Press, 1999.
Robinson, Michael G., ed. "Lois & Clark: What's New About *The New Adventures of Superman.*" *Studies in Popular Culture* 21, no. 1 (1998).
Rodnitzky, Jerry, ed. "Amerika, the Miniseries: Television's Last Cold War Gasp." *Studies in the Social Sciences* 36, no.25 (1999).
Sarantakes, Nicholas Evan, ed. "Cold War Pop Culture and the Image of U.S. Foreign Policy: The Perspective of the Original *Star Trek* Series." *Journal of Cold War Studies* 7, no. 4 (Fall 2005): 74–103.
Sardar, Ziauddin, and Sean Cubitt, eds. *Aliens R Us: The Other in Science Fiction Cinema.* London: Pluto Press, 2002.
Schumer, Arlen, ed. *Visions from* The Twilight Zone. San Francisco: Chronicle, 1990.
Scodari, Christine, ed. "Resistance Re-Examined: Gender, Fan Practices, and Science Fiction Television." *Popular Communication* 1, no.2 (2003): 111–130.
Silbergleid, Robin, ed. "'The Truth We Both Know': Reader Desire and Heteronarrative in *The X-Files.*" *Studies in Popular Culture* (2003).
Simpson, Paul, ed. *The Rough Guide to Cult TV.* London: Rough Guides.
Stevenson, Gregory. *Televised Morality: The Case of* Buffy the Vampire Slayer. Lanham, MD: Hamilton Books, 2004.
Tellote, J. P., ed. *The Essential Science Fiction Television Reader.* Lexington: University Press of Kentucky, 2008.
Tulloch, John, and Henry Jenkins, eds. *Science Fiction Audiences: Watching* Doctor Who *and* Star Trek. London: Routledge, 1995.
Tyrrell, William Blake, ed. "*Star Trek* as Myth and Television as Mythmaker." *Journal of Popular Culture* 10, no. 4 (Spring 1977): 711–719.
Urbanski, Heather. *Plagues, Apocalypses and Bug-Eyed Monsters: How Speculative Fiction Shows Us Our Nightmares.* Jefferson, NC: McFarland, 2007.
Wagner, Jon, and Jan Lundeen, eds. *Deep Space and Sacred Time:* Star Trek *in the American Mythos.* Westport, CT: Praeger, 1998.
Wilcox, Rhonda, ed. *Why Buffy Matters: the Art of* Buffy the Vampire Slayer. London and New York: I.B. Tauris, 2005.
_____, and David Lavery, eds. *Fighting the Forces: What's at Stake in* Buffy the Vampire Slayer. Lanham, MD: Rowman & Littlefield, 2002.
William, Cassidy, Susan Schwartz, and Ross Shepard Kraemer, eds. *Religions of* Star Trek. Boulder, CO: Westview Press, 2002.
Worland, Rick, ed. "Captain Kirk: Cold Warrior." *Journal of Popular Film and Television* 16, no. 3 (Fall 1988): 109–117.
_____. "From the New Frontier to the Final Frontier: *Star Trek* from Kennedy to Gorbachev." *Film and History* 24 no. 1–2 (1994): 19–35.
Zicree, Marc Scott, ed. The Twilight Zone *Companion,* 2d ed. Los Angeles: Silman-James Press, 1989.

Contributors

Allan W. Austin is an associate professor of history at Misericordia University in Dallas, Pennsylvania. He has published *From Concentration Camp to Campus: Japanese American Students and World War II* (University of Illinois Press, 2004) along with essays on Japanese American history during and after World War II as well as film history. He has also published *Asian American History and Culture: An Encyclopedia* (with Huping Ling and M.E. Sharpe, 2010). His next monograph, *American Friends Service Committee, Quakers and Race in the United States, 1917–1950*, is under contract with the University of Illinois Press.

Randall Clark is an assistant professor of communication and media studies at Clayton State University. He is the author of *At a Theater or Drive-In Near You: The History, Politics, and Culture of the American Exploitation Film* (Garland, 1995). He has published articles on the television series *Charmed* and *Perry Mason*; the films of Pam Grier; the Freddy the Pig children's books; and the French novel and film *Baise Moi*.

Korcaighe P. Hale is an assistant professor of history at the Zanesville branch of Ohio University. Her primary field of research is modern Irish history, and specifically the study of Irish neutrality. She has published "The Limits of Diplomatic Pressure: Operation Safehaven and the Search for German Assets in Ireland" (*Irish Historical Studies*, May 2009) and "'What he is speaks so loud that I can't hear what he's saying': R.W. Scott McLeod and the long shadow of Joseph McCarthy" (forthcoming). Her current research focuses on the efforts of Operation Safehaven in Denmark, 1944–1949.

Antony Keen is an associate lecturer and research associate at Open University. He received his M.A. in ancient history and Greek at the University of Edinburgh and his Ph.D. at the University of Manchester. He published his dissertation, "A Political History of Lycia and Its Relations with Foreign Powers during the 'Dynastic' Period," in 1998. His various teaching areas include Roman and Greek history and culture, Greek language and literature, and archaeology. His current research interests are Graeco–Roman classics and science fiction. He has published an article on *Babylon 5* in *Foundation: The International Review of Science Fiction*.

Judith Lancioni is an associate professor in the Department of Radio, Television, and Film at Rowan University in Glassboro, New Jersey, where she teaches courses in media research and criticism, television scriptwriting, and images of women in film. Her research interests include historical documentary and popular culture. She has published articles on Ken Burns' *The Civil War*, *Billy Elliot* as fairytale, and the ethical implications of *Survivor*. She is editor of *Fix Me Up*, a collection of essays on dating and makeover television shows published by McFarland in 2009. Currently she is researching the construction of the historical process in documentaries.

Novotny Lawrence is an assistant professor of race, media, and popular culture in the Radio-Television Department at Southern Illinois University–Carbondale where he teaches courses such as media and society, the history of African American images in film and television, and documenting the black experience. He is the author of *Blaxploitation Films of the 1970s: Blackness and Genre* (Routledge, 2007) and his essays "Fear of a Blaxploitation Monster: Blackness as Generic Revision in AIP's *Blacula*" and "The Detective Film as Genre" were published in *Film International* and *Screening Noir*, respectively. His current research focuses on independent films that exhibit a "neo–race film" aesthetic. Additionally, he is also working on a project on black documentary cinema.

Daryl Lee is an assistant professor of humanities at the State University of New York Institute of Technology at Utica-Rome where among the courses he teaches is a cultural history of monsters, robots, and cyborgs. He is currently working on a manuscript on the cultural and intellectual history of suicide in the nineteenth-century West, part of which has been published in *Intellectual History Review*.

Kendra Preston Leonard received a bachelor of music degree in cello performance at the Peabody Conservatory of Music, a certificate of advanced studies at Guildhall School of Music and Drama, and a master's degree in cello performance at the University of Miami. Her postgraduate studies in historical musicology were at the University of Cincinnati College Conservatory of Music. Leonard teaches at Westminster Choir College of Rider University in Princeton, New Jersey. She is a newsletter editor and webmaster for the North American British Music Studies Association. Her current research is on the use of music in film and television.

Janice Liedl is an associate professor of history at Laurentian University in Sudbury, Ontario. She has co-edited *Love and Death in the Renaissance* (Dovehouse, 1991) and published on Tudor English literary history. She is editing *The Encyclopedia of Elizabethan England* (forthcoming). Presently she is working on historical memory and popular culture since the nineteenth century including such subjects as the Norse voyages to America and the history behind *Twilight* and *Harry Potter*.

Bryan E. Vizzini is an associate professor of history at West Texas A&M University. His recent publications include "Cold War Fears, Cold War Passions: Conservatives and Liberals Square Off in 1950s Science Fiction" (*Quarterly Review of Film and Video*, 2009), and "Hero and Holocaust: Graphic Novels in the Undergraduate History Classroom," a chapter in the forthcoming MLA volume *Approaches to Teaching the Graphic Novel*. His current research focuses on how film, television, and graphic storytelling reflected the changes in cultural norms that accompanied 9–11 and its aftermath.

David C. Wright, Jr., is an associate professor and chair of the History and Government Department at Misericordia University where he teaches courses in modern French history, European intellectual history, European cultural history, and film and history. He has given conference papers and published in French history. His recent scholarship, presented at a variety of conferences, has focused on popular culture, analyzing representations of spatiality, utopianism, historical memory, nostalgia, and leaving home in science fiction, fantasy, and rock and roll music. He is currently working on a book that examines the poetics of rock and roll music lyrics.

Index

Abbott, John 37
ABC 29, 36–37, 41n, 86
The Abominable Snowmen 107
The Adventures of Ozzie and Harriet 49
Africa 70, 72, 164
Alabama 20
Alexander, Denise 14
Alien 25, 166
Alien Nation 29
Allen, Irwin 29, 32, 41
Alvarado, Manuel 109
America Divided: The Civil War of the 1960s 13, 22
Amos 'n' Andy 21
"The Amphibians" 39
Amy-Chinn, Dee 184
Andersen, Hans Christian 103, 105
Anderson, Gerry 32,102
Anderson, Sylvia 32
Andrews, Edward 13
Apollo space program 4, 82–84
The Armageddon Factor 109
Army-McCarthy hearings 44
"Arrival" 46–47, 57
Arthur, Robert Allan 10
Asia 36, 72, 74, 77, 121, 141, 175, 178, 180–181, 184
"Assignment Earth" 140–141, 154n
Astronautics 88
Atkins, Claude 17
Atomic Café 26n
Atwater, Barry 17
Atwill, William 83
Austin, Allan W. 4, 152n, 215
Austin, Steve 82, 85–87, 91–92, 94–95
The Avengers 43–45, 53
The Aztecs 101

Babylon 5 157, 215
Baker, Bob 108
Baker, Tom 108
Baldwin, James 151
Bar Kochbar 112n

Barbera, Joseph 32
Barnouw, Erik 25
Barthes, Roland 58
"Bastille Day" 196
Battle of Culloden 119–121
Battlefield 110
Battlestar Galactica 1, 3, 6, 25, 189–207
Battlestar Galactica (1978–1979) 85
Baudrillard, Jean 58
BBC 102–104, 113n
Becker, Carl 156–157, 169n
Ben-Hur 102
Berger, Arthur 86–87
Berlin 123
Berlioz, Hector 105
Bernardi, Daniel 65, 71–73, 132–133, 136–137
Berry, Dennis 126
Bernstein, Elmer 176
Bessie, Alvah 16
Beulah 21
Bhabha, Homi 195
Bhagavad Gita 119
Biberman, Herbert 16
"Big Bar Fight" 179
"The Big Goodbye" 155n
"The Big Tall Wish" 21–22
Bigfoot 86
The Bionic Woman 86
black power 62
Bond, James 31
Booker, M. Keith 2, 67, 71
Booth, John Wilkes 159–160
Boyd, Katrina 132
The Brain of Morbius 109
Breisach, Ernst 129n
Britain 408 AD 100
Britton, Wesley 45
Brown, Oliver 19, 22
Brown, Royal S. 175–176
Brown v. the Topeka Board of Education 19–20, 27n
Buffett, Jimmy 162

219

Index

Buffy the Vampire Slayer 116, 174
Buono, Victor 42n
Burke, Edmund 123
Burns, Ken 1, 124

"The Cage" 134, 141, 154n
Caidin, Martin 86
California 33, 38, 175
Cameron, James 163
Campbell, Joseph 59n
Capra, Frank 129n
Carry On 102
Carry On Cleo 102–103, 111n
Cash, Johnny 160
CBS 11–12
Chafe, William 61–64
Chaffey, Don 46
Chayefsky, Paddy 10, 25n
"Cheeseburger in Paradise" 162
Chicago 20, 63
Chicago Daily News 12
Childress, Alvin 21
"The Chimes of Big Ben" 43, 47–48, 57
China 15, 31, 36; *see also* Chinese
Chinese 174–175, 178–179, 181, 184; *see also* China
Churchill, Winston 103, 132, 159, 169n
"City on the Edge of Forever" 137–138, 150, 154n
Civil Rights Movement 19–21, 23, 25, 62, 71, 117
Civil War 117, 159, 175, 177
Clark, Randall 3, 215
Cleopatra 111n
Clynes, Manfred 88–90
Coen brothers 109
"Cold Comfort" 164
Cold War 2–3, 4, 9, 13–15, 19, 25–26n, 30–33, 35–36, 38–40, 43, 45, 47, 49, 54, 57, 61–64, 67–68, 70–71, 75, 82–83, 109, 136, 140
Cole, Lester 16
Colonialism 2, 6, 174, 186
"The Colony" 59n
Colossus: The Forbin Project 97n
Combat 41n
"The Comedian" 10
comic books 31
The Committee: The Extraordinary Career of the House on Un-American Activities 16
Connell, John 176
"Conspiracy" 103
Cook, David 176
Cooper, Gary 16
Cotton, Donald 104–105, 112n
Crane, Stephen 159
"The Creature" 39

A Critical History of Television's The Twilight Zone, 1959–1964 9
"Crossroads, Part II" 193
The Crucible 17
Chrysler building 10
Csicsery-Ronay, Istvan 146, 151
Cuban Missile Crisis 34, 38, 161
"The Cyborg" 39
Cyborg 86
Cyborg 2087 97n
"Cyborgs and Space" 88

The Daemons 107–108
Dale, Jim 103
The Dalek's Masterplan 106
Daly, Dan 159
"Dance of the Dead" 49–51, 57
Dances with Wolves 128n
Danger Man 44–46, 48, 53, 59n
Dante, Joe 25
Dark Angel 3, 6, 156–158, 163–165, 167–168, 171n; pilot episode 156
"The Dark Side of Earth" 10
"Day of Evil" 39
Dayton Accords 170n
"The Deadly Cloud" 39
"Deadly Dolls" 39
Deadly Invasion" 40
Dean, Joan 84–85
"Dear Doctor" 133, 155n
"Death's Head Revisited" 22
Deighton, Len 31
Democratic National Convention (1968) 63
Discipline and Power 58
Dixon, Ivan 21
Dixon, Roger 112n
Dixon Hill (character) 135
Dmytrk, Edward 16
Dr. Strangelove, Or: How I Learned to Stop Worrying and Love the Bomb 37, 45, 69, 79n
Doctor Who 3, 5, 100–115
Douglas, Susan 75
"Downloaded" 198
Dozier, William 11
Dragnet 65
Dudziak, Mary L. 70

Easy Rider 51
Ebola 164, 171n
Eccleston, Christopher 110
Edlund, Ben 182–183
Edmonson, Greg 176–177, 179, 181–182, 184–185
Egbee, Charles 163
Eick, David 189
Eisenhower, Dwight D. 62, 70

"Elementary Dear Data" 155n
Engel, Joel 66
England 45, 182; see also Great Britain
U.S.S. *Enterprise* 51, 84, 131, 133–134, 136, 139–140
Equilibrium 25
Erickson, Christian 201
Ermath, Elizabeth 151
Erway, Ben 17
Europe 36, 121–124, 162, 183
"Eye of Gorgon" 110
"The Eye of Jupiter" 204
"Eyes" 156

Fail Safe 37, 97n
"Fall Out" 55–57
fantasy 1–2, 5, 7, 9, 11, 25, 89, 193
"Far Beyond the Stars" 132, 142–148, 150–151, 155n
Farscape 116
Father Knows Best 23, 49
The Feminine Mystique 23–24
Feminist Movement 25
Fields, W.C. 160
Fire and Power: The American Space Program as Postmodern Narrative 83
Firefly 1, 3, 6, 167, 174–188
"The Fires of Pompeii" 110
"A Fistful of Datas" 135, 155n, 176
A Fistful of Dollars 176
"Flesh and Bone" 197
"Folsom Prison Blues" 160
Fontana, Dorothy 76
Ford Motor Company 10
Foucault, Michel 58–59n
Fox Network 174
France 45, 120
Francis, Derek 101–102
Frankenstein 108, 109
"Free for All" 49–50, 55, 57
French Resistance 123
Fried, Richard M. 13, 15–16, 18
Friedan, Betty 22–24
Frost, K.T. 107
Froug, William 24
A Funny Thing Happened on the Way to the Forum 102
"Future's End I & II" 140, 155n

Gangbusters 59n
Gay Liberation Movement 23
Gelbart, Larry 102
gender 2, 23, 25, 64–65, 75–78
Geraghty, Lincoln 131–132, 150
Germany 39, 117, 123, 139
Get Smart 44, 141
Gibson, Chris 176
"The Gift" 22

"The Girl Who Was Death" 51–54, 57
Gismondi, Italo 102
Goldberg, Whoopi 72
"The Good Death" 162
Goodman, Walter 16
Gould, Jack 12
Grade, Lew 44–45
Great Britain 169n; see also England
Great Depression 158, 163
Great Society 64
Great War 123; see also World War I
Greece 104–108, 110, 161
Greenberg, Drew Z. 181
Gregory, Chris 43, 59n
Grewell, Greg 193
Guadalcanal 159, 169n
The Gunfighters 103

Hale, Korcaighe P. 6, 215
Hall, Adam 31
Hamer, Fannie Lou 22
Hancock, Tony 102
"The Hand of God" 198–201
Handzlik, Jan 17
Hanna, William 32
The Happening 25
Haraway, Donna 85
Harvey, David 146
Have Gun Will Travel 59n
Hayden, Serling 18
Hayles, Katherine 88, 94
"The Heat Monster" 40
"Heavyweight" 10
Hedison, David 34
Hegel 190
Heinlein, Robert A. 132
Helford, Elyce Rae 72, 76
Henry V 159
"The Hero of Canton" 182
"Hide and Seek" 162
Highlander: The Series 3, 5–6, 116–130
The Highlanders 106
Hill, Adrienne 106
Hisama, Ellie M. 183–184
Hiss, Alger 44
history and memory 6, 126–127, 157, 190; and post-modernism 4–6, 51, 117, 125, 132, 134, 144–145, 147–149, 151; and television 1, 2, 124, 126, 131–133, 135–136, 140–141, 146, 157–158, 160
Hodgson, Godfrey 79n
Hollywood Ten 16, 44
Holocaust 124
Homer 112n, 159
Hoover, J. Edgar 68
The Horns of Nimon 100, 109–110
Horowitz, Daniel 23
"Hot Line" 37, 40

House Un-American Activities Committee 16, 18
How We Became Posthuman 88
Huggan, Graham 195
Hughes, Langston 151
Hulke, Malcolm 100
"The Hunted" 136, 155n
Hurston, Zora Neale 151
Hutcheon, Linda 198

"I Am Night — Color Me Black" 22
I, Claudius 102
Iliad 159
"Image in the Sand" 143–144, 155n
imperialism 120, 124
"The Invaders" 23–24
Ireland 119–120, 215
Irish 120, 124, 178, 181, 215
Irwin Allen Television Productions, 1964– 1970 37
Isserman, Maurice 13, 15, 22
Italy 161
It's a Wonderful Life 129n

James, Sid 102
Jameson, Frederic 146, 149
Japan 11, 73, 175, 178, 183, 185
Jaws 166
"Jaynestown" 182–183, 187n
Jensen, Pete 11, 12
Jeremiah 3, 6, 156–158, 165–168
Jet Pilot 59n
Johnson, Lyndon B. 62–64, 70
Johnson-Smith, Jan 2, 72–74
Johnston, June 22
Jonny Quest 32
Joyce, James 109

Kaczynski, Ted 164
Kazin, Michael 13, 15, 22
Keen, Tony 5, 215
Kennedy, John F. 34, 62, 70, 161, 170n
Kenney, Robert F. 63
"Key to Time" 109
The Killer Angels 175
"The Killing Game I & II" 140, 150, 155n
King, Martin Luther, Jr. 20, 22, 63, 70, 72
Kiss Me Deadly 59
Kline, Nathan 88–90
"Kobol's Last Gleaming I" 198
Korean War 15
Kraft Television Theater 9–10
Kubrick, Stanley 45, 69
Kuhn, Annette 147

LaFeber, Walter 63
Lagon, Mark 137
Lakota Sioux 122

Lambek, Michael 125
Lambert, Verity 102
Lancioni, Judith 5–6, 216
Land of the Giants 29–30, 35, 41
Landis, John 25
The Lantern Bearers 101
Lardner, Ring, Jr. 16
"The Last Lap of Luxury" 162
Laughton, Charles 102
Lawrence, Novotny 3, 216
Lawson, John Howard 16
Leary, Timothy 92
Leave It to Beaver 23, 49
Le Carré, John 45, 48
Lee, Daryl 4, 216
Lehman, Ernest 10
Leonard, Kendra Preston 6, 216
LeRoy, Mervyn 102
"Let That Be Your Last Battlefield" 136, 149–150, 154n
Letts, Barry 107
Libya 161–162; *see also* Libyans
Libyans 161–162, 170n
Liedl, Janice 6, 216
The Lieutenant 65
"Litmus" 196
"Little Green Men" 135, 155n
"The Living Doll" 23–24
"Living in Harmony" 51–54, 57
Locke, Ralph P. 183
Lockerbie, Scotland 161
Logan's Run 29
London Blitz 169
The Lone Ranger 59n
Los Angeles Times 12
Lost in Space 29–30, 35, 41n
Luce, J.V. 107
Lyotard, Jean-Francois 117–118

Macpherson, C.B. 88
Mad Max 166
The Magnificent Seven 176
Maltz, Albert 16
The Man from U.N.C.L.E. 31, 43
Manchurian Candidate 45, 59n
Marco Polo 101
"The Mark of Gideon" 136, 149, 154n
Markstein, George 46
Maross, Joe 13
Marshall, Thurgood 19, 22
Martin, Andrew 108
Martin, Dave 108
May, Elaine Tyler 75
Mayer, Louis B. 16
McCarthy, Joseph R. 15, 26–27n; *see also* McCarthyism
McCarthyism 19, 25, 68–69; *see also* McCarthy, Joseph R.

McCoy, Sylvester 110
McCurdy, Howard 84
McDaniel, Hattie 21
McGee, Marty 9, 11
McGoohan, Patrick 43–60
McHale's Navy 41n
McKern, Leo 54–55
McPherson, C.B. 88
"Meow" 164
Mercury Project 14, 29n
Merril, Judith 132
The Mike Wallace Show 11
Miller, Arthur 17
Miller, Toby 44, 57, 59n
The Mind Robber 107, 109
Mission: Impossible 43
Mississippi 20
"The Mist of Silence" 37
Mr. District Attorney 65
model minority 72–73
"Monster from Space" 39
"The Monsters Are Due on Maple Street" 17–19
Moore, Ronald D. 189
Morgan, Glen 169n
Morricone, Ennio 176
"Mortal Sins" 123
"Mother of Invention" 166
Mount, Paul 103
My Favorite Martian 31
My Geisha 183
My Son John 59n
The Myth Makers 100, 103–106, 109–110, 112n

Napoleonic Wars 117, 121
NASA 64, 83–84, 91
Nathan-Turner, John 109
nationalism 68–69, 124
Native American 122, 128n, 133, 136
NBC 66, 72
"Never No More" 159
New Jersey 216
New Orleans 147
The New Twilight Zone (1985–1989) 25
New York (City) 10, 137, 142, 146
New York Times 12, 83
Newman, Kim 105–106
Nightmare in Red: The McCarthy Era in Perspective 13
1984 44, 57, 59n
Nixon, Richard 63
North America 186
"Number Twelve Looks Just Like You" 24–25
Nye, David 84

O Brother Where Art Though? 109
"Occupation" 201

"The Old Man in the Cave" 26n
"The Omega Glory" 4, 61–81, 152n
"Once Upon a Time" 54–55
"One More Pallbearer" 26n
Ornitz, Samuel 16
Orwell, George 44, 57
"Our Mrs. Reynolds" 180–182, 187n
The Outer Limits 30–31

Panzer, Bill 126
Paris 104, 121, 123
Parker, Suzy 24
"Past Tense I & II" 138, 150, 155n
"Patterns" 9–10
"Patterns of Force" 139–140, 150, 154n
Peltz, Richard 136
Pennsylvania 122, 215
Perry, Steven 21
Pertwee, John 107–108
"The Phantom Strikes" 39
Pidgeon, Walter 32
"A Piece of the Action" 135, 154n
Planet of the Apes 29
Plato 107
Playhouse 90 9–10, 20
The Postmodern Condition 117
Post-Traumatic Stress Syndrome 125
Presnell, Don 9, 11
The Prisoner 3–4, 43–60, 59n
"A Private Little War" 136, 154n
"Prodigy" 164

"A Quality of Mercy" 22
Quo Vadis 101–102, 111n

race 2, 64–65, 70–72, 74, 77, 195, 205
racism 3, 25, 62, 65–66, 70, 77, 124, 136, 151, 191–192
"The Rank and File" 10
Ranke, Leopold von 169n
"Rapture" (*Battlestar Galactica*) 204
"Rapture" (*Star Trek: Deep Space Nine*) 142, 147–148, 155n
"Razor" 194, 203
Read, Anthony 108–109
Reagan, Ronald 16
Reconstruction Era 175
Red Channels 18, 27n
"Red River Valley" 180
Redmond, Sean 137
"Requiem for a Heavyweight" 9–10
"Return of the Phantom" 39
Rhodes, Sonny 177
"Ring-a-Ding Girl" 23–24
"The River of Stars" 159
Robinson, Edward G. 18
The Robots of Death 108
Rod Serling: Submitted for Your Approval 10

224 Index

Roddenberry, Gene 61–81
Rogin, Michael 58n
Rollins, Peter 2
The Romans 100, 101–106, 111n
Rome (Roman Empire) 102–104, 110, 120
Ronson lighters 10
Roosevelt, Franklin D. 159, 169n
Roots 124
Rosenberg, Julius 44
Rota, Nino 176
Rowley, Christina 183
Russia 36, 75, 117, 123

"Safe" 180–182, 187n
Said, Edward 6, 190
The Saint 43, 45
The Sarah Jane Adventure 110
Sarantakes, Nicholas 137
"Sarek" 134, 155n
Sayonara 183
Schrecker, Ellen 68
science fiction 1–2, 7, 9, 11, 25, 29, 38, 44, 61, 65, 84–85, 126, 131–132, 146–147, 157, 193
Scots 117, 119–120, 181; *see also* Scotland
Scotland 106, 120, 128n, 161, 182; *see also* Scots
Scott, Adrian 16
Scott, Derek 184
Screen Actors Guild 18
Screen Directors Guild 18
"seaQuest" 169n
seaQuest DSV/2032 3, 6, 156–158, 160–165, 167–168, 171
Seattle 164
Seaview 41n
"Second Chance" 161
Secret Agent Man 45
Serenity 174, 179–180
"Serenity" 177, 188n
Serling, Rod 3, 9–25, 31
Seven Days in May 45
"The Seven Million Dollar Man" 96
The Seven Samurai 175
sexuality 3
Shaara, Michael 175
"Shadowmen" 39
"Shadows and Symbols" 132, 143–148, 151, 155n
Shakespeare, William 103–105, 159
Shatner, William 162
Shelley, Mary 109
Sherlock Holmes 108, 135
Shevelove, Burt 102
Shimpach, Shawn 116
"Shindig" 179, 188n
"Shortie's in Love" 164
The Sign of the Cross 102

The Six Million Dollar Man 3–5, 82–99; pilot episode 91–95
"The Sky Is Falling" 40
"The Sky's on Fire" 41n
Sloman, Robert 107, 113n
Smith, Cecil 12
Sobchak, Vivian 147–148
"Something in the Air" 156
Sommers, Jaime 86
Sondergaard, Gale 18
Sondheim, Stephen 102
South America 170n
Soviet Union 13, 15, 18, 38, 62–64
Soylent Green 25
Space: Above and Beyond 3, 6, 156–160, 167–168, 171n
Spanish Civil War 117
"Specter of the Gun" 51
Spooner, Dennis 101–104, 111n
Sputnik 34, 75
The Spy Who Came In from the Cold 59n
"Star Dust" 159
Star Trek (the original series) 3–6, 25, 30, 51, 61–81, 79n, 85, 127n, 131; franchise 3, 5, 131–155
Star Trek: Deep Space Nine 3, 5–6, 131–133, 141–149, 151
Star Trek: Enterprise 131, 133
Star Trek: The Next Generation 72, 131,133, 135
Star Trek: Voyager 131, 133
Star Wars 84, 166
Starman 29
"The State of the Union" 156
Sterling, John 132
Stern, Megan 84
Stevenson, Robert Louis 159
Stewart, Patrick 177
Stingray 32, 102
"Storm Front I & II" 139–140, 155n
Straczynski, J. Michael 167
Sturge, John 176
Sutcliff, Rosemary 101
Swiss Family Robinson 41n

Takei, George 73
"A Taste of Armageddon" 136, 154n
"Tattoo" 136–137, 155n
Taussig, Michael 198
Taylor, Robert 16
television documentaries 1, 124, 126
television industry 10, 67–68, 72, 77
"Tell Our Moms We Done Our Best" 159
"Temple of Secrets" 105
Tennant, David 110
The Terminator 90
That Was the Week That Was 32
"Third from the Sun" 13–14

Third Programme 104
Thompson, William Irwin 83–84
Till, Emmett 20
"The Time Element" 11–12
"Time Enough at Last" 26n
The Time Monster 100, 107–109, 112n
The Time Tunnel 29–30, 35–36
"To Be or Not to Be" 161
Tokyo 159
Tomlin, David 46
Tosh, Donald 106
totalitarianism 123
"A Town Has Turned to Dust" 10
"Toy Soldiers" 159
"The Train Job" 178–179, 188n
"Treasures of the Mind" 161
"Trials and Tribbleations" 134, 155n
Troilus and Cressida 104
Trojan War 104, 109
Troughton, Patrick 106
Troy 112n
Les Troyens 105
Trpcic, Shawna 175
Truman, Harry S 62, 70
Trumbo, Dalton 16
Tulloch, John 109
Turim, Maureen 126
Turner, Terry 12
Twelve O'Clock High 41n
The Twilight Zone 1, 3–4, 9–25, 26n, 30–31
The Twilight Zone (2002–2003) 25
The Twilight Zone Companion 10
The Twilight Zone: The Movie 25
2001: A Space Odyssey 84

Ulysses 109
"Under the Big Black Sun" 160
Underground Railroad 122
The Underwater Menace 107
Underworld 100, 108–110, 113n
"Unification I & II" 134, 155n
The Untouchables 59n
Ustinov, Peter 102

V for Vendetta 25
Vietnam War 4, 34, 45, 52, 61–62, 70, 83, 136–137, 159
"Village of Guilt" 40
Vinson, Fred 19
Vizzini, Bryan E. 4, 217
von Ranke, Leopold 169n
Voyage to the Bottom of the Sea 1, 3–4, 29–42, 41n; the film 32

The War Games 104, 107
Warner, Jack 16

Warren, Earl 19–20
Washington, D.C. 37
"Water" 196
"The Wax Men" 39
Waxman, Franz 183
Wayne, John 159
Weaver, Fritz 13
Weston, Jack 17
Westworld 29
"Whale Song" 162
"What You Leave Behind" 148–149, 151, 155n
Whedon, Joss 167, 174–175, 177, 186
"Where is Everybody?" 12
Whitaker, David 103
Whitfield, Stephen 71–73
Wiener, Norbert 87–88, 90, 92
Wilcox, Collin 24
Wild, Harry 14
The Wild, Wild West 43, 53
Wiles, John 106
Williams, Graham 108
Williams, Kenneth 102
Williams, Spencer 21
Wilson, Donald 102
"Wine, Women, and War" 95, 98n
Wolfe, Gary 132
Wolfe, Peter 25
Women's Liberation Movement 22–23, 25, 62, 75
Wong, James 169n
Wood, John 105
Woodstock 162; Woodstock II 162, 170n
World War I 33, 39, 117, 123, 159; see also Great War
World War II 13, 33, 41n, 65, 73, 75, 117, 123, 137–140, 159, 169–170n, 175; see also Guadalcanal
Worth, Harry 102
"The Wrath of Kali" 120–121
Wright, David C., Jr. 5, 217
Wright, Richard 151
Wright, Will 176

X 160
X-Games 171n
Xena: Warrior Princess 116

yellow peril 74
Yojimbo 176
Y2K 163
Yugoslavian Civil War 162, 170n

Zicree, Marc Scott 10, 25

www.ingramcontent.com/pod-product-compliance
Ingram Content Group UK Ltd.
Pitfield, Milton Keynes, MK11 3LW, UK
UKHW041951140426
5217IPUK00015B/752